The Kingdom Of God

Samuel N. Greene, *Ph. D.*

GP

Glory Publishing, Inc.

Glory Publishing, Inc
1301-16 Monument Road
Jacksonville, FL 32225
GloryPublishingInc.com

About the author:
www.Brother-Sam.org

Printed in the United States of America
ISBN 978-1-937199-65-4
Copyright © 2014. All Rights Reserved

All Scriptures used in this book were taken from the King James Version.
Also, we have decided not to capitalize any names of the devil and his kingdom.

Foreword

Dear friends, Jesus said in Matthew 6:10, in teaching His disciples how to pray, "*Thy Kingdom come, thy will be done on earth as it is in heaven.*" Thy Kingdom come – This manual will deal exclusively with the Kingdom of God. What is the Kingdom of God? The Kingdom of God is about making Jesus sit upon the throne of our hearts and allowing Him to rule and reign within us by His grace. It is not a bunch of rules and regulations. It is all about Jesus reigning and ruling upon the throne of our hearts. The Kingdom of God is when you and I live under the rulership of Jesus Christ. The Kingdom of God is not a democracy, ruled by the opinions of people. It is a theocracy, ruled and reigned by God. It is interesting to note that the last church mentioned in the book of Revelation is the Laodicean church. The Laodicean is a type of the last day's church and the word Laodicea means, "a democracy, opinion of the people; ruled by the people." Therefore the last day's church is a church that will be pushing for democracy and rulership by the people and not by the Lord. This reminds us of what happened in Saul's day when the people wanted a king, even though God wanted to be their king. However, there is no Scriptural precedent for this. God is supposed to be the King of the Kingdom.

Concerning the Kingdom of God, Jesus said in Mark 4:11, "*Unto you it is given to know the mystery of the kingdom of God.*" We are supposed to know the mysteries of the Kingdom of God. It is not supposed to be something that we cannot attain to or understand. It has been given to us to know the mysteries of the Kingdom.

Just a quick perusal of the Scriptures can give us some answers to what the Kingdom of God is. Acts 14:22 says, "*We must through much tribulation enter into the kingdom of God.*" This means that through much tribulation we make Jesus the Lord of our lives. In Romans 14:17, it says, "*For the kingdom of God is not meat and drink; but righteousness, and peace, and joy in the Holy Ghost.*" The Kingdom of God here is not speaking of laws, rules, regulations, nor meats or drinks. But it is about righteousness (right standing with God), the peace of God ruling in our hearts and the joy of the Holy Ghost. We are to live an abundant life.

Paul said in II Thessalonians 1:5, "*...that ye may be counted worthy of the kingdom of God.*" There is an accounting worthy to be in the Kingdom of God. The Kingdom of heaven and the Kingdom of God are different in that the Kingdom of heaven deals with heaven, but the Kingdom of God deals with God rulership in His people on the earth right now. Thy Kingdom come, thy will be done, in earth, Jesus prayed.

I Corinthians 15:50 says, "*Now this I say, brethren, that flesh and blood cannot inherit the kingdom of God.*" One of the things we find out is that the carnal nature, the carnal mind and worldly pursuits will not be a part the Kingdom of God. As a matter of fact, Jesus said in Luke 9:62, "*No man, having put his hand to the plough, and looking back, is fit for the kingdom of God.*" Therefore, there is a becoming fit and an accounting worthy. Looking back into our past will not make us ready for the Kingdom of God.

This manual is dedicated to the glory of God. As Jesus did, we want to, as found in Acts 28:31, "*preaching and teaching the kingdom of God, and teaching those things which concern the Lord Jesus Christ, with all confidence, no man forbidding him.*" That is what we are doing. That is what the Kingdom of God is. It is teaching the things concerning the Lord Jesus. May God bless you and enlighten your eyes, as Psalms 119:130 says, "*The entrance of thy words giveth light; it giveth understanding unto the simple.*" I pray that you not only receive this revelation of the Kingdom of God, but begin to walk in it. God bless you as you do so.

All my love,

Papa Sam

The Kingdom Of God

Chapter 1
What Is The Kingdom Of God?

The gospel of Christ is the gospel of the Kingdom of God. It is not just the message of salvation. It is the message of the ruler-ship of God in His people. The Kingdom of God is the kingly rule of God in the lives of His people. It refers to the recognition of the authority of God. The Kingdom of God comes into being wherever the kingly authority of God is acknowledged. Entering into (or inheriting) the Kingdom of God is the privilege of those who are born again, have received Jesus as their Savior, have been filled with the Holy Ghost, and who acknowledge and live by the rule of God.

I.   What Is The Kingdom Of God?

   A.   Word Definition

      1.   Kingdom in Hebrew – a rule, dominion, an empire, a realm; it comes from a root – to reign, to ascend the throne, to set up a king or induct into royalty. It is the realm, the dominion, the place of God's ruler-ship upon His throne. We willingly induct Him into that royalty as His people.
      2.   Kingdom in Greek – royalty, rule, realm; it comes from a root – a foundation of power, a sovereign

   A.   Scriptures Defining the Kingdom of God

      1.   Romans 14:17, "*17For the kingdom of God is not meat and drink; but righteousness, and peace, and joy in the Holy Ghost.*"

The Kingdom of God is righteousness. What does that mean? Righteousness is our salvation, our right standing with God. The Kingdom of God is allowing the rule of God and His righteousness to come forth in our lives. It's a revelation that all who we are, is bound up in His life. If we are in the Kingdom of God and Jesus is reigning in our life, we will be free from condemnation and guilt; we will be in right standing with God. It's a revelation that we are no longer sinners but have the righteousness of God within us; because, the sinless one lives within us. The only time I sin is when I turn from Him and embrace something of this world. So the Kingdom of God is living by the faith of the Son of God, because "*I am crucified with Christ: nevertheless I live; yet not I, but Christ liveth in me*" (Galatians 2:20).

The Kingdom of God is also peace. Isaiah 32:17 says, *"And the work of righteousness shall be peace; and the effect of righteousness quietness and assurance forever."* Righteousness creates within us the peace of God. Moreover, Romans 5:1 tells us, *"Therefore being justified by faith, we have peace with God through our Lord Jesus Christ."* When we allow the rule of God in our lives, peace will reign within us.

Thirdly, Romans 14 tells us that the Kingdom of God is *"joy in the Holy Ghost."* Jesus came that *"they might have life, and that they might have it more abundantly."* Jesus wants us to have joy and life abundantly in this life. Joy is different from happiness. Happiness is dependent upon circumstances. Happiness is temporal. Joy, on the other hand, is eternal because it is *"in the Holy Ghost."* Joy is not in our soulish members, but in our spirits. When we allow the rule of God in our lives, we can immediately enter into His presence and glory. We should never be far from the manifest presence of God. The word for presence in the Hebrew literally means that God is turning His face towards us and looking at us. When you are in the Kingdom of God, you are allowing that face to look at you continually. You are not going to do something dark and ugly if you know He is looking at you. We can experience His joy and glory in His Kingdom!

2. Luke 13:18-22 – *"¹⁸Then said he, Unto what is the kingdom of God like? and whereunto shall I resemble it? ¹⁹It is like a grain of mustard seed, which a man took, and cast into his garden; and it grew, and waxed a great tree; and the fowls of the air lodged in the branches of it. ²⁰And again he said, Whereunto shall I liken the kingdom of God? ²¹It is like leaven, which a woman took and hid in three measures of meal, till the whole was leavened. ²²And he went through the cities and villages, teaching, and journeying toward Jerusalem."*

3. I Corinthians 4:20 – *"For the kingdom of God is not in word, but in power."*

4. Luke 17:20-21 – *"²⁰And when he was demanded of the Pharisees, when the kingdom of God should come, he answered them and said, The kingdom of God cometh not with observation: ²¹Neither shall they say, Lo here! or, lo there! for, behold, the kingdom of God is within you."*

5. I Thessalonians 2:12 – *"That ye would walk worthy of God, who hath called you unto his kingdom and glory."*

6. I Corinthians 15:50 – *"Now this I say, brethren, that flesh and blood cannot inherit the kingdom of God; neither doth corruption inherit incorruption."*

7. Matthew 6:27-33 – *"²⁷Which of you by taking thought can add one cubit unto his stature? ²⁸And why take ye thought for raiment? Consider the lilies of the field, how they grow; they toil not, neither do they spin: ²⁹And yet I say unto you, That even Solomon in all his glory was not arrayed like one of these. ³⁰Wherefore, if God so clothe the grass of the field, which to day is, and to morrow is cast into the oven, shall he not much more clothe you, O ye of little faith? ³¹Therefore take no thought, saying, What shall we eat? or, What shall we drink? or, Wherewithal shall we be clothed? ³²(For after all these things do the Gentiles seek:) for your heavenly Father knoweth that ye have need of all these things. ³³But seek ye first the kingdom of God, and his righteousness; and all these things shall be added unto you."*

8. Mark 4:11 – *"And he said unto them, Unto you it is given to know the mystery of the kingdom of God: but unto them that are without, all these things are done in parables"*

9. Matthew 6:10 – *"Thy kingdom come. Thy will be done in earth, as it is in heaven."*

10. I John 4:17 – *"Herein is our love made perfect, that we may have boldness in the day of judgment: because as he is, so are we in this world."*

11. Luke 9:1-6 – *"¹Then he called his twelve disciples together, and gave them power and authority over all devils, and to cure diseases. ²And he sent them to preach the kingdom of God, and to heal the sick. ³And he said unto them, Take nothing for your journey, neither staves, nor scrip, neither bread, neither money; neither have two coats apiece. ⁴And whatsoever house ye enter into, there abide, and thence depart. ⁵And whosoever will not receive you, when ye go out of that city, shake off the very dust from your feet for a testimony against them. ⁶And they departed, and went through the towns, preaching the gospel, and healing every where."*

12. Luke 8:1 – *"And it came to pass afterward, that he went throughout every city and village, preaching and shewing the glad tidings of the kingdom of God: and the twelve were with him"*

13. Acts 14:22 – *"Confirming the souls of the disciples, and exhorting them to continue in the faith, and that we must through much tribulation enter into the kingdom of God."*

Through much trials, testing and affliction we enter into the Kingdom of God. The Kingdom of God is about a people who are overcoming the flesh, world and devil. They have learned through the trials of life to be free from guilt and condemnation, to live by His Grace and allow Him to rule within them completely.

14. Esther 4:13-14 – *"¹³Then Mordecai commanded to answer Esther, Think not with thyself that thou shalt escape in the king's house, more than all the Jews. ¹⁴For if thou altogether holdest thy peace at this time, then shall there enlargement and deliverance arise to the Jews from another place; but thou and thy father's house shall be destroyed: and who knoweth whether thou art come to the kingdom for such a time as this?"*

15. Luke 9:62 – *"And Jesus said unto him, No man, having put his hand to the plough, and looking back, is fit for the kingdom of God."*

If we are looking back, giving ourselves to sin and things we shouldn't be doing; then, we cannot walk in Kingdom principles. As believers, we can walk free from that. Sin is not to have dominion over us. This doesn't mean we lose our salvation, but we can lose our reward of brideship. What a man sows, the same shall he also reap. We will be judged by the things we have done. On the other hand, all we have to do is to allow what God has already done in us. We have been born of incorruptible seed. We just need to let the seed of God grow up inside of us and it will keep us!

B. What The Kingdom Of God Is Not

1. Romans 14:13-17 – *"¹³Let us not therefore judge one another any more: but judge this rather, that no man put a stumblingblock or an occasion to fall in his brother's way. ¹⁴I know, and am persuaded by the Lord Jesus, that there is nothing unclean of itself: but to him that esteemeth any thing to be unclean, to him it is unclean. ¹⁵But if thy brother be grieved with thy meat, now walkest thou not charitably. Destroy not him with thy meat, for whom Christ died. ¹⁶Let not then your good be evil spoken of: ¹⁷For the kingdom of God is not meat and drink; but righteousness, and peace, and joy in the Holy Ghost."*

When Paul is talking about meat and drink here, he is speaking of the rules and regulations that came under the law. However, the Kingdom of God is a kingdom of liberty, a kingdom of peace, righteousness and joy in the Holy Ghost. That is why it is so important to be baptized in the Holy Ghost. You cannot know the Holy Ghost in the kind of way God wants you to know Him if you are not baptized in the Holy Ghost.

2. Colossians 2:4, 8, 14, 16-17, 19-23 – *"⁴And this I say, lest any man should beguile you with enticing words...⁸Beware lest any man spoil you through philosophy and vain deceit, after the tradition of men, after the rudiments of the world, and not after Christ...¹⁴Blotting out the handwriting of ordinances that was against us, which was contrary to us, and took it out of the way, nailing it to his cross;...¹⁶Let no man therefore judge you in meat, or in drink, or in respect of an holyday, or of the new moon, or of the sabbath days: ¹⁷Which are a shadow of things to come; but the body is of Christ...¹⁹And not holding the Head, from which all the body by joints and bands having nourishment ministered, and knit together, increaseth with the increase of God ²⁰Wherefore if ye be dead with Christ from the rudiments of the world, why, as though living in the world, are ye subject to ordinances, ²¹(Touch not; taste not; handle not; ²²Which all are to perish with the using;) after the commandments and doctrines of men? ²³Which things have indeed a shew of wisdom in will worship, and humility, and neglecting of the body; not in any honour to the satisfying of the flesh."*

When we get so involved with rules and regulations, we forget Jesus. When we let go of the head (Jesus), we frustrate the grace of God. When we do that, grace can't help us in our fight against sin because we are trying on our own. However, man has already proven he cannot keep the law on his own. We must understand the revelation that apart from the grace of God, we are nothing. It's impossible for us to keep the law!

    a.   Titus 3:5-7 – "*5Not by works of righteousness which we have done, but according to his mercy he saved us, by the washing of regeneration, and renewing of the Holy Ghost; 6Which he shed on us abundantly through Jesus Christ our Saviour; 7That being justified by his grace, we should be made heirs according to the hope of eternal life.*"

    b.   Ephesians 2:8-9 – "*8For by grace are ye saved through faith; and that not of yourselves: it is the gift of God: 9Not of works, lest any man should boast.*"

    c.   I Timothy 4:1-8 – "*1Now the Spirit speaketh expressly, that in the latter times some shall depart from the faith, giving heed to seducing spirits, and doctrines of devils; 2Speaking lies in hypocrisy; having their conscience seared with a hot iron; 3Forbidding to marry, and commanding to abstain from meats, which God hath created to be received with thanksgiving of them which believe and know the truth. 4For every creature of God is good, and nothing to be refused, if it be received with thanksgiving: 5For it is sanctified by the word of God and prayer. 6If thou put the brethren in remembrance of these things, thou shalt be a good minister of Jesus Christ, nourished up in the words of faith and of good doctrine, whereunto thou hast attained. 7But refuse profane and old wives' fables, and exercise thyself rather unto godliness. 8For bodily exercise profiteth little: but godliness is profitable unto all things, having promise of the life that now is, and of that which is to come.*"

People telling us what we should and should not eat or drink is exactly what Paul is talking about in Colossians 2. The Kingdom of God is not rules and regulations or the traditions of men. It is the rule of God in the hearts of His people. This rule of the Kingdom comes under one title: Jesus. We don't sin anymore because Jesus lives in our hearts. Instead of trying to follow the law to not commit adultery, we do not commit adultery because Jesus lives in our hearts. We don't have to fall into sin anymore because we love Jesus. We don't need a law anymore telling us not to do anything because Jesus lives in us and the Spirit of God tells us not to sin. As Hebrews 8:10 states "*I will put my laws into their mind, and write them in their hearts: and I will be to them a God, and they shall be to me a people.*"

We have to be delivered from the law which says, touch not, taste not, handle not. Jesus said it is not what goes in a man that defiles him, but that which comes out of him (Matthew 15:11). Therefore, instead of trying to follow rules and regulations, we come into the revelation that it is a good thing that the heart be established with grace.

As God's people we are delivered from the traditions and rules of men. I believe many in the body of Christ have been deceived by a spirit of anti-Christ that tells us that as soon as we are saved, we have to start following all kinds of rules and regulations. We are told that if we do not follow them, we are in danger of losing the thing we just received. We could do nothing to get saved. We can do nothing to lose our salvation. We must understand that in the Kingdom of God grace triumphs over works!

    d.   Hebrews 9:7-12 – "*7But into the second went the high priest alone once every year, not without blood, which he offered for himself, and for the errors of the people: 8The Holy Ghost this signifying, that the way into the holiest of all was not yet made manifest, while as the first tabernacle was yet standing: 9Which was a figure for the time then present, in which were offered both gifts and sacrifices, that could not make him that did the service perfect, as pertaining to the conscience; 10Which stood only in meats and drinks, and divers washings, and carnal ordinances, imposed on them until the time of reformation. 11But Christ being come an high priest of good things to come, by a greater and more perfect tabernacle, not made with hands, that is to say, not of this building; 12Neither by the blood of goats and calves, but by his own blood he entered in once into the holy place, having obtained eternal redemption for us."*

    e.   Hebrews 13:9 – *"Be not carried about with divers and strange doctrines. For it is a good thing that the heart be established with grace; not with meats, which have not profited them that have been occupied therein."*

Those that were occupied therein were the priests who were given over to eating and drinking under the law. John 1:17 says, *"For the law was given by Moses, but grace and truth came by Jesus Christ."* Other translations of this verse are:

"Moses gave us only the law with its rigid demands and merciless justice, while Jesus Christ brought us loving forgiveness as well."
"For while the Law was given through Moses, grace (unearned, undeserved favor and spiritual blessing) and truth came through Jesus Christ."
"Because the law, through the intermediate agency of Moses was given, but the aforementioned grace and truth came through Jesus Christ."

"Intermediate agency" means that the law was given for a time, not to be an eternal truth. The law was given for one simple reason: In the Old Testament they didn't have a Savior that would tell them immediately if something were wrong. They didn't have a witness of the Spirit like we have now.

All of us have a hole in us that longs for order, for direction, and for somebody to be our ruler. But like the little colt upon whom never a man sat, we were never meant to be ridden by a man. God never wanted Israel to have a king; because, He was their king. Adam didn't need Eve; but, God granted it. Eve was in Adam already; man was both male and female at that time. What happened was that God was not enough for Adam. God has never proven to be enough for anybody. But somehow, someday, somewhere, some way, there will come forth a people who will say to Him, "All my springs are in thee. All that I am and ever want to be is bound up in You, the bundle of life." That is what we need, not more rules and regulations. So that it is no longer I that liveth, but Christ that liveth in me. He is the only one with authority; therefore we are not ruling our lives, but He is!

Right now God is trying to get a people, a remnant, who will allow Him to rule and reign. He is trying to get His Kingdom operating in our lives. Every day we allow the rule of God and let Him sit on the throne of our hearts. Anything that rises up that is going to take Him off the throne, we put it down. It is that simple. We start by making Him the sovereign. That means He is the only King and Potentate, the only ruler in our lives.

Religion wants men to control you. The word itself means "to bind." All religion seeks is to control you. Jeremiah says, the priests bear rule by their means and my people love to have it so. The priests control us and manipulate us and we just love it. Because, then we don't have to be responsible. We let somebody else be responsible for our lives. We don't have to take ownership for anything. We can blame the pastor, the elders, but ultimately the blame is ours. We were the ones who chose to come under that blind leader. At some point, there has got to be a reformation in the Body of Christ. A revolution of truth. We have got to stop being politically correct and not saying things because they might hurt somebody. Because if we don't say the truth they might just lose brideship, which is our reward. And for eternity there will be weeping and gnashing of teeth because they will not have entered into what they could have received, had somebody told them.

Babylon is God's arch enemy and it lives in the Body of Christ. Men manipulating God's people and saying something contrary to what God is saying. The Sons of God are led by the spirit of God, not by the words of men.

So the Kingdom of God is not about following rules and regulations anymore, meats and drink, and the laws and traditions of men. Jesus invites us in Matthew 11:29-30 to *"Take my yoke upon you, and learn of me; for I am meek and lowly in heart: and ye shall find rest unto your souls. [30]For my yoke is easy, and my burden is light."* We might not be perfect now, totally victorious and abiding in His Kingdom; but, we see the place afar off. We see a perfect day coming when you and I by the grace of God enter into fullness, enter into son-ship, enter into the Kingdom of God. All that we need has been provided for by our sovereign ruler. Jesus is King of kings and Lord of lords. The Kingdom of God is about making Jesus sit upon the throne of our hearts and allowing Him to rule and reign within us by His grace. We don't need a bunch of rules and regulations anymore. All we need is Jesus on the throne. If He is on the throne, then we can walk in all God ever wants for our lives! The Kingdom of God is when we live under the rulership of Jesus Christ!

Chapter 2
Principles Of The Kingdom Of God

I.   Scriptures Defining And Illuminating The Kingdom of God

A.   Matthew 21:28-32 - "*28But what think ye? A certain man had two sons; and he came to the first, and said, Son, go work to day in my vineyard. 29He answered and said, I will not: but afterward he repented, and went. 30And he came to the second, and said likewise. And he answered and said, I go, sir: and went not. 31Whether of them twain did the will of his father? They say unto him, The first. Jesus saith unto them, Verily I say unto you, That the publicans and the harlots go into the kingdom of God before you. 32For John came unto you in the way of righteousness, and ye believed him not: but the publicans and the harlots believed him: and ye, when ye had seen it, repented not afterward, that ye might believe him.*"

We find in life that there are those that say they will do and never do it, and those that seemingly do not want to do it but end up doing what is on God's heart anyway. A true kingdom person is always going to have the heart of the kingdom rather than their own selfishness. It is not those who say, but those who do that will experience the Kingdom of God. They will have a meek and lowly heart. A heart to do, to submit, and to serve. Jesus said I did not come to be ministered unto but to minister. The prevailing wind in the body of Christ, however, is to be ministered unto, rather than to minister. What is so amazing about this passage in Matthew is that a person so seemingly horrible as a publican or a harlot is greater than someone who may appear to espouse to great spiritual truths simply because they did the will of God by repenting and believing Jesus. Kingdom people ultimately show God by their actions. God is going to only have people in the Kingdom of God who have allowed God to rule and reign in their lives.

Scriptures that declare God is a God of knowledge and God looks at what we do more than just what we say. God wants us to have Kingdom hearts that do not just say, but do.

1.   I Samuel 2:3 - "*Talk no more so exceeding proudly; let not arrogancy come out of your mouth: for the Lord is a God of knowledge, and by him actions are weighed.*"

2.   I John 2:6 - "*He that saith he abideth in him ought himself also so to walk, even as he walked.*"

3.   II Corinthians 8:10-11 – "*And herein I give my advice: for this is expedient for you, who have begun before, not only to do, but also to be forward a year ago. 11Now therefore perform the doing*

of it; that as there was a readiness to will, so there may be a performance also out of that which ye have."

4. Acts 17:30 - *"And the times of this ignorance God winked at; but now commandeth all men every where to repent."*
5. Matthew 26:39 – *"And he went a little further, and fell on his face, and prayed, saying O my Father, if it be possible, let this cup pass from me: nevertheless not as I will, but as thou wilt."* Jesus in the garden of Gethsemane.

B. Matthew 6:24-33 - *"³¹Therefore take no thought, saying, What shall we eat? Or, What shall we drink? Or, Wherewithal shall we be clothed? ³²(For after all these things do the Gentiles seek:) for your heavenly Father knoweth that ye have need of all these things. ³³But seek ye first the kingdom of God, and his righteousness; and all these things shall be added unto you."*

This Scripture teaches us that all of the things we need for our lives (both naturally and spiritually), the things we eat, the clothes we wear, etc., will be provided by our heavenly Father if we seek first His Kingdom and righteousness. Take no thought for your life. This is the true Kingdom Heart. Kingdom people serve and seek God and not this world's goods or acceptance from this world. We must not concern ourselves constantly with earthly, natural things. We are exhorted to not take thought for our life, our provision and sustenance.

Jesus said in Luke 12:15, *"For a man's life consisteth not in the abundance of the things which he possesseth."* What happens is that the world gets mixed in with the church and I believe this mixture is there today. Babylon and the religious system is all about prosperity. Babylon is all about you having all kinds of blessings, money and prosperity. Jesus did not die on the cross just so we could be rich and have money. If we are going to be in the Kingdom of God, we need to stop being burdened down with our natural lives and things pertaining to what we eat, drink and put on, how we are going to pay our bills, how we are going to survive, etc. At some point we must stop and first begin to seek His Kingdom. God will allow situations in our lives where we are forced to believe Him for our provision. Operating in the Kingdom of God is being in a position of intimacy with the Lord where we first go to Him and rest in His provision for our lives. Kingdom people are sure about their God! They know God has taken care of them. As I John 4:16 tells us, *"And we have known and believed the love that God hath to us."* Below are ample Scriptures that encourage us that if we would seek the Lord, our needs will be met.

1. Philippians 4:19 - *"But my God shall supply all your need according to his riches in glory by Christ Jesus."*
2. Psalms 84:11 - *"For the Lord God is a sun and shield: the Lord will give grace and glory: no good thing will he withhold from them that walk uprightly."*
3. II Peter 1:3-4 - *"³According as his divine power hath given unto us all things that pertain unto life and godliness, through the knowledge of him that hath called us to glory and virtue: ⁴Whereby are given unto us exceeding great and precious promises: that by these ye might be partakers of the divine nature, having escaped the corruption that is in the world through lust."*
4. Psalms 23:1 - *"The Lord is my shepherd; I shall not want."*
5. Psalms 34:9-10 - *"⁹O fear the Lord, ye his saints: for there is no want to them that fear him. ¹⁰The young lions do lack, and suffer hunger: but they that seek the Lord shall not want any good thing."*
6. II Corinthians 9:8-12 - *"⁸And God is able to make all grace abound toward you; that ye, always having all sufficiency in all things, may abound to every good work: ⁹(As it is written, He hath dispersed abroad; he hath given to the poor: his righteousness remaineth for ever. ¹⁰Now he that ministereth seed to the sower both minister bread for your food, and multiply your seed sown, and increase the fruits of your righteousness;) ¹¹Being enriched in every thing to all bountifulness, which causeth through us thanksgiving to God. ¹²For the administration of this service not only supplieth the want of the saints, but is abundant also by many thanksgivings unto God."*
7. Deuteronomy 8:6-9 - *"...⁹A land wherein thou shalt eat bread without scarceness, thou shalt not lack any thing in it; a land whose stones are iron, and out of whose hills thou mayest dig brass."*

8. Psalms 37:25-26 - "*25I have been young, and now am old; yet have I not seen the righteous forsaken, nor his seed begging bread. 26He is ever merciful, and lendeth; and his seed is blessed.*"

C. Matthew 19:16-24 - "*21Jesus said unto him, If thou wilt be perfect, go and sell that thou hast, and give to the poor, and thou shalt have treasure in heaven: and come and follow me... 24And again I say unto you, It is easier for a camel to go through the eye of a needle, than for a rich man to enter into the kingdom of God.*"

This was a proverb in common use among the Jews and is still common among the Arabians. It denoted that a thing is impossible or exceedingly difficult. It's not to be taken literally. It simply points out the difficulty of a rich man to be in the Kingdom. The reason for this is because most people do not possess their riches; they allow their riches to possess them. Being rich is not a sin. The sin is loving money and making it an idol in our lives.

1. I John 2:15 - "*Love not the world, neither the things that are in the world. If any man love the world, the love of the Father is not in him.*"

   a. Luke 16:15 - "*And he said unto them, Ye are they which justify yourselves before men; but God knoweth your hearts: for that which is highly esteemed among men is abomination in the sight of God.*"
   b. Luke 6:20-26 - "*20And he lifted up his eyes on his disciples, and said, Blessed be ye poor: for yours is the kingdom of God...*"
   c. I Timothy 6:17-19 - "*17Charge them that are rich in this world, that they be not highminded, nor trust in uncertain riches, but in the living God, who giveth us richly all things to enjoy; 18That they do good, that they be rich in good works, ready to distribute, willing to communicate; 19Laying up in store for themselves a good foundation against the time to come, that they may lay hold on eternal life.*"
   d. James 1:9-11 - "*9Let the brother of low degree rejoice in that he is exalted: 10But the rich, in that he is made low: because as the flower of the grass he shall pass away. 11For the sun is no sooner risen with a burning heat, but it withereth the grass, and the flower thereof falleth, and the grace of the fashion of it perisheth: so also shall the rich man fade away in his ways.*"
   e. James 5:1-3 - "*5Go to now, ye rich men, weep and howl for your miseries that shall come upon you. 2Your riches are corrupted, and your garments are motheaten. 3Your gold and silver is cankered; and the rust of them shall be a witness against you, and shall eat your flesh as it were fire. Ye have heaped treasure together for the last days.*"

2. Proverbs 30:8-9 - "*8Remove far from me vanity and lies: give me neither poverty nor riches; feed me with food convenient for me: 9Lest I be full, and deny thee, and say, Who is the Lord? or lest I be poor, and steal, and take the name of my God in vain.*"
3. A camel is a beast of burden carrying burdens. He is the rich man. His riches constitute a burden. His riches come from others, he spends it for others and must ultimately leave it for others. We must unburden ourselves from the things of the world and seek and concentrate on the "Kingdom of God" or the needs and riches of others. This is the true heart of a Kingdom disciple, where it's not about him, but others.
4. Proverbs 23:4-5 - "*4Labour not to be rich: cease from thine own wisdom. 5Wilt thou set thine eyes upon that which is not? for riches certainly make themselves wings; they fly away as an eagle toward heaven.*"
5. Proverbs 28:20-22 - "*20A faithful man shall abound with blessings: but he that maketh haste to be rich shall not be innocent. 21To have respect of persons is not good: because for a piece of bread that man will transgress. 22He that hasteth to be rich hath an evil eye, and considereth not that poverty shall come upon him.*"
6. Jeremiah 9:23-24 - "*23Thus saith the Lord, Let not the wise man glory in his wisdom, neither let the mighty man glory in his might, let not the rich man glory in his riches: 24But let him that*

glorieth glory in this, that he understandeth and knoweth me, that I am the Lord which exercise lovingkindness, judgment, and righteousness, in the earth: for in these things I delight, saith the Lord."

7. I Timothy 6:5-12 - "...*9*But they that will be rich fall into temptation and a snare, and into many foolish and hurtful lusts, which drown men in destruction and perdition."

8. James 2:5-6 - "*5*Hearken, my beloved brethren, Hath not God chosen the poor of this world rich in faith, and heirs of the kingdom which he hath promised to them that love him? *6*But ye have despised the poor. Do not rich men oppress you, and draw you before the judgment seats?"

9. Mark 4:18-19 - "*18*And these are they which are sown among thorns; such as hear the word, *19*And the cares of this world, and the deceitfulness of riches, and the lusts of other things entering in, choke the word, and it becometh unfruitful."

10. Proverbs 27:24 - "For riches are not for ever: and doth the crown endure to every generation?"

11. Proverbs 11:28 - "He that trusteth in his riches shall fall: but the righteous shall flourish as a branch."

12. Psalms 62:10 - "Trust not in oppression, and become not vain in robbery: if riches increase, set not your heart upon them."

13. Psalms 49:6-12 – "They that trust in their wealth, and boast themselves in the multitude of their riches; *7*None of them can by any means redeem his brother, nor give to God a ransom for him: *8*(For the redemption of their soul is precious, and it ceaseth for ever:) *9*That he should still live for ever, and not see corruption. *10*For he seeth that wise men die, likewise the fool and the brutish person perish, and leave their wealth to others. *11*Their inward thought is, that their houses shall continue for ever, and their dwelling places to all generations; they call their lands after their own names. *12*Nevertheless man being in honour abideth not: he is like the beasts that perish."

14. II Chronicles 1:8-12 - "*8*And Solomon said unto God, Thou hast shewed great mercy unto David my father, and hast made me to reign in his stead. *9*Now, O Lord God, let thy promise unto David my father be established: for thou hast made me king over a people like the dust of the earth in multitude. *10*Give me now wisdom and knowledge, that I may go out and come in before this people: for who can judge this thy people, that is so great? *11*And God said to Solomon, Because this was in thine heart, and thou hast not asked riches, wealth, or honour, nor the life of thine enemies, neither yet hast asked long life; but hast asked wisdom and knowledge for thyself, that thou mayest judge my people, over whom I have made thee king: *12*Wisdom and knowledge is granted unto thee; and I will give thee riches, and wealth, and honour, such as none of the kings have had that have been before thee, neither shall there any after thee have the like."

Chapter 3
The King Of This Kingdom

As we are learning, the Kingdom of God is not a natural, outward kingdom; moreover it is a spiritual one in the lives of His people. However, not everyone in the body of Christ is walking in this Kingdom. It is for those who are bowing to the Lordship of Jesus and His Kingdom. His Kingdom is coming on earth as it is in heaven. When we really start living like Jesus on earth, His Kingdom will come and then His Will can be done. God wants us to walk in His Kingdom on earth and not just when we get to heaven. Jesus is coming back for a people who will crown Him King. Many believe that a rapture will save them while they are just holding on. But for the sons of God, we are looking for His Kingdom to be alive and operating on this earth.

In this lesson, we will look specifically at the King of the Kingdom. Since the Kingdom of God is within us, I believe there is a stirring and a hunger for not just more of God, but for His rule, His dominion in our lives completely in the earth. If you and I do not allow Jesus to be King of His Kingdom, then nothing is going to take place and His Kingdom will not come.

The Kingdom is the Lord's and not ours. A lot of the preaching that's done today makes it seem like the Kingdom is ours. Many have the mindset that it's all about us and what we get in the Kingdom. However, is He truly Lord over our lives? Does He have dominion? Can He walk into our lives and say "do this" and you do it? What if He says "I want that thing, give it to me now" or "I don't like the way you've been acting. Cut it out."? What happens in us when Jesus wants to be Lord in every area of our lives? Dominion means He dominates our life. I can't think of anyone in the universe I'd want to dominate me other than Jesus. There's only room for one king. It has to be, it must be, we've got to let it be Jesus.

I. Psalms 22:28-31 – "*28For the kingdom is the Lord's: and he is the governor among the nations. 29All they that be fat upon earth shall eat and worship: all they that go down to the dust shall bow before him: and none can keep alive his own soul. 30A seed shall serve him; it shall be accounted to the Lord for a generation. 31They shall come, and shall declare his righteousness unto a people that shall be born, that he hath done this.*"

   A. Word definitions:

      1) Governor in Hebrew – in the sense of massing, a foreign nation, troop of animals, flight of locusts

2) Kingdom in Hebrew – something ruled, a realm

B. Other translations of verse 28:

"For the kingship and the kingdom are the Lord's, and He is ruler over the nations."
"God has taken charge; from now on He has the last word."
"For dominion belongs to the Lord and He rules over the nations."
"For royal power belongs to the Lord...and He shall have dominion over the nations."

The Kingdom is the Lord's and He is the governor among the nations. A lot of people will disagree and say that satan is the god of this world, as 2 Corinthians 4:4 refers to satan as the *"god of this world."* In the Greek, however, the passage should read that satan is the "god of this age". An age has a beginning and an end. And whatever he did have rule over, Jesus triumphed over him and made an open show of him on the cross. Jesus took the keys of hell and death back from satan. Therefore, satan is in control of nothing, except for the things we allow him. We must believe that the Kingdom is truly the Lord's. Satan cannot have authority over those who abide in Jesus. So when we make Jesus the King of our lives, all other rule and dominion have no more power over us.

Jesus is the governor among the nations. God wants to send His people to the nations to make disciples of the nations. We can go in His authority as long as we are under His authority. We must be under godly authority (i.e. father ministry) and under the King of king's authority. When we are, we can put our foot down everywhere and it will belong to us. I remember what God spoke to me as I started traveling to the nations. He quoted to me Joshua 1:3, *"Every place that the sole of your foot shall tread upon, that have I given unto you."* So as I travel, I know that Jesus is the Governor of the nations. Every demon in those countries must bow because the Kingdom of God is here. His rule is inside of us and we must expand that Kingdom throughout the earth.

C. Companion Scriptures Extolling the King:

1. Psalms 45:6-11 – *"[6]Thy throne, O God, is for ever and ever: the sceptre of thy kingdom is a right sceptre. [7]Thou lovest righteousness, and hatest wickedness: therefore God, thy God, hath anointed thee with the oil of gladness above thy fellows. [8]All thy garments smell of myrrh, and aloes, and cassia, out of the ivory palaces, whereby they have made thee glad. [9]Kings' daughters were among thy honourable women: upon thy right hand did stand the queen in gold of Ophir. [10]Hearken, O daughter, and consider, and incline thine ear; forget also thine own people, and thy father's house; [11]So shall the king greatly desire thy beauty: for he is thy Lord; and worship thou him."*

   a. Psalms 45 is quoted in Hebrews 1:8, which, when read in context, explains that Jesus is God and King because He is called that by the Father. *"But unto the Son he saith, Thy throne, O God, is for ever and ever: a scepter of righteousness is the scepter of thy kingdom."* (Hebrews 1:8) Moreover, Jesus has a scepter, which speaks of His authority and rule.

   b. Word definitions:

      1) Throne in Hebrew – properly covered, canopied, seat, stools; it comes from a root that means – to plump up, fill up the hollow places, to cover, to overwhelm
      2) Sceptre in Hebrew – a branch or stick, for ruling, punishing, fighting, or walking

   c. Other translations of verse 6:

   "Your throne is God's throne, the scepter of your royal rule measures right living."
   "Thy throne, O God, is age enduring, and for ever; a sceptre of uprightness is the sceptre of thy kingdom."

"Your throne, God, will last for ever and ever; you rule your kingdom with a sceptre of equity (justice)."
"God your throne will last forever; you rule your kingdom with fairness."
"Your throne O God is permanent; the sceptre of your kingdom is a sceptre of justice."
"Your seat of power O God is for ever, and ever, the rod of your kingdom is a rod of honor."

1) Scriptures For His Scepter: (His Authority)

    a) Genesis 49:10 – *"The sceptre shall not depart from Judah, nor a lawgiver from between his feet, until Shiloh come; and unto him shall the gathering of the people be."*

I believe Jesus wants to give His authority to a people. I believe this Scripture is saying that if we are true worshippers (and prove that over years of faithfulness in our worship to Him; no matter the circumstances or how we feel, we just keep worshipping our King in every area of our lives), then God will slip into our hands His scepter, His authority.

    b) Hebrews 1:8 – *"The scepter of righteousness is the scepter of thy kingdom."*

His scepter is a scepter of righteousness and uprightness. It speaks of right-living and honor. We cannot get His scepter unless we walk uprightly, unless we honor God, unless we are living right. When Jesus spoke, it says of Him in John 7:46, *"Never man spake like this man."* Also, Mark 1:27 states of Jesus' words and authority, *"For with authority commandeth he even the unclean spirits, and they do obey him."* Jesus was carrying the scepter everywhere He went. His words were backed with power and authority.

    c) Esther 5:2 – *"And it was so, when the king saw Esther the queen standing in the court, that she obtained favour in his sight: and the king held out to Esther the golden sceptre that was in his hand. So Esther drew near, and touched the top of the sceptre."*

If we want the scepter, the authority of God in our life, then we must lose ourselves. We have to die to our ambitions, wants, desires and will! We must say *"Thy kingdom come. Thy will be done in earth"* (Matthew 6:10). That earth speaks of our lives. There has to be a cry in all of us that wants King Jesus to rule, reign and have dominion in us! If we get serious enough, then He will hear us and come and truly reign through us.

d. Jesus Is The King Of The Kingdom

    1) Psalms 2:6-12 – *"[6]Yet have I set my king upon my holy hill of Zion. [7]I will declare the decree: the Lord hath said unto me, Thou art my Son; this day have I begotten thee. [8]Ask of me, and I shall give thee the heathen for thine inheritance, and the uttermost parts of the earth for thy possession. [9]Thou shalt break them with a rod of iron; thou shalt dash them in pieces like a potter's vessel. [10]Be wise now therefore, O ye kings: be instructed, ye judges of the earth. [11]Serve the Lord with fear, and rejoice with trembling. [12]Kiss the Son, lest he be angry, and ye perish from the way, when his wrath is kindled but a little. Blessed are all they that put their trust in him."*

    2) Psalms 10:16 – *"The Lord is King for ever and ever: the heathen are perished out of his land."*

    3) Psalms 24:7-10 – *"[7]Lift up your heads, O ye gates; and be ye lift up, ye everlasting doors; and the King of glory shall come in. [8]Who is this King of glory? The Lord strong and mighty, the Lord mighty in battle. [9]Lift up your heads, O ye gates; even lift them up, ye everlasting doors; and the King of glory shall come in. [10]Who is this King of glory? The Lord of hosts, he is the King of glory. Selah."*

What is the gate that we must open? It is the gate of our hearts, our true selves, the areas of our souls where we never let anyone in. That is the gate we must open up and say, "The King of glory shall come in and I shall bow to Him from this moment on."

Jesus is the King of glory! The glory doesn't come in our lives to bless us. It comes because Jesus wants to come and reign. The glory of God is the essence of who He is. Are we going to invite the King of glory to become the governor, to have dominion and rule in our lives?

4) Psalms 29:10 – *"The Lord sitteth upon the flood; yea, the Lord sitteth King for ever."*

What does it mean when it says that God sits upon the flood? The floods speak of His glory and presence as well as a multitude of people. John 7:38 says, *"Out of his belly shall flow rivers of living water."* Jesus sits upon that glory as it flows out of us. This is Him reigning as we worship and praise Him. Then, He can begin to operate within us. The Kingdom of God is more than just going to church. It is the reality of where we live in His abiding presence.

5) Psalms 47:2-9 – *"2For the Lord most high is terrible; he is a great King over all the earth. 3He shall subdue the people under us, and the nations under our feet. 4He shall choose our inheritance for us, the excellency of Jacob whom he loved. Selah. 5God is gone up with a shout, the Lord with the sound of a trumpet. 6Sing praises to God, sing praises: sing praises unto our King, sing praises. 7For God is the King of all the earth: sing ye praises with understanding. 8God reigneth over the heathen: God sitteth upon the throne of his holiness. 9The princes of the people are gathered together, even the people of the God of Abraham: for the shields of the earth belong unto God: he is greatly exalted."*

a) Terrible in Hebrew – to fear; morally, to revere; cause to frighten, to be afraid, to put in fear, to dread, to be held in reverence

(1) Scriptures Concerning God As Terrible:

(a) Deuteronomy 7:21 – *"Thou shalt not be affrighted at them: for the Lord thy God is among you, a mighty God and terrible."*

(b) Deuteronomy 10:17 – *"For the Lord your God is God of gods, and Lord of lords, a great God, a mighty, and a terrible, which regardeth not persons, nor taketh reward"*

(c) Nehemiah 9:32 – *"Now therefore, our God, the great, the mighty, and the terrible God, who keepest covenant and mercy, let not all the trouble seem little before thee, that hath come upon us, on our kings, on our princes, and on our priests, and on our prophets, and on our fathers, and on all thy people, since the time of the kings of Assyria unto this day."*

(d) Psalms 66:3-8 – *"3Say unto God, How terrible art thou in thy works! through the greatness of thy power shall thine enemies submit themselves unto thee. 4All the earth shall worship thee, and shall sing unto thee; they shall sing to thy name. Selah. 5Come and see the works of God: he is terrible in his doing toward the children of men. 6He turned the sea into dry land: they went through the flood on foot: there did we rejoice in him. 7He ruleth by his power for ever; his eyes behold the nations: let not the rebellious exalt themselves. Selah. 8O bless our God, ye people, and make the voice of his praise to be heard."*

(e) Psalms 68:35 – *"O God, thou art terrible out of thy holy places: the God of Israel is he that giveth strength and power unto his people. Blessed be God."*

(f) Psalms 99:1-5 – "*¹The Lord reigneth; let the people tremble: he sitteth between the cherubims; let the earth be moved. ²The Lord is great in Zion; and he is high above all the people. ³Let them praise thy great and terrible name; for it is holy. ⁴The king's strength also loveth judgment; thou dost establish equity, thou executest judgment and righteousness in Jacob. ⁵Exalt ye the Lord our God, and worship at his footstool; for he is holy.*"

(g) Jeremiah 20:11 – "*But the Lord is with me as a mighty terrible one: therefore my persecutors shall stumble, and they shall not prevail: they shall be greatly ashamed; for they shall not prosper: their everlasting confusion shall never be forgotten.*"

(h) Joel 2:11 – "*And the Lord shall utter his voice before his army: for his camp is very great: for he is strong that executeth his word: for the day of the Lord is great and very terrible; and who can abide it?*"

(i) Isaiah 64:3 – "*When thou didst terrible things which we looked not for, thou camest down, the mountains flowed down at thy presence.*"

6) Psalms 48:1-3 – "*¹Great is the Lord, and greatly to be praised in the city of our God, in the mountain of his holiness. ²Beautiful for situation, the joy of the whole earth, is mount Zion, on the sides of the north, the city of the great King. ³God is known in her palaces for a refuge.*"

7) Psalms 95:3 – "*For the Lord is a great God, and a great King above all gods.*"

8) Psalms 149:2 – "*Let Israel rejoice in him that made him: let the children of Zion be joyful in their King.*"

9) Proverbs 20:28 – "*Mercy and truth preserve the king: and his throne is upholden by mercy.*"

10) Proverbs 24:21 – "*My son, fear thou the Lord and the king: and meddle not with them that are given to change*"

11) Song of Solomon 1:4 – "*Draw me, we will run after thee: the king hath brought me into his chambers: we will be glad and rejoice in thee, we will remember thy love more than wine: the upright love thee.*"

12) Isaiah 6:1-8 "*In the year that king Uzziah died I saw also the Lord sitting upon a throne, high and lifted up, and his train filled the temple...*"

II. More Scriptures On His Kingdom:

A. Psalms 103:19 – "*The Lord hath prepared his throne in the heavens; and his kingdom ruleth over all.*"

B. Psalms 145:10-13 – "*¹⁰All thy works shall praise thee, O Lord; and thy saints shall bless thee. ¹¹They shall speak of the glory of thy kingdom, and talk of thy power; ¹²To make known to the sons of men his mighty acts, and the glorious majesty of his kingdom. ¹³Thy kingdom is an everlasting kingdom, and thy dominion endureth throughout all generations.*"

C. Daniel 4:17, 25 – "*¹⁷This matter is by the decree of the watchers, and the demand by the word of the holy ones: to the intent that the living may know that the most High ruleth in the kingdom of men, and giveth it to whomsoever he will, and setteth up over it the basest of men...²⁵That they shall drive thee from men, and thy dwelling shall be with the beasts of the field, and they shall make thee to eat grass as oxen, and they shall wet thee with the dew of heaven, and seven times shall pass over thee, till thou know that the most High ruleth in the kingdom of men, and giveth it to whomsoever he will.*"

God wants us to walk in His authority as well. Jesus promised to us in John 14:12, "*He that believeth on me, the words that I do shall he so also; and greater works than these shall he do; because I go unto my father.*" Why don't we see these greater works? I believe it is because there is not a people humble enough to handle the greatness of God working through them. We must die to ourselves, so that He can live through us. It's not just about talk anymore. The Kingdom must be the Lord's! Our ministry should never be ours. It should be His and His alone. There is a place in God where we can be so enveloped in Him and His glory that our lives will be transformed and we will start living free from sin and begin to walk in real, God-given authority. We, like Jesus, are to be "*a kingdom of priests, and a holy nation*" (Exodus 19:6). When we allow what God is right now in glory to live in our lives, then that is the Kingdom of God. As we allow that to continue in our lives, it will continue to grow and prosper in our lives. It will then agitate and infect other people till the kingdom begins to grow. When we worship together as a people, we form a throne. Then, King Jesus comes and sits upon that throne, as Psalms 50:2 states, "*Out of Zion, the perfection of beauty, God hath shined.*"

Chapter 4
My Kingdom Is Not Of This World

We want to look in this lesson at the truth that the Kingdom of God is not of this world. Actually, the Kingdom of God has very little to do with this world at all. *"The kingdom of God is not meat and drink; but righteousness, and peace, and joy in the Holy Ghost,"* Romans 14:17 tells us. It has nothing to do with natural things. His kingdom is a spiritual one. One of the things we find in Scriptures is that people were looking for God's kingdom to come naturally. It says in Luke 17:20, *"And when he was demanded of the Pharisees, when the kingdom of God should come..."* They were looking for a natural kingdom to be restored to their nation. But Jesus answered, *"The kingdom of God cometh not with observation"* (verse 20). This means that all you can see is the effects of the kingdom manifested in somebody's life, as they are operating under the anointing and Spirit of God. We need to stop looking for it naturally. For those who are looking for things to happen with natural Israel and for another rebuilt temple and sacrifices, I believe they are in great error. For one thing, Jesus is the lamb slain before the foundation of the whole earth. To go back to the slaying of animals again would be sacrilegious. The Kingdom of God has nothing to do with these things naturally, for *"The kingdom of God is within you"* (Luke 17:21).

Jesus finishes answering the Pharisees demand of the coming of the kingdom in Luke 17:24, by saying, *"For as lightning, that lighteneth out of the one part under heaven, shineth unto the other part under heaven; so shall also the Son of man be in his day."* The day of the Son of man is the day of the manifestation of the sons of God. Jesus has done everything He is ever going to do. He sat down at the right hand of God the Father. He is now expecting a people to come forth to perfection in His name. Therefore, Jesus is saying that you will miss the day of the Son of man and not see it when you are looking for things to take place naturally. The coming of His Kingdom is the unseen Jesus coming forth inside of His people, changing their soulish man into His glorious image.

Moreover, since the Kingdom of God is not natural, I feel our emphasis in the body of Christ should never be over natural things, such as politics, the government and things that pertain unto this life. Of course we are to *"Render to Caesar the things that are Caesar's, and to God the things that are God's"* (Mark 12:17). We are to be good citizens and fulfill our duties in this earth. But with true kingdom people comes the revelation that the Kingdom of God has nothing to do with this life. II Corinthians 4:18 states, *"While we look not at the things which are seen, but at the things which are not seen: for the things which are seen are temporal* [Greek = subject to change]; *but the things which are not seen are eternal."* True kingdom people have their eyes fixed upon a spiritual kingdom with Jesus ruling and reigning in their lives. And the closer they get to Jesus, the further away they are from the systems and things of this world. As Jesus said of satan in John 14:30, *"The prince of this world cometh, and hath nothing in me."* One translation reads, *"The prince of this world cometh, and hath nothing in common with me."* As His people begin walking in His Kingdom, the enemy and the things of this world will not have anything more in common with them. Therefore, this lesson is devoted to looking at this principle – that the Kingdom of God is not of this world.

I.   John 18:36 – *"Jesus answered, My kingdom is not of this world: if my kingdom were of this world, then would my servants fight, that I should not be delivered to the Jews: but now is my kingdom not from hence."*

Jesus is saying His kingdom is not of this world and that if it was, then His servants would fight naturally. II Corinthians 10:4 states, *"For the weapons of our warfare are not carnal, but mighty through God to the pulling down of strong holds."*

   A.   Other translations:

"Jesus answered, My Kingdom, Kingship, royal power belongs not to this world...But as it is, My Kingdom is not from this world, it has no such origin or source."
"My Kingdom, said Jesus, doesn't consist of what you see around you...But, I am not that kind of King, not the world's kind of King"
"My Kingdom is not an earthly Kingdom..." "I am not an earthly King...But my Kingdom is not of the world."
"But now my Kingdom is from another place"
"My Kingship does not derive it's authority from this world's order of things."
"My Kingdom does not belong to this world."
"My Kingdom doesn't have it's origin on earth."
"No, My Kingdom does not belong here."

   B. Word Definition For World

      1. Greek Word For World – *kosmos* – an orderly arrangement or system of things.

Babylon is not only a religious system; Babylon is a worldly system. Any system or orderly arrangement of things is something we need to be careful of because it is outside the anointing of God and the things of God. Even in our church meetings and gatherings, we need to not get locked into a system and a way of doing things where we cut off the Spirit of God from flowing freely among us.

The Kingdom of God is not a democracy, ruled by the opinions of people. It is a theocracy, ruled and reigned by God. It is interesting to note that the last church mentioned in the book of Revelation is the Laodicean church. The Laodicean church is a type of the last day's church. The word Laodicea means, "a democracy, opinion of the people, ruled by the people." So the last day's church is a church that will be pushing for democracy and ruled by the people. For example, there is no Scriptural precedent for a congregation voting a pastor of a church into their congregation. The Bible clearly says that God appoints and sets the members and the leadership (Numbers 27:16, Ephesians 4:11, I Corinthians 12:18). We leave God out of it because we have an orderly arrangement and a system of doing things.

   B.   A Look At What The Kingdom Of God Is Like Scripturally

      1.   Romans 14:17 – *"For the kingdom of God is not meat and drink; but righteousness, and peace, and joy in the Holy Ghost."*
      2.   Psalms 145:10-13 – *"10All thy works shall praise thee, O Lord; and thy saints shall bless thee. 11They shall speak of the glory of thy kingdom, and talk of thy power; 12To make known to the*

sons of men his mighty acts, and the glorious majesty of his kingdom. ¹³Thy kingdom is an everlasting kingdom, and thy dominion endureth throughout all generations."

The Kingdom of God deals with the glory of God. It is beautiful and wonderful, something beyond this world. That is why you cannot understand the things of the Kingdom of God intellectually. Jesus told Peter, *"Flesh and blood hath not revealed it unto thee, but my Father which is in heaven"* (Matthew 16:17). It takes the Spirit of revelation to understand what God is saying. It is just like Nicodemus trying to understand naturally about a man entering again into his mother's womb about being born again. Jesus was speaking of being born again by the Spirit of God and the Word of God. Another example is in Acts 1:3, where it says that Jesus, *"being seen of them forty days and speaking of the things pertaining to the kingdom of God."* After He spoke to them of the Kingdom of God, they still took it naturally and asked Him, *"Lord, wilt thou at this time restore again the kingdom to Israel"* (Acts 1:6). They were still thinking about natural Israel; but, He was trying to communicate to them glorious truths of the Kingdom of God. He responded in verse 8, *"But ye shall receive power, after that the Holy Ghost is come upon you."* The Kingdom of God is not about a natural people anymore, but spiritual Israel, the new Jerusalem, being an everlasting Kingdom, full of the glory of God. Jesus was saying the Kingdom of God is about the baptism of the Holy Ghost and not about the kingdom being restored to natural Israel anymore.

3. Micah 4:8 – *"And thou, O tower of the flock, the strong hold of the daughter of Zion, unto thee shall it come, even the first dominion; the kingdom shall come to the daughter of Jerusalem."*

What is the first dominion? Genesis1:26 states, *"And God said, Let us make man in our image, after our likeness: and let them have dominion over the fish of the sea, and over the fowl of the air, and over the cattle, and over all the earth, and over every creeping thing that creepeth upon the earth."* This dominion that God originally destined for man to walk in is going to be given to the daughter of Zion. Zion is going to get back everything that Adam lost. That is the Kingdom of God.

4. Obadiah 17-21 – *"¹⁷But upon mount Zion shall be deliverance, and there shall be holiness; and the house of Jacob shall possess their possessions. ¹⁸And the house of Jacob shall be a fire, and the house of Joseph a flame, and the house of Esau for stubble, and they shall kindle in them, and devour them; and there shall not be any remaining of the house of Esau; for the Lord hath spoken it. ¹⁹And they of the south shall possess the mount of Esau; and they of the plain the Philistines: and they shall possess the fields of Ephraim, and the fields of Samaria: and Benjamin shall possess Gilead. ²⁰And the captivity of this host of the children of Israel shall possess that of the Canaanites, even unto Zarephath; and the captivity of Jerusalem, which is in Sepharad, shall possess the cities of the south. ²¹And saviours shall come up on mount Zion to judge the mount of Esau; and the kingdom shall be the Lord's."*

God is going to have a people who are like Him and have nothing in common anymore to this world. God calls them *"saviours"* in verse 21. Psalms 82:6 says, *"I have said, Ye are gods; and all of you are children of the most High."* This is not saying that we will be Jesus; but, we will be like Him. The world will be grateful one day when the sons of God come and bring the Kingdom of God to them.

5. Matthew 6:10 – *"Thy kingdom come. Thy will be done in earth, as it is in heaven."*

The Kingdom of God is a heavenly kingdom and not an earthly one. It is spiritual. The Kingdom of God is the unseen realm all around us. Most people put their attention on the visible realm. We should be putting our efforts and devoting our lives to the invisible, spiritual realm, with the glory and majesty of God. We must let the things of His Kingdom have rule and dominion over us rather than the things of this world if we want to see His Kingdom come.

a. II Timothy 4:18 – *"And the Lord shall deliver me from every evil work, and will preserve me unto his heavenly kingdom: to whom be glory for ever and ever. Amen."*

6. Matthew 9:35-39 – "*35And Jesus went about all the cities and villages, teaching in their synagogues, and preaching the gospel of the kingdom, and healing every sickness and every disease among the people. 36But when he saw the multitudes, he was moved with compassion on them, because they fainted, and were scattered abroad, as sheep having no shepherd. 37Then saith he unto his disciples, The harvest truly is plenteous, but the labourers are few; 38Pray ye therefore the Lord of the harvest, that he will send forth labourers into his harvest.*"

7. Matthew 20:20-28 – "*20Then came to him the mother of Zebedee's children with her sons, worshipping him, and desiring a certain thing of him. 21And he said unto her, What wilt thou? She saith unto him, Grant that these my two sons may sit, the one on thy right hand, and the other on the left, in thy kingdom. 22But Jesus answered and said, Ye know not what ye ask. Are ye able to drink of the cup that I shall drink of, and to be baptized with the baptism that I am baptized with? They say unto him, We are able. 23And he saith unto them, Ye shall drink indeed of my cup, and be baptized with the baptism that I am baptized with: but to sit on my right hand, and on my left, is not mine to give, but it shall be given to them for whom it is prepared of my Father. 24And when the ten heard it, they were moved with indignation against the two brethren. 25But Jesus called them unto him, and said, Ye know that the princes of the Gentiles exercise dominion over them, and they that are great exercise authority upon them. 26But it shall not be so among you: but whosoever will be great among you, let him be your minister; 27And whosoever will be chief among you, let him be your servant: 28Even as the Son of man came not to be ministered unto, but to minister, and to give his life a ransom for many.*"

Jesus sits at the right hand of God the Father. But there will be a people who will sit at the right hand of Jesus. The one who sits next to Jesus at his right hand is the bride. Psalms 45:9 states, "*Upon thy right hand did stand the queen in gold of Ophir.*" The coming kingdom is about brideship. It is about His glory and ruling and reining with Him.

8. Mark 4:10-13 – "*10And when he was alone, they that were about him with the twelve asked of him the parable. 11And he said unto them, Unto you it is given to know the mystery of the kingdom of God: but unto them that are without, all these things are done in parables: 12That seeing they may see, and not perceive; and hearing they may hear, and not understand; lest at any time they should be converted, and their sins should be forgiven them. 13And he said unto them, Know ye not this parable? and how then will ye know all parables?*"

The Kingdom of God deals with the invisible mystery of God. We are supposed to know His mysteries. Many people love to glory in the fact that things are a mystery, but Jesus wants to reveal His mysteries to us.

a. Greek for mystery – *musterion* – to shut the mouth because of a secret; that which is known only by the initiated

This definition tells us that God's mysteries are known only by those who are initiated into them. Moreover, there are some things that we cannot tell others because they are not initiated into those mysteries. In order to be initiated by God into the mysteries of God, we must show our selves approved un to Him. II Timothy 2:15 states, "*Study to shew thyself approved unto God, a workman that needeth not to be ashamed, rightly dividing the word of truth.*" Deuteronomy 29:29 also states, "*The secret things belong unto the LORD our God: but those things which are revealed belong unto us and to our children forever.*"

9. Mark 9:47 – "*And if thine eye offend thee, pluck it out: it is better for thee to enter into the kingdom of God with one eye, than having two eyes to be cast into hell fire:*"

Jesus is not telling us to actually cut out our physical eye. What He is telling us is to have a single eye, an eye that is fixed on one thing. In other words, if we have an eye that is roaming around and looking at worldly things, we need to cut that thing out of our lives. If what we are seeing is offensive to the Spirit of

God, we need to cease from seeing those things. We cannot enter into the Kingdom of God with double vision, being double minded, because *"a double minded man is unstable in all his ways."* Being double minded affects every area of our lives. If we are not singly minded on Jesus, our whole life will be out of order.

    a. Matthew 6:22 – *"The light of the body is the eye: if therefore thine eye be single, thy whole body shall be full of light."*

    b. Song of Solomon 1:15 – *"Behold, thou art fair, my love; behold, thou art fair; thou hast doves' eyes."* – Doves have single vision. They can only see one thing at a time.

10. Mark 10:21-26 – *"²¹Then Jesus beholding him loved him, and said unto him, One thing thou lackest: go thy way, sell whatsoever thou hast, and give to the poor, and thou shalt have treasure in heaven: and come, take up the cross, and follow me. ²²And he was sad at that saying, and went away grieved: for he had great possessions. ²³And Jesus looked round about, and saith unto his disciples, How hardly shall they that have riches enter into the kingdom of God! ²⁴And the disciples were astonished at his words. But Jesus answereth again, and saith unto them, Children, how hard is it for them that trust in riches to enter into the kingdom of God! ²⁵It is easier for a camel to go through the eye of a needle, than for a rich man to enter into the kingdom of God. ²⁶And they were astonished out of measure, saying among themselves, Who then can be saved?"*

The problem with this rich young ruler was that his possessions possessed him. There is nothing wrong with having things as long as we are in control of them. When it controls us, that is the time we must let those things go.

Jesus then turned to His disciples and said that it is very hard for those that trust in riches to enter into the Kingdom of God. Jesus is trying to tell them that riches of this life have nothing to do with the Kingdom of God.

    a. Luke 16:15 – *"And he said unto them, Ye are they which justify yourselves before men; but God knoweth your hearts: for that which is highly esteemed among men is abomination in the sight of God."*

        1) Abomination in Greek – *bdelugma* – to be disgusted, to abhor, detest, to stink

What men and the world esteem, God says that it stinks.

    b. Luke 6:20-24 – *"²⁰And he lifted up his eyes on his disciples, and said, Blessed be ye poor: for yours is the kingdom of God. ²¹Blessed are ye that hunger now: for ye shall be filled. Blessed are ye that weep now: for ye shall laugh. ²²Blessed are ye, when men shall hate you, and when they shall separate you from their company, and shall reproach you, and cast out your name as evil, for the Son of man's sake. ²³Rejoice ye in that day, and leap for joy: for, behold, your reward is great in heaven: for in the like manner did their fathers unto the prophets. ²⁴But woe unto you that are rich! for ye have received your consolation."*

The things that Jesus mentions in these verses are the opposite of what the world thinks we should be doing. James 2:5 says, *"Hath not God chosen the poor of this world rich in faith, and heirs of the kingdom which he hath promised to them that love him?"* Acts 14:22 says, *"We must through much tribulation enter into the kingdom of God."*

11. Luke 17:20-21 – *"²⁰And when he was demanded of the Pharisees, when the kingdom of God should come, he answered them and said, The kingdom of God cometh not with observation: ²¹Neither shall they say, Lo here! or, lo there! for, behold, the kingdom of God is within you."*
12. John 3:3-12 – *"³Jesus answered and said unto him, Verily, verily, I say unto thee, Except a man be born again, he cannot see the kingdom of God. ⁴Nicodemus saith unto him, How can a man be*

born when he is old? can he enter the second time into his mother's womb, and be born? ⁵Jesus answered, Verily, verily, I say unto thee, Except a man be born of water and of the Spirit, he cannot enter into the kingdom of God. ⁶That which is born of the flesh is flesh; and that which is born of the Spirit is spirit. ⁷Marvel not that I said unto thee, Ye must be born again. ⁸The wind bloweth where it listeth, and thou hearest the sound thereof, but canst not tell whence it cometh, and whither it goeth: so is every one that is born of the Spirit. ⁹Nicodemus answered and said unto him, How can these things be? ¹⁰Jesus answered and said unto him, Art thou a master of Israel, and knowest not these things? ¹¹Verily, verily, I say unto thee, We speak that we do know, and testify that we have seen; and ye receive not our witness. ¹²If I have told you earthly things, and ye believe not, how shall ye believe, if I tell you of heavenly things?"

13. Acts 1:6-8 – "*⁶When they therefore were come together, they asked of him, saying, Lord, wilt thou at this time restore again the kingdom to Israel? ⁷And he said unto them, It is not for you to know the times or the seasons, which the Father hath put in his own power. ⁸But ye shall receive power, after that the Holy Ghost is come upon you: and ye shall be witnesses unto me both in Jerusalem, and in all Judaea, and in Samaria, and unto the uttermost part of the earth.*"

14. I Corinthians 4:20 – "*For the kingdom of God is not in word, but in power.*"

The word for power is *dunamis* which means, "miraculous force." Luke 11:20 states, "*But if I with the finger of God cast out devils, no doubt the kingdom of God is come upon you.*" When Jesus did something that normally doesn't happen in this earth, such as heal the sick and cast out devils, then you know that the Kingdom of God has come. The Kingdom of God is the unseen realm where the miraculous power of God is pulsating. We don't just need the Word of God, but the power of God that backs up the word of God. Mark 16:20 states, "*And they went forth, and preached every where, the Lord working with them, and confirming the word with signs following.*"

15. I Thessalonians 2:12 – "*That ye would walk worthy of God, who hath called you unto his kingdom and glory.*" The Kingdom of God is about the glory of God and His manifest presence.

16. Revelation 12:10-11 – "*¹⁰And I heard a loud voice saying in heaven, Now is come salvation, and strength, and the kingdom of our God, and the power of his Christ: for the accuser of our brethren is cast down, which accused them before our God day and night. ¹¹And they overcame him by the blood of the Lamb, and by the word of their testimony; and they loved not their lives unto the death.*"

When the sons of God possess and enter into the Kingdom of God (Obadiah 17-21), then will come salvation, strength, and the Kingdom of God and the power of His anointed. This will happen to the sons of God because they overcame the devil by the blood of the lamb, by the word of their testimony and they loved not their own carnal, soulish life unto the death. They died daily, like the apostle Paul (I Corinthians 15:31).

If you want to enter into the Kingdom of God, you must get the revelation that it is about dying daily to the things of this world. Once you start that dying process in your life, you become like John was on the isle of Patmos ("my killing") and will ultimately receive the revelation of Jesus Christ. The reason people do not have the glory or the anointing or true revelation in their lives is because they are not dying every day to their own wants, opinions and carnal desires.

His Kingdom is not of this world. We must get our minds, our souls, our lives and all who we are off of the things of this world and onto the things of His Spirit and kingdom.

 a. Greek word for power here is – *exousia* – authority, tonken of control, delegated influence, mastery; superhuman ability.

C. A Look At What The Scripture Says About The World

1. II Corinthians 4:4 – *"In whom the god of this world hath blinded the minds of them which believe not, lest the light of the glorious gospel of Christ, who is the image of God, should shine unto them."*

   a. The Greek word for *"world"* – *aion* – an age. This is different than the Greek word *kosmos*, which is the word for the actual world itself. The actual world belongs to God (Psalms 24:1 *"The earth is the Lord's, and the fullness thereof."*) Satan is not the god of this world, but the god of this "age", which is a time period that has a beginning and an end. Jesus said that satan has had his hour, in Luke 22:53, *"This is your hour, and the power of darkness."* And his hour is almost up.

   b. Ephesians 2:2 – *"Wherein in time past ye walked according to the course of this world, according to the prince of the power of the air, the spirit that now worketh in the children of disobedience:"*

2. John 17:11-16 – *"11And now I am no more in the world, but these are in the world, and I come to thee. Holy Father, keep through thine own name those whom thou hast given me, that they may be one, as we are. 12While I was with them in the world, I kept them in thy name: those that thou gavest me I have kept, and none of them is lost, but the son of perdition; that the scripture might be fulfilled. 13And now come I to thee; and these things I speak in the world, that they might have my joy fulfilled in themselves. 14I have given them thy word; and the world hath hated them, because they are not of the world, even as I am not of the world. 15I pray not that thou shouldest take them out of the world, but that thou shouldest keep them from the evil. 16They are not of the world, even as I am not of the world."*

3. The world is the visible realm. The Kingdom is the invisible realm.

4. The world (*kosmos* in Greek – orderly arrangement of things or system) is what we live in, even in the church (system of religion).

The Kingdom of God, however, deals with God's nature, God's Spirit, God's laws, God's Word and will. The Spirit of God has an altogether different standard and order that comes out of the heavenly, invisible realm (Rom. 1:15-17). The world is a negative thing in relation to God because it is a system organized outside of the anointing of God. Any system or arrangement of things that is organized and the anointing of God is not involved in it is not the Kingdom of God. Where Jesus is not the King, it is not the Kingdom of God; but, it is something of this world.

5. I John 5:19 – *"And we know that we are of God, and the whole world lieth in wickedness."*

   a. Greek for wickedness – "wicked one"
   b. Revelation 12:9 – *"....Satan, which deceiveth the whole world..."*

6. Galatians 1:4 – *"Who gave himself for our sins, that he might deliver us from this present evil world, according to the will of God and our Father:"*

7. Romans 8:1-15 – The carnal mind is an enemy of God.

8. James 4:4 – *"Ye adulterers and adulteresses, know ye not that the friendship of the world is enmity with God? whosoever therefore will be a friend of the world is the enemy of God."*

9. I John 2:15-17 – *"15Love not the world, neither the things that are in the world. If any man love the world, the love of the Father is not in him. 16For all that is in the world, the lust of the flesh, and the lust of the eyes, and the pride of life, is not of the Father, but is of the world. 17And the world passeth away, and the lust thereof: but he that doeth the will of God abideth for ever."*

If we love the world, the love of the Father is not in us. That does not mean that God does not love us. It means that we don't have a love of the Father because we have another love, another idol. The things that are of this world are the lust of the flesh, the lust of the eyes, and the pride of life.

10. John 12:25 – *"He that loveth his life shall lose it; and he that hateth his life in this world shall keep it unto life eternal."* Everything in this world is catered for us to love our soulish life. However, we must hate our soulish life (Greek = *psuche* – soulish life) that we may inherit life eternal (Greek = *zoe* – life as God is living it now).

11. The world is the visible realm, while the Kingdom of God deals with the invisible.

D. We Walk In His Kingdom By Faith And Are Not Of This World, For The Kingdom Of God Is Within Us And We Live In It.

1. Psalms 89:15-18 – *"15Blessed is the people that know the joyful sound: they shall walk, O Lord, in the light of thy countenance. 16In thy name shall they rejoice all the day: and in thy righteousness shall they be exalted. 17For thou art the glory of their strength: and in thy favour our horn shall be exalted. 18For the Lord is our defence; and the Holy One of Israel is our king."*

True kingdom people hear a sound that no one else hears. We sense the presence of God and witness to the things of His kingdom that no one understands.

2. Psalms 16:11 – *"Thou wilt shew me the path of life: in thy presence is fulness of joy; at thy right hand there are pleasures for evermore."* In His presence we experience the fullness of joy and eternal pleasures.

3. Psalms 17:15 – *"As for me, I will behold thy face in righteousness: I shall be satisfied, when I awake, with thy likeness."* One day we will see His face.

4. II Corinthians 3:18 – *"But we all, with open face beholding as in a glass the glory of the Lord, are changed into the same image from glory to glory, even as by the Spirit of the Lord."*

5. Psalms 27:4 – *"One thing have I desired of the Lord, that will I seek after; that I may dwell in the house of the Lord all the days of my life, to behold the beauty of the Lord, and to inquire in his temple."*

6. I Corinthians 15:31 – *"I protest by your rejoicing which I have in Christ Jesus our Lord, I die daily."*

7. Galatians 2:20 – *"I am crucified with Christ: nevertheless I live; yet not I, but Christ liveth in me: and the life which I now live in the flesh I live by the faith of the Son of God, who loved me, and gave himself for me."*

8. I John 5:4 – *"For whatsoever is born of God overcometh the world: and this is the victory that overcometh the world, even our faith."*

9. II Peter 1:4 – *"Whereby are given unto us exceeding great and precious promises: that by these ye might be partakers of the divine nature, having escaped the corruption that is in the world through lust."*

10. Psalms 102:16-18 – *"16When the Lord shall build up Zion, he shall appear in his glory. 17He will regard the prayer of the destitute, and not despise their prayer. 18This shall be written for the generation to come: and the people which shall be created shall praise the Lord."*

11. II Corinthians 10:3-6 – *"3For though we walk in the flesh, we do not war after the flesh: 4(For the weapons of our warfare are not carnal, but mighty through God to the pulling down of strong holds;) 5Casting down imaginations, and every high thing that exalteth itself against the knowledge of God, and bringing into captivity every thought to the obedience of Christ; 6And having in a readiness to revenge all disobedience, when your obedience is fulfilled."*

12. Ephesians 6:10-18 – *"10Finally, my brethren, be strong in the Lord, and in the power of his might. 11Put on the whole armour of God, that ye may be able to stand against the wiles of the devil. 12For we wrestle not against flesh and blood, but against principalities, against powers, against the rulers of the darkness of this world, against spiritual wickedness in high places. 13Wherefore take unto you the whole armour of God, that ye may be able to withstand in the evil day, and having done all, to stand. 14Stand therefore, having your loins girt about with truth, and having on the breastplate of righteousness; 15And your feet shod with the preparation of the gospel of peace; 16Above all, taking the shield of faith, wherewith ye shall be able to quench all the fiery darts of*

the wicked. [17]And take the helmet of salvation, and the sword of the Spirit, which is the word of God: [18]Praying always with all prayer and supplication in the Spirit, and watching thereunto with all perseverance and supplication for all saints;"

II.   People Always Look For An Outward Sign Of The Kingdom

A.   Scriptures

1.   Luke 17:20-24 – *"[20]And when he was demanded of the Pharisees, when the kingdom of God should come, he answered them and said, The kingdom of God cometh not with observation: [21]Neither shall they say, Lo here! or, lo there! for, behold, the kingdom of God is within you. [22]And he said unto the disciples, The days will come, when ye shall desire to see one of the days of the Son of man, and ye shall not see it. [23]And they shall say to you, See here; or, see there: go not after them, nor follow them. [24]For as the lightning, that lighteneth out of the one part under heaven, shineth unto the other part under heaven; so shall also the Son of man be in his day."*

Their whole idea of the Kingdom of God was wrong. The Pharisees were looking for a natural kingdom to be restored to them. The day of the Son of man is the manifestation of the sons of God, which is Jesus coming forth within a people. It is likened to lightning. Lightning is simply a flash of revelation and His power being released. It is seen instantly; and, then it is gone. If you are not careful, you can miss the Kingdom of God. You can miss the power of God being released and a visitation of the Lord, simply because you are looking in the wrong direction or looking at something natural or something you should not be looking for, as these Pharisees were doing.

In our personal lives, we might be expecting something to happen to us naturally in this life. Rather, we should concentrate on worshipping, studying the Word of God and being faithful to Jesus and knowing Him intimately.

2.   John 6:28-71 – *"Then said they unto him, What shall we do, that we might work the works of God? [29]Jesus answered and said unto them, This is the work of God, that ye believe on him whom he hath sent. [30]They said therefore unto him, What sign shewest thou then, that we may see, and believe thee? what dost thou work? [31]Our fathers did eat manna in the desert; as it is written, He gave them bread from heaven to eat. [32]Then Jesus said unto them, Verily, verily, I say unto you, Moses gave you not that bread from heaven; but my Father giveth you the true bread from heaven. [33]For the bread of God is he which cometh down from heaven, and giveth life unto the world. [34]Then said they unto him, Lord, evermore give us this bread. [35]And Jesus said unto them, I am the bread of life: he that cometh to me shall never hunger; and he that believeth on me shall never thirst. [36]But I said unto you, That ye also have seen me, and believe not... [41]The Jews then murmured at him, because he said, I am the bread which came down from heaven. [42]And they said, Is not this Jesus, the son of Joseph, whose father and mother we know? how is it then that he saith, I came down from heaven? [43]Jesus therefore answered and said unto them, Murmur not among yourselves. [44]No man can come to me, except the Father which hath sent me draw him: and I will raise him up at the last day."*

They wanted to see something before they believed. However, we must believe first in order to see. So many people are like this. They want a sign. They want to see something so they can believe. Jesus said in Matthew 12:39-40, *"An evil and adulterous generation seeketh after a sign; and there shall no sign be given to it, but the sign of the prophet Jonas: [40]For as Jonas was three days and three nights in the whale's belly; so shall the Son of man be three days and three nights in the heart of the earth."* The only sign God gave was the gift of Jesus to the world and everything that is of God now is centered around Jesus. The Kingdom of God is about the King of the kingdom, Jesus.

They wanted to know the work of God. They said to Jesus that their fathers ate manna from heaven. They were making a reference to Moses, who made a sign that everybody saw. Therefore, they wanted Jesus to make a sign for everybody to see. Jesus responded to them by saying that He was the true Bread was from heaven.

They did not really want the Bread, when they said for Him to give them that bread; because, verse 41 says they murmured when Jesus said that He was the Bread which came down from heaven. When Jesus told them the truth, they did not receive the truth and then reasoned among themselves in the natural about who Jesus was, by saying He was the son of Joseph. In the last days, many people will mock and murmur as they did to Jesus here because they will just accuse God's people of being simply a human being, not knowing the Kingdom of God is within them. Likewise, the order of Melchizedek is going to be a company of people who have divested themselves from their own families and their own heritage. They no longer live according to the dictates of this world. They get a revelation that their true citizenship is in heaven. God is their Father and they are seated with Him in heavenly places in Christ Jesus.

Even in John 6:52, the Jews were still striving among themselves, saying, "*How can this man give us his flesh to eat?*" Again, they were thinking things naturally and not understanding Jesus was speaking of the spiritual truths of the Kingdom of God. Jesus finished what He was saying to them in verse 63, "*It is the spirit that quickeneth; the flesh profiteth nothing: the words that I speak unto you, they are spirit and they are life.*"

Therefore, this story shows how many of the people wanted Jesus to show them a sign, as Moses did. They wanted Jesus to show them some kind of miracle so that they can believe.

3. John 18:33-38 – "*³³Then Pilate entered into the judgment hall again, and called Jesus, and said unto him, Art thou the King of the Jews? ³⁴Jesus answered him, Sayest thou this thing of thyself, or did others tell it thee of me? ³⁵Pilate answered, Am I a Jew? Thine own nation and the chief priests have delivered thee unto me: what hast thou done? ³⁶Jesus answered, My kingdom is not of this world: if my kingdom were of this world, then would my servants fight, that I should not be delivered to the Jews: but now is my kingdom not from hence. ³⁷Pilate therefore said unto him, Art thou a king then? Jesus answered, Thou sayest that I am a king. To this end was I born, and for this cause came I into the world, that I should bear witness unto the truth. Every one that is of the truth heareth my voice. ³⁸ Pilate saith unto him, What is truth? And when he had said this, he went out again unto the Jews, and saith unto them, I find in him no fault at all.*"

Pilate was even asking Jesus that if He were a king, then perhaps He can show him something to prove it. He then asks Jesus "*What is truth?*" Truth isn't something you see, but something you hear. How do you hear the truth? You hear it through the Word of God that is spoken. Romans 10:17 states, "*So then faith cometh by hearing, and hearing by the word of God.*" Truth finds a home not in something we see, but in something we hear, in something that resonates deep within us. However, most people want to see something rather than believe in something. Jesus said to Thomas in John 20:27-29, "*Reach hither thy finger, and behold my hands; and reach hither thy hand, and thrust it into my side: and be not faithless, but believing... ²⁹Thomas, because thou hast seen me, thou hast believed: blessed are they that have not seen, and yet have believed.*"

For example, I did not get saved because I saw some miracle. I got saved when I heard a man preach the gospel in my high school auditorium. He spoke about how the love of God changed his life when he was without hope and desperate. When I heard it, something deep inside of me was begging for that and hungry for some true substance. My life was passing before my eyes and I knew that I needed to respond. I got up on my knees before my entire school and prayed the prayer of salvation on the stage and I got gloriously saved.

4. John 7:1-5 – "*¹After these things Jesus walked in Galilee: for he would not walk in Jewry, because the Jews sought to kill him. ²Now the Jews' feast of tabernacles was at hand. ³His brethren therefore said unto him, Depart hence, and go into Judaea, that thy disciples also may see the*

works that thou doest. ⁴For there is no man that doeth any thing in secret, and he himself seeketh to be known openly. If thou do these things, shew thyself to the world. ⁵For neither did his brethren believe in him."

Jesus must have had at least five siblings in his family. And for the first 30 years of His life, He did nothing. He did not heal anybody, neither did He teach or preach one message. He just submitted to his family for those 30 years. He allowed the dealings of God in His life for those 30 years just for a 3 ½ year ministry.

When His brethren were speaking to Him here, they were basically saying for Him to show them something. They were saying that if He were truly the Son of God, then show the people that you are. Nobody does something in secret. Show yourself openly! They did not even believe in Him. They were with the disciples in the upper room on the day of Pentecost. Acts 1:14 says, *"These all continued with one accord in prayer and supplication, with the women, and Mary the mother of Jesus, and with his brethren."* So at least their hearts were eventually touched by Him.

Our own families may hate and criticize us. But we must be an example to them of everyday walking with Jesus. We must not love our lives unto the death and be an example by the word of our testimony and eventually they will see our faithfulness; they will eventually see the true Jesus in our life. Then they will truly know that Jesus lives because He lives in us.

5. Acts 1:1-11 – *"...³To whom also he shewed himself alive after his passion by many infallible proofs, being seen of them forty days, and speaking of the things pertaining to the kingdom of God...⁶When they therefore were come together, they asked of him, saying, Lord, wilt thou at this time restore again the kingdom to Israel? ⁷And he said unto them, It is not for you to know the times or the seasons, which the Father hath put in his own power...⁹And when he had spoken these things, while they beheld, he was taken up; and a cloud received him out of their sight. ¹⁰And while they looked stedfastly toward heaven as he went up, behold, two men stood by them in white apparel; ¹¹Which also said, Ye men of Galilee, why stand ye gazing up into heaven? this same Jesus, which is taken up from you into heaven, shall so come in like manner as ye have seen him go into heaven."*

After all of those 3 ½ years of walking with Him and after those 40 days of seeing many infallible proofs and of Him teaching the things concerning the Kingdom of God, the first thing they ask Him is if He were going to bring the natural kingdom back to Israel. Like them, we must stop looking at the natural. Jesus was saying that the whole purpose of the Kingdom of God is for a people to receive the King and His power (the baptism of the Holy Ghost). The Kingdom of God in action is a people in whom the King is truly living in them. We are not looking for a kingdom anymore. We have already found it and King Jesus is already living in our hearts.

6. John 6:14-15 – *"¹⁴Then those men, when they had seen the miracle that Jesus did, said, This is of a truth that prophet that should come into the world. ¹⁵When Jesus therefore perceived that they would come and take him by force, to make him a king, he departed again into a mountain himself alone."*

Those men wanted to make Jesus an actual king. They responded by thinking naturally. They did not see that Jesus was a king of a kingdom that cannot be seen. There are many people today who believe that Jesus is going to come and sit on a natural throne in Jerusalem. Jesus already sits upon the throne in mount Zion when we worship Him. What is truly important is not some natural throne, but that Jesus is sitting upon the throne of our hearts.

7. Luke 11:14-20 – *"¹⁴And he was casting out a devil, and it was dumb. And it came to pass, when the devil was gone out, the dumb spake; and the people wondered. ¹⁵But some of them said, He*

casteth out devils through Beelzebub the chief of the devils. [16]And others, tempting him, sought of him a sign from heaven. [17]But he, knowing their thoughts, said unto them, Every kingdom divided against itself is brought to desolation; and a house divided against a house falleth. [18]If Satan also be divided against himself, how shall his kingdom stand? because ye say that I cast out devils through Beelzebub. [19]And if I by Beelzebub cast out devils, by whom do your sons cast them out? therefore shall they be your judges. [20]But if I with the finger of God cast out devils, no doubt the kingdom of God is come upon you." The Kingdom of God is come when deliverance and healing is taking place.

8. Matthew 11:1-5 – "*[1]And it came to pass, when Jesus had made an end of commanding his twelve disciples, he departed thence to teach and to preach in their cities. [2]Now when John had heard in the prison the works of Christ, he sent two of his disciples, [3]And said unto him, Art thou he that should come, or do we look for another? [4]Jesus answered and said unto them, Go and shew John again those things which ye do hear and see: [5]The blind receive their sight, and the lame walk, the lepers are cleansed, and the deaf hear, the dead are raised up, and the poor have the gospel preached to them.*"

The first problem John had was that he still had disciples. When Jesus came on the scene, he should have told his disciples to go follow Jesus now. If the Lamb of God has come, we need to let our disciples go and we must go follow Him ourselves. Our ministry should be over at that time. But John was in prison now because he was still ministering and getting involved with political concerns, by talking about Herod's wife.

At the beginning, John was the one who saw Jesus and proclaimed His coming. But now John is saying here, "*Art thou he that should come?*" He was looking for proof to see something. He was questioning what was true. His eyes were not on Jesus anymore, but on his ministry and his own life. Jesus responded by saying that the Kingdom of God is already here, for the blind are receiving their sight, the lame are walking, the lepers are cleansed, the deaf hear, the dead are being raised and the poor have the gospel preached to them.

9. Luke 17:11-19 – "*[11]And it came to pass, as he went to Jerusalem, that he passed through the midst of Samaria and Galilee. [12]And as he entered into a certain village, there met him ten men that were lepers, which stood afar off: [13]And they lifted up their voices, and said, Jesus, Master, have mercy on us. [14]And when he saw them, he said unto them, Go shew yourselves unto the priests. And it came to pass, that, as they went, they were cleansed. [15]And one of them, when he saw that he was healed, turned back, and with a loud voice glorified God, [16]And fell down on his face at his feet, giving him thanks: and he was a Samaritan. [17]And Jesus answering said, Were there not ten cleansed? but where are the nine? [18]There are not found that returned to give glory to God, save this stranger. [19]And he said unto him, Arise, go thy way: thy faith hath made thee whole.*"

B. We Walk By Faith

1. II Corinthians 5:7 – "*(For we walk by faith, not by sight:)*" - We don't need natural things to confirm spiritual truths.
2. John 20:29 – "*Jesus saith unto him, Thomas, because thou hast seen me, thou hast believed: blessed are they that have not seen, and yet have believed.*"
3. Hebrews 11:1 – "*Now faith is the substance of things hoped for, the evidence of things not seen.*"
4. II Corinthians 4:18 – "*While we look not at the things which are seen, but at the things which are not seen: for the things which are seen are temporal; but the things which are not seen are eternal.*"

How many people spend most of their effort and time on things of this world? God doesn't want His people looking always at the natural. He wants them to get more in tuned to the realm of the spirit so that when they walk through the veil, it will feel like home to them. This life is to prepare us for the Kingdom of God that is coming.

5. Romans 8:24-25 – "*24For we are saved by hope: but hope that is seen is not hope: for what a man seeth, why doth he yet hope for? 25But if we hope for that we see not, then do we with patience wait for it.*"

6. Hebrews 11:1-13 – "*Now faith is the substance of things hoped for, the evidence of things not seen...6But without faith it is impossible to please him: for he that cometh to God must believe that he is, and that he is a rewarder of them that diligently seek him. 7By faith Noah, being warned of God of things not seen as yet, moved with fear, prepared an ark to the saving of his house; by the which he condemned the world, and became heir of the righteousness which is by faith. 8By faith Abraham, when he was called to go out into a place which he should after receive for an inheritance, obeyed; and he went out, not knowing whither he went. 9By faith he sojourned in the land of promise, as in a strange country, dwelling in tabernacles with Isaac and Jacob, the heirs with him of the same promise: 10For he looked for a city which hath foundations, whose builder and maker is God. 11Through faith also Sara herself received strength to conceive seed, and was delivered of a child when she was past age, because she judged him faithful who had promised. 12Therefore sprang there even of one, and him as good as dead, so many as the stars of the sky in multitude, and as the sand which is by the sea shore innumerable. 13These all died in faith, not having received the promises, but having seen them afar off, and were persuaded of them, and embraced them, and confessed that they were strangers and pilgrims on the earth.*"

   a. Faith is a substance and it is evidence of things we hope for and do not see naturally. Our faith needs to be so alive and active that our belief becomes the actual evidence and thing for which we are believing.

   b. In verse 7 it says that by faith Noah was moved by things he had not yet seen. In Noah's day, nobody had ever seen rain yet. Nobody knew what it was. But, he was moved by fear and prepared an ark through faith.

   c. Abraham left everything he knew; not knowing where he was going. The principle here is that Abraham did not have any natural thing to put in his mind. He walked by faith and not by what he saw.

   d. Sarah was well past her child bearing years. Again, there was nothing seen, of this world, that was able to cause her to bear seed. Nevertheless she judged Him faithful who promised.

Chapter 5
Teaching And Preaching The Kingdom Of God

I would like to look at this principle of what happens when you teach or preach a kingdom message as well as the kind of responses you will get from religious people, factions and groups within the body of Christ. I would like to look, as well, at what our responses to them should be.

Many people in the body of Christ have an idea of the way we are supposed to teach and preach. Perhaps we are taught on hermeneutics and different ways to minister. But if you read the gospels, the Old Testament and the book of Acts, you find that those who were really called were not really passive people, nor were they people who just gently stood there, never ruffling anyone's feathers. When it comes to teaching and preaching the gospel of the Kingdom of God, you just can't expect people to readily believe what you are saying. Teaching and preaching the gospel of the Kingdom of God is not just speaking of having a salvation experience and going to heaven. It is about the principles of the Kingdom of God, which is the sovereign Lord Jesus ruling within the lives of His people. Sometimes we need to persuade and dispute the things of the Kingdom of God.

First of all, we should always respond as much as we possibly can to people in the love of God. We always want to react in a loving and reconciling way. But there is a limit, many times, to this and we will look at how Jesus and others reacted to certain people, especially to those whose hearts were hardened and believed not.

One thing we have to understand is that not everybody is going to be a disciple. Remember, Jesus had the multitudes. Then He had the 12. Within the 12, He had the 3, Peter, James and John. And of the three, He had John, the beloved disciple, who laid his head on the breast of Jesus and to whom was given the revelation of Jesus Christ.

Many people, when they hear the word of salvation, will receive it and respond. When they hear a message on healing or deliverance, they will respond. As long as you speak on things that everybody likes and everyone wants to hear, they will love you, support you and come to your church. As long as you prophesy sweet things, it is good. But when it comes to discipleship and having to tell people the truth, it is another story entirely. Of course you always teach things as people are able to hear them, but you should never compromise the truth.

Remember the story in John 6, when the multitudes were following Him because He had just blessed and fed them? Then, as the multitude was following, Jesus turned to them all and said in John 6:53, *"Verily, verily, I say unto you, Except ye eat the flesh of the Son of man, and drink his blood, ye have no life in you."* After hearing this, it says in verse 66, *"From that time many of his disciples went back, and walked no more with him."* Jesus then even turned to His 12 disciples and asked, *"Will ye also go away?"* (verse 67) So, when teaching and preaching about things like discipleship and true messages of the Kingdom of God, I find that many have trouble receiving the message.

There are always people who are pioneers that have the word of the Lord, who go before hand. As they enter in to those things, they will experience great difficulty. Anytime God has moved in the earth and brought something new, it was not received. Even Jesus was *"despised and rejected of men"* (Isaiah 53:3). If you are going to come teaching and preaching a kingdom message, a message where King Jesus is the absolute ruler and has total dominion in the lives of His people, we must understand these things.

When I travel and minister, I find that when I mention things like eternal salvation, the manifestation of the sons of God and the bride (the remnant), I find many responses from many people. Some receive it with joy and gladness, and full of glory. Other times I find great opposition from people. Sometimes people are very ignorant and will have no idea what I am talking about. Other times, people get very angry and hardened; and, they will believe not. They will not search the Scriptures to see whether these things are so (Acts 17:11). Therefore, in this lesson, we will look Scripturally at teaching and preaching a true kingdom message, which is beyond glorious, yet not received by so many.

I. Differing Principles To Consider

A. Acts 28:23, 31 – *"23And when they had appointed him a day, there came many to him into his lodging; to whom he expounded and testified the kingdom of God, persuading them concerning Jesus, both out of the law of Moses, and out of the prophets, from morning till evening…31Preaching the kingdom of God, and teaching those things which concern the Lord Jesus Christ, with all confidence, no man forbidding him."*

1. Paul testifies and expounds about the kingdom.
2. "Persuading them concerning Jesus" – It is a choice we have to be persuaded about him.
3. "Teaching those things which concern the Lord Jesus" – The central message of the Kingdom of God is the King of the kingdom, Jesus.

4. Out Of The Scriptures

a. Luke 24:25-27 – *"…27And beginning at Moses and all the prophets, he expounded unto them in all the scriptures the things concerning himself."*
b. Hebrews 10:7 – *"Then said I, Lo, I come (in the volume of the book it is written of me,) to do thy will, O God."*
c. John 5:39 – *"Search the scriptures; for in them ye think ye have eternal life: and they are they which testify of me."*
d. Hebrews 1:1-2 – *"1God, who at sundry times and in divers manners spake in time past unto the fathers by the prophets, 2Hath in these last days spoken unto us by his Son, whom he hath appointed heir of all things, by whom also he made the worlds;"*
e. Jeremiah 2:8 – *"The priests said not, Where is the Lord? and they that handle the law knew me not: the pastors also transgressed against me, and the prophets prophesied by Baal, and walked after things that do not profit."*
f. John 1:45 – *"Philip findeth Nathanael, and saith unto him, We have found him, of whom Moses in the law, and the prophets, did write, Jesus of Nazareth, the son of Joseph."*
g. Matthew 5:17 – *"Think not that I am come to destroy the law, or the prophets: I am not come to destroy, but to fulfil."*

h. Revelation 19:13 – *"And he was clothed with a vesture dipped in blood: and his name is called The Word of God."*

i. I John 5:7 – *"For there are three that bear record in heaven, the Father, the Word, and the Holy Ghost: and these three are one."*

j. John 1:1, 14, 17 – *"¹In the beginning was the Word, and the Word was with God, and the Word was God...¹⁴And the Word was made flesh, and dwelt among us, (and we beheld his glory, the glory as of the only begotten of the Father,) full of grace and truth...¹⁷For the law was given by Moses, but grace and truth came by Jesus Christ."*

k. Acts 26:22-23 – *"²²Having therefore obtained help of God, I continue unto this day, witnessing both to small and great, saying none other things than those which the prophets and Moses did say should come: ²³That Christ should suffer, and that he should be the first that should rise from the dead, and should shew light unto the people, and to the Gentiles."*

l. Acts 8:35 – *"Then Philip opened his mouth, and began at the same scripture, and preached unto him Jesus."*

m. I Corinthians 1:30 – *"But of him are ye in Christ Jesus, who of God is made unto us wisdom, and righteousness, and sanctification, and redemption:"*

n. II Peter 3:18 – *"But grow in grace, and in the knowledge of our Lord and Saviour Jesus Christ. To him be glory both now and for ever. Amen."*

B. Acts 19:8-10 – *"⁸And he went into the synagogue, and spake boldly for the space of three months, disputing and persuading the things concerning the kingdom of God. ⁹But when divers were hardened, and believed not, but spake evil of that way before the multitude, he departed from them, and separated the disciples, disputing daily in the school of one Tyrannus. ¹⁰And this continued by the space of two years; so that all they which dwelt in Asia heard the word of the Lord Jesus, both Jews and Greeks."*

You have to dispute and persuade when it comes to things concerning the Kingdom of God. You cannot expect people to just automatically believe what you have to say. We are not talking about the kingdom of heaven, a salvation message, but the principles of the Kingdom of God, the sovereign Lord ruling in the lives of his people. People are not going to receive that so readily. We need to know how to minister when it comes to the kingdom of God, and how we are to give this message that is so powerful and so glorious, but yet not received by so many.

Many times you will find that as you are ministering, you have to dispute the things people say. That is why you need to know the Word of God, so that you need to know how to answer them.

1. Disputing And Persuading The Things Concerning The Kingdom Of God

When we teach and preach the gospel of the Kingdom of God, we want to follow Paul's example of what he did here. He persuaded and disputed the things concerning the Kingdom of God. Moreover, when many were hardened in their hearts, it says that Paul separated the disciples. I believe there comes a time when we have to separate ourselves from nominal Christians and unbelievers to devote ourselves to true discipleship. We need to learn how to dispute and persuade the things concerning the Kingdom of God. We need to be taught the Word of God so that we can dispute and answer the things we believe. I believe, as we get to know the Lord intimately, we can convince the gainsayers and those that oppose the truth. Paul said in II Corinthians 5: 11, *"Knowing therefore the terror of the Lord, we persuade men."* We are not just persuading the world, but Christians as well. Once Christians realize what they could have had and for which they did not pay a price, there will be weeping and gnashing of teeth. Heaven is assured to believers, but brideship and entering into all that God has destined for us in the Kingdom of God is something for which we must attain. Paul also said in I Corinthians 9:11, *"Woe is unto me, if I preach not the gospel!"*

The Bible also says that teachers and preachers of the Word of God will receive a greater judgment both on what they teach and on things they do not teach. James 3:1 says, *"My brethren, be not many masters, knowing that we shall receive the greater condemnation."* Also, Revelation 22 says:

> *"If any man shall add unto these things, God shall add unto him the plagues that are written in this book: ¹⁹And if any man shall take away from the words of the book of this prophecy, God shall take away his part out of the book of life, and out of the holy city, and from the things which are written in this book."* (Revelation 22:18-19)

God forbid that we do not teach and preach things because we are fearful of what people will say. People in the Bible were persecuted and even martyred for what they believed. I believe a revolution must take place in the leadership of the body of Christ, where men and women of God become radical for Jesus, radical for the things of God, radical for the sheep, and radical for the propagation of the Kingdom of God. Or else we are going to continue, as we are right now, availing and achieving nothing and never really bringing great change to people's lives.

    a.   Disputing

        1)   Disputing in Greek – *dialegomai* – *to* say thoroughly, to discuss in argument or exhortation, to preach to, reason with, speak.

We must be able to say thoroughly what we believe, by showing people out of the Word of God. II Corinthians 13:1 says, *"In the mouth of two or three witnesses shall every word be established."* We must show them throughout the Scriptures the truths we are teaching and not just pointing to one verse of Scripture where they can gainsay against. We must be living epistles, *"known and read of all men"* (II Corinthians 3:2). God told His people in Isaiah 1:18, *"Come now, and let us reason together."* God is looking for people who are sound in the faith, sound in doctrine to be able to disciple the nations.

        2)   Same Greek words translated disputing:

            a)   Acts 17:1-4 – Paul at Thessalonica – *"...²And Paul, as his manner was, went in unto them (synagogue of the Jews), and three sabbath days <u>reasoned with</u> them out of the scriptures..."*

We do not argue the Word of God, we present the truth to them from a place of peace. II Timothy 2:24-25 states, *"And the servant of the Lord must not strive; but be gentle unto all men, apt to teach, patient, ²⁵In meekness instructing those that oppose themselves."* We must be in the spirit and not in the flesh.

Moreover, after we have shown to people throughout the Scriptures the truth of a matter, it is up to them to believe it or not. Paul said in Titus 3:10, *"A man that is an heretick* [one who is involved with heresy or some heretical belief] *after the first and second admonition reject."* It does not mean we reject them and cut them off; but, it means we have to move on because there is nothing more to say to them. We do not have to prove anything to anybody. The Word of God can do that itself, because *"faith cometh by hearing, and hearing by the word of God"* (Romans 10:17). We must just speak the Word of God, because the Word of God carries within it the faith to believe what you and I are saying. It is the convincing argument itself.

            b)   Acts 17:16-17 – Paul at Athens – *"¹⁶Now while Paul waited for them at Athens, his spirit was stirred in him, when he saw the city wholly given to idolatry. ¹⁷Therefore <u>disputed</u> he in the synagogue with the Jews, and with the devout persons, and in the market daily with them that met with him."*

            c)   Acts 18:1-6 – Paul at Corinth – *"...⁴And he <u>reasoned</u> in the synagogue every sabbath, and persuaded the Jews and the Greeks...⁶And when they opposed* *themselves, and blasphemed, he shook his raiment, and said unto them, Your blood be upon your own heads; I am clean: from henceforth I will go unto the Gentiles."*

    d)   Acts 18:19 – Paul at Ephesus – *"...but he himself entered into the synagogue, and <u>reasoned with</u> the Jews."*

    e)   Acts 20:6-9 – Paul at Troas – *"...⁷And upon the first day of the week, when the disciples came together to break bread, Paul <u>preached</u> unto them, ready to depart on the morrow; and continued his speech until midnight...⁹And there sat in a window a certain young man named Eutychus, being fallen into a deep sleep: and as Paul was <u>long preaching</u>, he sunk down with sleep, and fell down from the third loft, and was taken up dead."*

Disputing is translated *"preaching"* in this verse. So disputing also means to preach. Preaching is not what we necessarily see on television today, which is just something that wants to excite people's flesh or getting people stirred up. Much of that charismatic behavior of preaching is just learned religious behavior. True preaching is bringing forth the true living Word of God and the gospel of the kingdom.

    f)   Acts 24:24-25 – Paul before Felix – *"...²⁵And as he <u>reasoned</u> of righteousness, temperance, and judgment to come Felix trembled, and answered, Go thy way for this time; when I have a convenient season, I will call for thee."*

    g)   Hebrews 12:5 – *"And ye have forgotten the exhortation which <u>speaketh</u> unto you as unto children, My son, despise not thou the chastening of the Lord, nor faint when thou art rebuked of him:"*

The word *"speaketh"* in this verse is also the same word for disputing. When you dispute, you are not yelling. You're speaking. We don't argue the Bible. We minister from a place where we don't lose our peace, bringing forth the principles of the Kingdom, even when we say things people don't want to hear.

    b.   Persuading

        1)   Persuading in Greek – *peitho* – to convince by argument, to rely by inward certainty, to cause to assent to evidence or authority

We believe what we believe because the Scriptures declare it. The sword of the Spirit is the Word of God (Ephesians 6:17). Jesus always answered others with *"It is written..."* (Matthew 4:4) or *"Have ye never read?"* (Matthew 21:16) Jesus always took them to the Word of God. You cannot do that if you do not know the Word of God. There is a big difference between having a cursory understanding of the Scriptures and being a disciple.

Also, we must have inward certainty on what we believe in order to minister to others. How can we be sure to others, if we are not sure ourselves? What a man believes rules him.

        a)   Acts 28:23 – Paul in Rome – *"And when they had appointed him a day, there came many to him into his lodging; to whom he expounded and testified the kingdom of God, persuading them concerning Jesus, both out of the law of Moses, and out of the prophets, from morning till evening."*

          (1) Same Greek word translated differently (word underlined):

(a) Acts 5:40 – "*And to him <u>they agreed</u>: and when they had called the apostles, and beaten them, they commanded that they should not speak in the name of Jesus, and let them go.*"

(b) Acts 12:20 – "*And Herod was highly displeased with them of Tyre and Sidon: but they came with one accord to him, and, <u>having made</u> Blastus the king's chamberlain their friend, desired peace; because their country was nourished by the king's country.*"

(c) Acts 17:4 – "*And some of them <u>believed</u>, and consorted with Paul and Silas; and of the devout Greeks a great multitude, and of the chief women not a few.*"

(d) Luke 11:22 – "*But when a stronger than he shall come upon him, and overcome him, he taketh from him all his armour wherein <u>he trusted</u>, and divideth his spoils.*"

(e) Acts 5:37 – "*After this man rose up Judas of Galilee in the days of the taxing, and drew away much people after him: he also perished; and all, even as many as <u>obeyed him</u>, were dispersed.*"

(f) Romans 2:19 – "*And <u>art confident</u> that thou thyself art a guide of the blind, a light of them which are in darkness,*"

(g) I John 3:19 – "*And hereby we know that we are of the truth, and shall <u>assure</u> our hearts before him.*"

We need to get people to agree and trust the Scriptures. We need to get people to believe and see that they can be confident and assured in what God has said. We need to dispute and persuade concerning the Kingdom of God.

    c.   Other Companion Scriptures

    1)   II Corinthians 5:11 – "*Knowing therefore the terror of the Lord, we persuade men; but we are made manifest unto God; and I trust also are made manifest in your consciences.*"

    2)   I Thessalonians 2:2 – "*But even after that we had suffered before, and were shamefully entreated, as ye know, at Philippi, we were bold in our God to speak unto you the gospel of God with much contention.*"

This Scripture says Paul spoke the gospel of God with much contention. He was authoritative in the way He spoke and had inward certainty on the things he was declaring. Sometimes when we speak there are demons in the room coming against us. Therefore, sometimes we have to "*earnestly contend for the faith, which was once delivered unto the saints*" (Jude 3). We contend for the faith because it is people's lives that are at stake and we have a love for them. Paul did not hide anything from the people to whom he was ministering to. In Acts 20:27, Paul says, "*For I have not shunned to declare unto you all the counsel of God.*" Paul told them all the truth, as the Scriptures declared.

    3)   Matthew 9:37-38 – "*[37]Then saith he unto his disciples, The harvest truly is plenteous, but the labourers are few; [38]Pray ye therefore the Lord of the harvest, that he will send forth labourers into his harvest.*" (Luke 10:2)

    a)   Labourers in Greek – a teacher

Plenty of people go out to evangelize; but, nobody wants to teach God's people and father them. A father has to say the things you do not want to hear. A father tells you the truth about yourself because he loves you, not because he is against you. And when you are a father, whether your child will like what you have to say or not, you love them enough to tell them anyway.

    d.   Concerning The Kingdom Of God

        1)   His message was one of Jesus being the one and only sovereign Lord of every life. And the principles of this new life and kingdom for which we are to aspire. The Kingdom of God is when the King Jesus is absolute ruler and has total dominion in the lives of His people. He is not a part-time king. He is not a part-time God.

2.   Many Were Hardened

    a.   Hardened in Greek – render stubborn. From a root – dry, hard or tough, fierce, harsh, severe

This speaks of people that when the truth comes to them, they do not care about the truth. They are hard, tough, dry and stubborn. We should have a love for the truth (II Thessalonians 2:10), even when that truth comes to us as an arrow and breaks us and deals with us. For others, though, it does not convict them, because, they do not ultimately care about the truth. Stephen says of those Pharisees who were ready to stone him to death, "*Ye stiffnecked and uncircumcised in heart and ears, ye do always resist the Holy Ghost: as your fathers did, so do ye*" (Acts 7:51).

Truth does not mean anything to us until we have walked through some serious trials and have suffered for it and have allowed it to deal with us. Only in the furnace of affliction does truth get married to our situation and that revelation then becomes a part of us now. When we have overcome and paid the price for truth; then, it becomes truly of great worth, and nobody can ever take it from us.

    b.   Hardened in Hebrew – to be dense, tough, or severe, be cruel, stiffnecked.

        1)   How does one become hardened scripturally?

We need to check out our own hearts and ask ourselves if we are doing anything that is going to cause our hearts to be hardened. If you cannot speak truth to yourself, you will never receive it from anybody else.

            a)   Hebrews 3:13-19 – "*13But exhort one another daily, while it is called To day; lest any of you be hardened through the deceitfulness of sin. 14For we are made partakers of Christ, if we hold the beginning of our confidence stedfast unto the end; 15While it is said, To day if ye will hear his voice, harden not your hearts, as in the provocation. 16For some, when they had heard, did provoke: howbeit not all that came out of Egypt by Moses. 17But with whom was he grieved forty years? was it not with them that had sinned, whose carcases fell in the wilderness? 18And to whom sware he that they should not enter into his rest, but to them that believed not? 19So we see that they could not enter in because of unbelief.*"

            (1) Exhort one another daily

We should be exhorting and encouraging each other. And even more so, we should learn to stir ourselves. When we do not stay stirred up, we are much more susceptible to sinning. I find in my life that if I refrain from reading my Bible for a couple days, I get susceptible to falling.

We must stay stirred personally. Isaiah 64:7 states, "*And there is none that calleth upon thy name, that stirreth up himself to take hold of thee.*" We are responsible for our own walk with God; as well as we should not allow other people to negatively affect us. We ought to be getting ourselves prepared more and more, as we see the day approaching, to enter into the Kingdom of God.

(2)   Hardened <u>through the deceitfulness of sin</u>

(3)   Hold our confidence in the Lord steadfast unto the end

(4)   Today hear His voice

(5)   Don't allow unbelief to enter in

2)   Nehemiah 9:16-17 – "*16But they and our fathers dealt proudly, and hardened their necks, and hearkened not to thy commandments, 17And refused to obey, neither were mindful of thy wonders that thou didst among them; but hardened their necks, and in their rebellion appointed a captain to return to their bondage: but thou art a God ready to pardon, gracious and merciful, slow to anger, and of great kindness, and forsookest them not.*"

In these verses of Scripture, Nehemiah is relaying the story of Moses and the journeying of the children of Israel. The people of Israel saw ten major miracles when they left Egypt. Even seeing all of the wonders of God did not make them believe. After that, they saw the Red Sea part when Moses lifted up his rod. In their journeys, they had the cloud by day and the pillar of fire by night to lead them and protect them every day for 40 years. Manna, supernatural bread, fell down every morning from heaven. However, out of all the children of Israel, only two people, Joshua and Caleb, made it through into the promise land.

Moreover, when God came down upon the mount (Exodus 20:18-21), there was thunder, smoke, lightning and the sound of the trumpet. In other words, this was God showing them who He really was. But when the people saw it, verse 18 says, "*they removed, and stood afar off.*" They wanted nothing to do with God. Psalms 50:3 says it is "*very tempestuous round about him.*" It is like the eye of a hurricane. If you just endure all of the wind blowing, all of the thunder and lightning and the sounds, then you make into the secret place of the Most High God. You end up right in the middle of the glory of God, at His throne. You have to get through all of that to get to the heart. In His glory is the greatest place to be in the whole universe. And once you have been there, you can never turn back. When you see God for who He is, you fall in love with Him.

However, the people of Israel stood away from God. They did not see Him for who He was and they truly did not love Him. Therefore, in this passage, Nehemiah explains how the children of Israel hardened their necks. Likewise, I believe that when we harden our hearts, we do not truly receive the kingdom message.

a)   Dealt proudly – We harden our hearts when we are full of pride

The reason people resist the truth about son-ship is because they are full of pride. They do not want to be told they have to change. They do not want to be told they are doing things wrong or that they are lazy. It is not easy hearing the truth about ourselves; but, it is the only way we will ever change. Pride is the hardest thing we have to fight in our lives every day. It is the number one thing that keeps us out of the kingdom of God. You will go to heaven, but you will not enter into the Kingdom of God, where the King rules and reigns. Therefore, we must fight to always have a soft and tender heart before Him.

b)   We harden our necks and hearts when we do not obey God's commands.

When our hearts are hard, we refuse to turn our necks to His will. When truth comes into our lives, we will not receive it. We must allow the Word of God to cleanse us and wash us continually or we can find ourselves hardening our necks.

c)   When we are not mindful of God's grace, miracles, and help.

When a trial comes up again in our lives, we must remember how He has always been gracious and kind to us. Remember, the disciples saw the miracles Jesus did. They saw Him feed the 5,000. But He still had to ask them in Mark 8:17, *"Have ye your heart yet hardened?"* They completely forgot what He has done in the midst of them.

In ministry, many times I have seen people rejoice with me and be a partaker of His glory time and time again. Then after five or seven years of sitting under the Word and experiencing His miraculous hand and glory, I have seen people leave my church, hardened in their hearts. They left because at some point God wanted something in their lives He was putting His finger on and they refused to deal with it. Their hearts became hardened and rather than bowing the knee and being mindful of what He has done for them, they just got up and left.

> (1) Exodus 32:1-8 – *"...⁸They have turned aside quickly out of the way which I commanded them: they have made them a molten calf, and have worshipped it, and have sacrificed thereunto, and said, <u>These be thy gods, O Israel, which have brought thee up out of the land of Egypt.</u>"*

d) When we are rebellious
e) We end up returning to our former bondage

3) Jeremiah 19:15 – *"Thus saith the Lord of hosts, the God of Israel; Behold, I will bring upon this city and upon all her towns all the evil that I have pronounced against it, because they have <u>hardened their necks</u>, that they might not hear my words."*

a) That they may not hear my words –We harden our necks in not receiving the Word of God because many times in obeying His Word it costs us something and we simply refuse to do it.

4) Daniel 5:20 – *"But when his heart was lifted up, and his mind <u>hardened in pride</u>, he was deposed from his kingly throne, and they took his glory from him."*

a) Heart lifted up

Do not ever let your heart be lifted up in thinking you are somebody. Always remember there is somebody that sings better than you, somebody that preaches better than you, somebody that teaches, and prophesies better than you. We should not be comparing ourselves.

b) Mind stubborn

Stubbornness is simply a refusal to bow. It is an attitude that say it is got to be your way or the highway. When someone is stubborn, they refuse to be dealt with.

c) Proud
d) He was deposed (Belshazzar)
e) Romans 12:3 – *"For I say, through the grace given unto me, to every man that is among you, not to think of himself more highly than he ought to think; but to think soberly, according as God hath dealt to every man the measure of faith."*

5) Mark 6:47-52 – *"⁴⁷And when even was come, the ship was in the midst of the sea, and he alone on the land. ⁴⁸And he saw them toiling in rowing; for the wind was contrary unto them: and about the fourth watch of the night he cometh unto them, walking upon the sea, and would have passed by them. ⁴⁹But when they saw him walking upon the sea, they supposed it had been a spirit, and cried out: ⁵⁰For they all saw him, and were troubled. And immediately he talked with them, and saith unto them, Be of good cheer:*

it is I; be not afraid. ⁵¹And he went up unto them into the ship; and the wind ceased: and they were sore amazed in themselves beyond measure, and wondered. ⁵²For they considered not the miracle of the loaves: <u>for their heart was hardened</u>."

a) Hardened in Greek – to petrify, to render stupid or callous, blind. From a root word that means a kind of stone.

b) These were disciples who allowed themselves to grow accustomed to God's presence and miraculous power and forget how great and what a privilege it is to know Him intimately.

6) Mark 8:14-21 – "*¹⁴Now the disciples had forgotten to take bread, neither had they in the ship with them more than one loaf. ¹⁵And he charged them, saying, Take heed, beware of the leaven of the Pharisees, and of the leaven of Herod. ¹⁶And they reasoned among themselves, saying, It is because we have no bread. ¹⁷And when Jesus knew it, he saith unto them, Why reason ye, because ye have no bread? perceive ye not yet, neither understand? <u>have ye your heart yet hardened</u>? ¹⁸Having eyes, see ye not? and having ears, hear ye not? and do ye not remember? ¹⁹When I brake the five loaves among five thousand, how many baskets full of fragments took ye up? They say unto him, Twelve. ²⁰And when the seven among four thousand, how many baskets full of fragments took ye up? And they said, Seven. ²¹And he said unto them, How is it that ye do not understand?"*

Notice in this passage that Jesus was speaking to His disciples. Jesus was talking about the teaching of the Pharisees and of Herod. He did not care about natural food; but, the disciples made a mistake and took Him the wrong way. He was not thinking in a carnal and petty way as they were thinking. The disciples had thought He was talking about something that He was not. They might have thought that He was going to be mad at them for not bringing any bread. They whispered among themselves and what arose in them were petty insecurities, foolish attitudes of rejection and an embarrassment for the mistakes that they made.

Therefore, I find in ministry that when you are insecure and are always feeling rejected, you propagate your rejected attitude on everybody with whom you come in contact. Then, you become overly sensitive around others and are watching everyone, waiting for them to confirm to you that they are rejecting you. This can cause you to never trust anyone and your heart becomes hardened so that you cannot receive. Then when God sets a man or woman of God in your life to teach you and help you, you become so full of rejection, insecurities and petty fear that you allow these attitudes and emotions rule you. We have got to learn to overcome it. We all have to overcome the voices, fears, insecurities, and inferiority in our lives. We cannot allow it to live in us so that our hearts become hardened.

7) John 12:37-43 – "*³⁷But though he had done so many miracles before them, yet they believed not on him: ³⁸That the saying of Esaias the prophet might be fulfilled, which he spake, Lord, who hath believed our report? and to whom hath the arm of the Lord been revealed? ³⁹Therefore they could not believe, because that Esaias said again, ⁴⁰He hath blinded their eyes, and <u>hardened their heart</u>; that they should not see with their eyes, nor understand with their heart, and be converted, and I should heal them. ⁴¹These things said Esaias, when he saw his glory, and spake of him. ⁴²Nevertheless among the chief rulers also many believed on him; but because of the Pharisees they did not confess him, lest they should be put out of the synagogue: ⁴³For they loved the praise of men more than the praise of God."*

a) Some will never believe.
b) God hardens some hearts (Pharaoh)
c) It must come by revelation (Matthew 16:17)
d) Only when we see His glory will we bow
e) Loved the praise of men more than the praise of God

3. Believed Not

They made a choice to not believe.

4. Spake Evil Of The Way (Kingdom Teaching)

When we preach or teach a kingdom message, this is the kind of response we may get from religious people and Pharisees. How are we to respond to this? We are always to respond in the love of God. We always want to react in love and in a reconciling way. But there is a limit. Even Jesus himself, as well as Paul, dealt with those who were hardened and did not believe. One thing we have to understand is that not everybody is going to be a disciple. Remember Jesus had the multitudes, then He had the 12, then the three, and then He had the one, John, the beloved disciple. John is the one whom Jesus loved, who laid his head upon his breast, and to whom He gave the revelation of Jesus Christ.

But many, when God truly reveals Himself, do not want anything to do with Him (Exodus 20:21). When people (Christians) hear a word of salvation or healing or deliverance, they'll respond. But when it comes to discipleship, it's not so readily received.

Remember in John 6, when Jesus said, "Unless you eat my flesh and drink my blood, you have no life in you." And they responded saying, "This is a hard saying. Who can hear this?" Then many of the disciples turned and walked no more with Him. Jesus' response was not to beg His own disciples to stay; but, He turned immediately to them, and asked, "Are you going too?"

Any time God moved in the earth and brought something new, it was not received. It was rejected initially. Even Jesus was despised and rejected of men (Isaiah 53:3). So if you are going to come teaching a kingdom message, this is what you can expect. As long as you say things that everybody likes and wants to hear, they love you and support you. As long as you say things that are pleasing and prophesy sweet things to them (Isaiah 30:10), it is good. But when you tell them the truth, they do not want to hear it. Jesus told people the truth all the time. He never hid anything or lied about anything or softened anything so they could receive it. You speak the word as they are able to hear it, but you never compromise truth. You never deceive people. What happens many times in churches is pastors do not say what they want to say because they know if they do, people will not stay. They will not come because they are being asked to be responsible. Discipleship is personal responsibility for your walk with God.

Many people love Jesus; but, they are not in love with Jesus. Many people love the things of God, but when it comes to really knowing Him and seeing Him and what He really wants from us, they do not want it. It is too much responsibility and it would cost them too much. The truth is too much for them. They are not interested in change. They do not want somebody pressuring them. The kingdom of God is all about the dealings of God and being changed every day of your life, dying daily. And if you do not want that, you will never make it. He does not want a part-time people. He does not want a people that halfway-loves Him.

5. Paul Departed From Them

There comes a time when we must separate ourselves from unbelievers and nominal Christians and give ourselves solely to those who desire to be disciples. Therefore, Paul departed from those whose hearts were hardened.

> a. Titus 3:9-11 – "⁹But avoid foolish questions, and genealogies, and contentions, and strivings about the law; for they are unprofitable and vain. ¹⁰A man that is an heretick after the first and second admonition reject; ¹¹Knowing that he that is such is subverted, and sinneth, being condemned of himself."

1) Admonition in Greek – *nouthesia* – warning
2) Reject in Greek – *paraiteomai* – keep out

3) I Corinthians 11:19 – "*For there must be also heresies among you, that they which are approved may be made manifest among you.*" God allows heresies on purpose so those who are not heretics and approved unto God may be made manifest.

   a) Heresies in Greek – *hairesis* – a choice, disunion. From a root – to take for oneself, to choose, to prefer, to sail away. A heresy is something that is sailing away from the Gospel, saying something that is not founded in the Scriptures.

4) II Peter 2:1-3 – "*¹But there were false prophets also among the people, even as there shall be false teachers among you, who privily shall bring in damnable heresies, even denying the Lord that bought them, and bring upon themselves swift destruction. ²And many shall follow their pernicious ways; by reason of whom the way of truth shall be evil spoken of. ³And through covetousness shall they with feigned words make merchandise of you: whose judgment now of a long time lingereth not, and their damnation slumbereth not.*"

Heresy is teaching held by a factional religious party or group which deny some aspect of established doctrine. New Testament writers gave no toleration to heresy in the church.

5) Galatians 1:6-12 – "*⁶I marvel that ye are so soon removed from him that called you into the grace of Christ unto <u>another gospel</u>: ⁷Which is not another; but there be some that trouble you, and would pervert the gospel of Christ. ⁸But though we, or an angel from heaven, preach any other gospel unto you than that which we have preached unto you, let him be accursed. ⁹As we said before, so say I now again, If any man preach <u>any other gospel</u> unto you than that ye have received, let him be accursed. ¹⁰For do I now persuade men, or God? or do I seek to please men? for if I yet pleased men, I should not be the servant of Christ. ¹¹But I certify you, brethren, that the gospel which was preached of me is not after man. ¹²For I neither received it of man, neither was I taught it, but by the revelation of Jesus Christ.*"

Those that are perverting the gospel are those who pervert the grace of God.

   a) II Corinthians 11:4 – "*For if he that cometh preacheth <u>another Jesus</u>, whom we have not preached, or if ye receive <u>another spirit</u>, which ye have not received, or <u>another gospel</u>, which ye have not accepted, ye might well bear with him.*"

There is another Jesus, another spirit and another gospel. Also, as II Peter 2:1-3 states, there are false teachers in these last days.

6) Romans 16:17 – "*Now I beseech you, brethren, <u>mark them</u> which cause divisions and offences contrary to the doctrine which ye have learned; and <u>avoid them</u>.*"
7) II Corinthians 6:14-18 – "*¹⁴Be ye not unequally yoked together with unbelievers: for what fellowship hath righteousness with unrighteousness? and what communion hath light with darkness? ¹⁵And what concord hath Christ with Belial? or what part hath he that believeth with an infidel? ¹⁶And what agreement hath the temple of God with idols? for ye are the temple of the living God; as God hath said, I will dwell in them, and walk in them; and I will be their God, and they shall be my people. ¹⁷<u>Wherefore come out from among them</u>, and be ye separate, saith the Lord, and touch not the unclean thing; and I will receive you, ¹⁸And will be a Father unto you, and ye shall be my sons and daughters, saith the Lord Almighty.*"

There comes a time when we need to get out of something because to stay in it will destroy us. One of the last words in the book of Revelation to His church is to come out of Babylon. Revelation 18:4 states, *"Come out of her, my people, that ye be not partakers of her sins, and that ye receive not of her plagues."* Moreover, verse 2 states that Babylon is, *"become the habitation of devils, and the hold of every foul spirit, and a cage of every unclean and hateful bird."* A little leaven leavens the whole lump. We can only deal with it by coming out and removing ourselves completely from it

8) II Corinthians 7:1 – *"Having therefore these promises, dearly beloved, <u>let us cleanse ourselves</u> from all filthiness of the flesh and spirit, perfecting holiness in the fear of God."*

9) Matthew 23:2-3, 13-39 – *"²Saying, The scribes and the Pharisees sit in Moses' seat: ³All therefore whatsoever they bid you observe, that observe and do; but do not ye after their works: for they say, and do not...¹³But woe unto you, scribes and Pharisees, hypocrites! for ye shut up the kingdom of heaven against men: for ye neither go in yourselves, neither suffer ye them that are entering to go in...²⁴Ye blind guides, which strain at a gnat, and swallow a camel...³⁹For I say unto you, Ye shall not see me henceforth, till ye shall say, Blessed is he that cometh in the name of the Lord."*

10) Matthew 21:12-14 – *"¹²And Jesus went into the temple of God, and <u>cast out all them that sold and bought in the temple</u>, and overthrew the tables of the moneychangers, and the seats of them that sold doves, ¹³And said unto them, It is written, My house shall be called the house of prayer; but ye have made it a den of thieves. ¹⁴And the blind and the lame came to him in the temple; and he healed them."*

Jesus was not just talking to anybody. He was speaking to those in the temple, such as the Levites and priests, who were selling doves and trinkets. Jesus didn't shy away. He actually went in and made a whip (John 2:15), knocked over their tables and ran the thieves out of the temple. Jesus actually whipped people out of the church. How much of this buying and selling is going on in the church today?

11) Acts 18:6 – Paul forsaking the Jews – *"And when they opposed themselves, and blasphemed, he shook his raiment, and said unto them, Your blood be upon your own heads; I am clean: from henceforth I will go unto the Gentiles."*

Paul loved his own people. Paul says in Romans 10:1, *"Brethren, my heart's and prayer to God for Israel is, that they might be saved."* But in this passage, Paul shook his raiment and departed from the Jews to go and preach the gospel to the Gentiles. What motivated Paul to act this way to his people? Every time Paul preached and taught to them, every time he disputed and persuaded, they believed not. Not only did they believe not, but they got very angry at Paul. At one time, a band of men gathered together and covenanted with each other to follow Paul wherever he went to torment him and trouble him. Acts 23:12 states, *"And when it was day, certain of the Jews banded together, and bound themselves under a curse, saying that they would neither eat nor drink till they had killed Paul."* Therefore, there came a time when even Paul had to depart from even his own people.

b. He Separated The Disciples – Disciples Are Different From The Multitudes

Discipleship is being responsible for your own walk with God. Many people love Jesus; but, they are not *in love* with Him. But there are people who are in love with him and desire more. They are desiring truth and real change in their lives. It is not enough for them to go to a meeting and get blessed; but, they also want the next day to be a different person.

1) Mark 6:45-46 – *"⁴⁵And straightway he constrained his disciples to get into the ship, and to go to the other side before unto Bethsaida, while he sent away the people. ⁴⁶And when he had sent them away, he departed into a mountain to pray."*

2) Isaiah 8:16 – *"Bind up the testimony, seal the law among my disciples."*

A disciple is one who has the testimony of God bound up within them and the Word of God sealed up in their lives.

3) Matthew 8:21-27 – "*21And another of his disciples said unto him, Lord, suffer me first to go and bury my father. 22But Jesus said unto him, Follow me; and let the dead bury their dead. 23And when he was entered into a ship, his disciples followed him. 24And, behold, there arose a great tempest in the sea, insomuch that the ship was covered with the waves: but he was asleep. 25And his disciples came to him, and awoke him, saying, Lord, save us: we perish. 26And he saith unto them, Why are ye fearful, O ye of little faith? Then he arose, and rebuked the winds and the sea; and there was a great calm. 27But the men marvelled, saying, What manner of man is this, that even the winds and the sea obey him!*"

4) Disciple in Hebrew – *limmud* – learned, taught, instructed, used. From a root – skillful, expert, accustomed to

5) Disciple in Greek – *mathetes* – a learner, a pupil, discipled one, student of the Word

6) Luke 6:40 – "*The disciple is not above his master: but every one that is perfect shall be as his master.*"

A true disciple wants to be as his master Jesus. It is not enough just to be saved. A disciple is not satisfied just to go to heaven. He wants to bear the image of his master.

7) Luke 14:27 – "*And whosoever doth not bear his cross, and come after me, cannot be my disciple.*"

8) Luke 14:33 – "*So likewise, whosoever he be of you that forsaketh not all that he hath, he cannot be my disciple.*"

We must show Jesus that nothing in this life, such as family, job, possessions, relationships, etc. owns us. Jesus must own everything we have. That is a true disciple.

9) Luke 14:26 – "*If any man come to me, and hate not his father, and mother, and wife, and children, and brethren, and sisters, yea, and his own life also, he cannot be my disciple.*"

a) Hate in Greek – to love less

To be a true disciple means that we must put our family in order. Jesus must come first.

10) Matthew 9:37-38 – "*37Then saith he unto his disciples, The harvest truly is plenteous, but the labourers are few; 38Pray ye therefore the Lord of the harvest, that he will send forth labourers into his harvest.*" Labourers in Greek – a toiler, a teacher

11) Mark 3:13-15 – "*13And he goeth up into a mountain, and calleth unto him whom he would: and they came unto him. 14And he ordained twelve, that they should be with him, and that he might send them forth to preach, 15And to have power to heal sicknesses, and to cast out devils:*"

A disciple's greatest calling is that they are to be with Him. A disciple must spend intimate time with Jesus every day. This is not just praying and asking Him for things, but to simply be with Him, to honor Him, glorify Him and know Him!

12) Matthew 14:15-21 – "*15And when it was evening, his disciples came to him, saying, This is a desert place, and the time is now past; send the multitude away, that they may go*

into the villages, and buy themselves victuals. [16]But Jesus said unto them, They need not depart; give ye them to eat. [17]And they say unto him, We have here but five loaves, and two fishes. [18]He said, Bring them hither to me. [19]And he commanded the multitude to sit down on the grass, and took the five loaves, and the two fishes, and looking up to heaven, he blessed, and brake, and <u>gave the loaves to his disciples, and the disciples to the multitude</u>. [20]And they did all eat, and were filled: and they took up of the fragments that remained twelve baskets full. [21]And they that had eaten were about five thousand men, beside women and children."

Only disciples can feed bread to the multitude because they got it directly broken for them by Jesus.

Chapter 6

What The Kingdom Of God Produces

In this lesson, I would like to look at the outworking of the Kingdom of God and what it produces within the lives of His people. Again, the Kingdom of God does not come with observation. You may not be able to see this kingdom, as Luke 17:20-21 states, "*The kingdom of God cometh not with observation: ²¹Neither shall they say, Lo here! or, lo there! For, behold, the kingdom of God is within you.*" The Kingdom of God is a spiritual kingdom within the sons of men. You won't necessarily see it. Rather, you will see the outworking of it and what it produces. When the earth sees the Kingdom of God manifesting itself through the sons of God, the new Jerusalem, then the true Kingdom of God will be realized in the earth.

Jesus is going to have a loyal and dedicated people, a precious and escaped portion, a remnant that have been through His dealings, have been through the darkest of dark and have prevailed and overcome. They won't have anything to boast about, except for the grace and mercy of God. The Kingdom of God will have been produced fully within them.

I. Scriptural Examples

    A. Mark 4:26-32 – "*²⁶And he said, So is the kingdom of God, as if a man should cast seed into the ground; ²⁷And should sleep, and rise night and day, and the seed should spring and grow up, he knoweth not how. ²⁸For the earth bringeth forth fruit of herself; first the blade, then the ear, after that the full corn in the ear. ²⁹But when the fruit is brought forth, immediately he putteth in the sickle, because the harvest is come. ³⁰And he said, Whereunto shall we liken the kingdom of God? or with what comparison shall we compare it? ³¹It is like a grain of mustard seed, which, when it is sown in the earth, is less than all the seeds that be in the earth: ³²But when it is sown, it groweth up, and becometh greater than all herbs, and shooteth out great branches; so that the fowls of the air may lodge under the shadow of it.*"

        1. The Kingdom of God is like a seed sown into the ground. I Peter 1:23 says that we have been born again of "*incorruptible* [seed], *by the word of God, which liveth and abideth for ever.*" Moreover, the angel Gabriel told Mary, in Luke 1:35, "*that holy thing which shall be born of thee shall be called the Son of God.*" Everything starts with a seed. God plants the seed within us. It grows up within our spirit and overflows into our soulish man. As our souls are sanctified completely by His word and presence, the glory then flows out into the physical realm and then

the harvest can come. The parable says that the sickle is immediately put forth when it reaches full ripeness. As soon as our physical bodies move into that Kingdom realm, it is over and the sons of God have been formed and a harvest can be gathered.

Therefore, this first parable explains that first is the blade, then the ear, and after that the full corn in the ear. These three areas speak of our three-fold nature: our spirit, soul and bodies.

2. The second parable of this passage is a picture of the Kingdom of God being likened unto a grain of mustard. What begins very small and miniscule becomes the greatest of all trees. Out of that seed, grows a great tree. What God is doing in His people is likened unto trees. Isaiah 61:3 states, *"that they might be called trees of righteousness, the planting of the Lord, that he might be glorified."* God plants the seed and then the seed begins to grow. God's people are to *"take root downward, and bear fruit upward."*

Many times, before God can build up His people, He must do what God called Jeremiah to do. Jeremiah 1:10, *"See, I have this day set thee over the nations and over the kingdoms, to root out, and to pull down, and to destroy, and to throw down, to build, and to plant."* God must first get rid of all the garbage in our lives and the things within us that are not of Him. But as God deals with His people, He can then begin to build up, plant and grow His Kingdom within them.

B. Luke 13:20-21 – *"20And again he said, Whereunto shall I liken the kingdom of God? 21It is like leaven, which a woman took and hid in three measures of meal, till the whole was leavened."*

1. The three measures of meal speak of the three-fold man. The Kingdom of God is to grow up, beginning in our spirits, then flow to out into our souls, until it reaches our bodies, every area of our lives comes under His Kingdom.
2. The problem is, many Christians feel that just getting born again in their spirits is enough. However, God wants every aspect of our being, our spirit, soul and body, to be conformed to His image. The Kingdom of God is within us and wants to fill us completely.

C. Psalms 145:10-13 – *"10All thy works shall praise thee, O Lord; and thy saints shall bless thee. 11They shall speak of the glory of thy kingdom, and talk of thy power; 12To make known to the sons of men his mighty acts, and the glorious majesty of his kingdom. 13Thy kingdom is an everlasting kingdom, and thy dominion endureth throughout all generations."*

How do you make known to the sons of men His mighty acts and the glorious majesty of His kingdom? I believe it will be made known as a people are truly walking in His kingdom. Jesus prayed in John 17:21 that His people, *"may be one; as thou Father, art in me, and I in thee, that they also may be on in us: that the world may believe that thou hast sent me."* Until we realize that the Kingdom of God is within us and wants to manifest itself within us, then we can truly begin to try to walk it out, where Jesus is truly exalted.

D. Daniel 7:18 – *"But the saints of the most High shall take the kingdom, and possess the kingdom for ever, even for ever and ever."*

It does not matter to me as to when this will take place; but, that it will take place. The sons of God will possess the Kingdom of God. Jesus will truly rule and reign within them.

E. Obadiah 17-21 – *"17But upon mount Zion shall be deliverance, and there shall be holiness; and the house of Jacob shall possess their possessions. 18And the house of Jacob shall be a fire, and the house of Joseph a flame, and the house of Esau for stubble, and they shall kindle in them, and devour them; and there shall not be any remaining of the house of Esau; for the Lord hath spoken it. 19And they of the south shall possess the mount of Esau; and they of the plain the Philistines: and they shall possess the fields of Ephraim, and the fields of Samaria: and Benjamin shall possess Gilead. ²⁰And the captivity of this host of the children of Israel shall possess that of the Canaanites, even unto Zarephath; and the captivity of Jerusalem, which is in Sepharad, shall possess the cities of the south. ²¹And saviours shall come up on mount Zion to judge the mount of Esau; and the kingdom shall be the Lord's."*

1. Hebrew word for deliverance – *peleytah* – "an escaped portion or remnant." Mount Zion is an escaped remnant, which travel that narrow way which leads to life.
2. Esau is a type of the flesh.
3. Jacob is a type of God's people who have not yet had a character change within them.
4. South always represents prosperity and blessing.
5. Philistines represent the enemies of God.
6. *"Saviours"* in verse 21 are the sons of God, who will be walking in total deliverance.

They will not have to pray or seek God about deliverance from sin and sickness in their lives anymore. They will be walking in divine health, purity and innocence again. They will possess the mount of Esau, the flesh. This is akin to Genesis 25:26, when Jacob came out of his mother's womb. Esau came out first, but Jacob reached out with his hand and took hold of Esau's heal. As the sons of God go through the womb, through the veil, the house of Jacob is going to put their hands upon the man of flesh and rule and reign over it. They will possess the mount of Esau.

It is interesting that God would use the term *"saviours"* to describe His people. This is like when Joseph was given an Egyptian name by Pharaoh. Pharaoh called Joseph *"Zaphnathpaaneah,"* which literally means, "savior of the age (or world)." He was given this name after he went through all of his dealings and time in prison. Psalms 105:19 says of Joseph, *"Until the time that his word came: the word of the Lord tried him."* His word came when Pharaoh called Joseph to stand before him. Joseph ended up saving the then known world from famine. Everybody had to go to Egypt to be fed during the famine. Joseph was a savior to the whole world.

7. The house of Jacob will also possess their possessions. I believe this means that their possessions will not possess them. That is the trouble with prosperity. It can get a hold of us and become bigger to us than it should. We need to get to the place as Paul did, when he says in Philippians 3:12, *"I know both how to be abased, and I know how to abound: every where and in all things I am instructed both to be full and to be hungry, both to abound and to suffer need."* We need to come to a place that riches mean nothing to us and do not change us. Also, poverty, the dealings of God and valley experiences, do not change us either. We need to remain consistent. God is doing this work within us, as Isaiah says,

> *"Every valley shall be exalted, and every mountain and hill shall be made low: and the crooked shall be made straight, and the rough places plain. ⁵And the glory of the Lord shall be revealed, and all flesh shall see it together."* (Isaiah 40:4-5)

F. Ezekiel 16:1-18 – *"⁸Now when I passed by thee, and looked upon thee, behold, thy time was the time of love; and I spread my skirt over thee, and covered thy nakedness: yea, I sware unto thee, and entered into a covenant with thee, saith the Lord God, and thou becamest mine... ¹³And thou was exceeding beautiful, and thou didst prosper into a kingdom."*

This is the story of the woman (who is a type of God's people) who was cast out into the open field. But God passed by and saved her. These verses, which have great spiritual significant, then tell of all the growth and ways that the Lord fashions the woman until she reaches fullness and ultimately prospers into a kingdom. This parable is a type of how God saves His people and then grow them up where the Kingdom of God finds its fulfillment in her life. As Exodus 19:6 states, we are called to be "*a kingdom of priests, and an holy nation.*"

G. Matthew 6:10 – "*Thy kingdom come. Thy will be done in earth, as it is in heaven.*"

I believe Jesus is speaking of the Kingdom of God coming not only in the actual earth, but in our flesh as well. In the earthen part of our lives, the Kingdom of God will rule within. Practically speaking, every day in our lives when we come across a temptation or some dealing, the Kingdom of God rules and causes us to overcome in the trial where we don't even acknowledge that temptation. In other words, the principles of the Kingdom of God become bone of our bone and flesh of our flesh. Jesus said in John 14:30, "*For the prince of this world cometh, and hath nothing in me.*" One translation says, "*The prince of this world cometh, and has nothing in common with me.*" Paul exhorts us in Ephesians 4:27, "*Neither give place to the devil.*"

Therefore, one by one, every chamber of our soul has been taken over by the Spirit of God and the Word of God and has been redeemed and changed into the likeness of Jesus. As Paul says in Galatians 2:20, "*I am crucified with Christ: nevertheless I live; yet not I, but Christ liveth in me: and the life which I now live in the flesh I live by the faith of the Son of God, who loved me, and gave himself for me.*" David says in Psalms 17:15, "*As for me, I will behold thy face in righteousness: I shall be satisfied, when I awake, with thy likeness.*" We are to be conformed to the image of the Son. We should prepare ourselves to walk through that veil into His glory.

H. 1 Thessalonians 2:12 – "*That ye would walk worthy of God, who hath called you unto his kingdom and glory.*"

II. God's Kingdom Is A Spiritual One

A. John 18:36 – "*Jesus answered, My kingdom is not of this world: if my kingdom were of this world, then would my servants fight, that I should not be delivered to the Jews: but now is my kingdom not from hence.*"

   1. Romans 14:17 – "*For the kingdom of God is not meat and drink; but righteousness, and peace, and joy in the Holy Ghost.*"
   2. Luke 17:20-21 – "*[20]And when he was demanded of the Pharisees, when the kingdom of God should come, he answered them and said, The kingdom of God cometh not with observation: [21]Neither shall they say, Lo here! or, lo there! for, behold, the kingdom of God is within you.*"
   3. II Peter 1:1-11 – "*[1]Simon Peter, a servant and an apostle of Jesus Christ, to them that have obtained like precious faith with us through the righteousness of God and our Saviour Jesus Christ: [2]Grace and peace be multiplied unto you through the knowledge of God, and of Jesus our Lord, [3]According as his divine power hath given unto us all things that pertain unto life and godliness, through the knowledge of him that hath called us to glory and virtue: [4]Whereby are given unto us exceeding great and precious promises: that by these ye might be partakers of the divine nature, having escaped the corruption that is in the world through lust. [5]And beside this, giving all diligence, add to your faith virtue; and to virtue knowledge; [6]And to knowledge temperance; and to temperance patience; and to patience godliness; [7]And to godliness brotherly kindness; and to brotherly kindness charity. [8]For if these things be in you, and abound, they make you that ye shall neither be barren nor unfruitful in the knowledge of our Lord Jesus Christ. [9]But he that lacketh these things is blind, and cannot see afar off, and hath forgotten that he was purged from his old sins. [10]Wherefore the rather, brethren, give diligence to make your calling and election sure: for if ye do these things, ye shall never fall: [11]For so an entrance shall be ministered unto you abundantly into the everlasting kingdom of our Lord and Saviour Jesus Christ.*"

      a. Virtue in Greek – *arete* – "manliness, excellence, valor"

      b. The promises in Scripture are given to us to be a partaker of His divine nature.

      c. Once you partake of the divine nature, it enters into you and you begin to take on His glorious nature. You actually become a little Christ, or anointed one, which is what the word Christian actually means. The highest you can go in God is being a partaker of His divine nature.

      d. Once you begin to partake of His nature, you can escape all the temptation and evil that is in this world through lust because our new nature in Him will reject that temptation.

      e. When King Jesus begins to move in His kingdom of priests, and the Kingdom of God becomes operative in our lives, then we can begin to manifest and show the real Jesus to the world.

      f. We must give diligence to this calling.

      g. Many people feel that faith is enough. However, we must add to our faith, then, virtue, knowledge, temperance, patience, godliness, and brotherly kindness. These are the characteristics of Jesus, the nature of God.

      h. Having the character of God means having shoulders strong enough to carry His glory within you.

      i. When we do these things mentioned in these verses and carry His character, an entrance shall be given into His everlasting Kingdom.

4. Luke 13:24-29 – "*24Strive to enter in at the strait gate: for many, I say unto you, will seek to enter in, and shall not be able. 25When once the master of the house is risen up, and hath shut to the door, and ye begin to stand without, and to knock at the door, saying, Lord, Lord, open unto us; and he shall answer and say unto you, I know you not whence ye are: 26Then shall ye begin to say, We have eaten and drunk in thy presence, and thou hast taught in our streets. 27But he shall say, I tell you, I know you not whence ye are; depart from me, all ye workers of iniquity. 28There shall be weeping and gnashing of teeth, when ye shall see Abraham, and Isaac, and Jacob, and all the prophets, in the kingdom of God, and you yourselves thrust out. 29And they shall come from the east, and from the west, and from the north, and from the south, and shall sit down in the kingdom of God.*"

      a. It does not matter if you have received great teaching or you can prophesy and move in the gifts of God. What matters is having His character and nature within you.

      b. It is sin in God's eyes to not know Him intimately.

      c. Knowing Him intimately is what the Kingdom of God is all about.

      d. Many will realize the horror when the door into the Kingdom of God is shut to those who do not know Him intimately.

5. I Corinthians 4:20 – "*For the kingdom of God is not in word, but in power.*"

Chapter 7
The Coming Of The Kingdom

In this lesson, I want to look at the coming of the Kingdom of God in the last days. Particularly, I want to start with a passage found in Micah:

> "*6In that day, saith the Lord, will I assemble her that halteth, and I will gather her that is driven out, and her that I have afflicted; 7And I will make her that halted a remnant, and her that was cast far off a strong nation: and the Lord shall reign over them in mount Zion from henceforth, even for ever. 8And thou, O tower of the flock, the strong hold of the daughter of Zion, unto thee shall it come, even the first dominion;* **the kingdom shall come to the daughter of Jerusalem**." (Micah 4:6-8)

"*In that day*" is speaking about the "day of the Lord" or the last days. I believe this passage is a picture of God's holy remnant and how the Kingdom of God will come and be established in the earth in the last days. The Kingdom of God is God's rule and reign completely within a people. As Jesus said in Luke 17:21, "*Behold, the kingdom of God is within you.*" This is going to come to a poor and afflicted people, as Micah declares.

God has a word for those that halt. He is not speaking to the "great ones." He is not talking to the super-spiritual or those that seem to have it all together. He wants the halt or those that can't walk on their own to have hope. He wants them to get the revelation that the Lord allowed the affliction and trials in their lives for a greater purpose. So if you do not have it all together today, hear the Word of the Lord.

God wants to make you part of His holy remnant. I believe the Scriptures are very clear that this remnant is not everybody in the body of Christ; but a people within a people. Consider this: Jesus had the multitude following Him. Then Jesus had the 70 that followed Him most of the time. After that, Jesus had the twelve disciples specifically chosen. Then out of the 12, He had the three (Peter, James, and John) who personally went with Jesus to do and experience greater things than the other nine. And finally, within the three, Jesus had the one disciple (John) who laid His head on Jesus' chest at the last supper of whom the Bible says twice that John was the disciple whom Jesus loved. This is the principle of the remnant.

Now let me say also that God is no respecter of persons. He loves everybody; but if the truth is told, not everybody has or desires to have an intimate relationship with Jesus. Therefore, out of the body of Christ is going to come forth a holy remnant, completely devoted and in love with the Lord Jesus. Yes, they may be halt; but the truth is without Jesus nobody can make it. Furthermore this remnant understands that apart from the grace of God they are nothing. You see in our weaknesses, God is made strong. He gets glory by working through our inabilities. And when God finally finds a people that allow Him to work through the issues in their lives, He will bring together a people that are broken and humbled prepared for the Kingdom of God.

Moreover, Micah says God will reign over this people in Mount Zion. God will have brought the halt to Mount Zion. Zion is a place, a people, a mountain, and a kingdom; but more than anything, Zion is a place in the spirit where God's corporate people come together and God's glory literally enthrones everybody's heart in worship. It is the place where God Himself reigns in a people on the earth. Therefore, it has nothing to do with a particular natural piece of land but everything to do with the hearts of God's holy remnant all over the earth.

Psalms 50:2 says, "*Out of Zion, the perfection of beauty, God hath shined.*" Zion is the place where the presence of God rests over the mercy seat and we come in and give Him glory. Out of this place, God shines. As a people we enter into Zion through worship creating with our hearts a throne for Him to come and dwell and a place for Him to rule and reign. This is the Zion the Lord is coming to in the last days. God wants to rule and reign out of a people. This people would have been halt; but now in Zion, they will be completely healed, delivered, and made free. They will be given the Spirit of God without measure like Jesus had. Everyone here will know the Lord intimately and out of this people God will rule and reign in the earth. This is the establishment of the coming Kingdom of God in the last days.

Lastly, God defines the coming of the Kingdom of God as a people having "*the first dominion.*" What does this mean? It means having dominion over God's creation like God originally gave Adam in the Garden of Eden. God wants us to have dominion over everything. The sons of God are going to have restored to them the first dominion and then "*the kingdom shall come to the daughter of Jerusalem.*" This passage is not speaking of natural Jerusalem, but God's spiritual Jerusalem.

There is a difference between the Kingdom of Heaven and the Kingdom of God. The Kingdom of God is the rule and governing principles of God operative on the earth. As Christians we are learning to live in the Kingdom of God right now. We are assured of the Kingdom of Heaven because of the sacrifice of Jesus. However, we are not assured of dwelling and living in the Kingdom of God. Jesus said, "*No man, having put his hand to the plough, and looking back, is fit for the kingdom of God*" (Luke 9:62). Jesus wasn't talking about the Kingdom of Heaven here, but the Kingdom of God. This is why we need to rightly divide the Word of God. As Christians, we can never lose our salvation because that was by grace alone. What we lose if we don't go on with God is our reward of the coming Kingdom of God.

Romans 14:17 says, "*The kingdom of God is not meat and drink.*" This is speaking of the Law. The Kingdom of God is not about laws; but it is "*righteousness, and peace, and joy in the Holy Ghost.*" In Luke 17:20-21 Jesus said, "*The kingdom of God cometh not with observation.*" I Corinthians 4:20 says, "*For the kingdom of God is not in word, but in power.*"

Jesus teaches us that our prayer should be, "*Thy kingdom come. Thy will be done in earth, as it is in heaven*" (Matthew 6:10). What God is trying to do on this side of the veil is get us ready for the other side of the veil. God wants what is happening in heaven to be manifested in the earth. We need to start living in how God is living right now "*because as he is, so are we in this world*" (I John 4:17). This is what is coming to God's remnant.

God is preparing us to live in the Kingdom of God and right now, you and I can begin to do it. No longer do we need to think of the Kingdom of God as something way off in the future because it is now. When Jesus walked the earth He preached, "*The Kingdom of God is at hand*" (Mark 1:15). God is waiting on you and me.

We need to stop talking and start doing the Word of God. And as we do, I believe we are going to find the struggles and sins in our lives falling off of us.

I Corinthians 15:50 says, "*flesh and blood cannot inherit the kingdom of God.*" All the fruits of the flesh mentioned in Galatians 5 cannot inherit the Kingdom of God. In other words, you and I will not be in the remnant or bride of Christ if we allow the flesh in our lives to rule and reign. Our flesh must be put under. We must have dominion over our flesh and the Holy Spirit will be the one who will do it for us. We need to simply make a decision that we will not be ruled by our flesh anymore and yield these things to the Holy Ghost. In the last days, the actual Kingdom of God on earth is going to live in a people. I believe this is going to happen in a remnant. As you will read below, the Scriptures declare this. It is that in what we are called.

I want to be a part of that remnant. How about you? But the truth is you can't be part of the remnant being a casual Christian and going to church 1-2 times a week. Hebrews 10:25 exhorts us, "*Not forsaking the assembling of ourselves together, as the manner of some is; but exhorting one another: and so much the more, as ye see the day approaching.*" The day of the coming of the Kingdom of God is fast approaching and now more than ever, Jesus needs to be everything to you. But yet in much of the body of Christ, the truth is Jesus is not the focus and most important thing. Most people visit Jesus when they want to and when it is convenient for them. Get rid of the convenience. Make Him Lord in everything in your life; because, the word kingdom means a rule and dominion. If Jesus does not rule your life now, how will the Kingdom ever come to you? It will not.

So allow the Scriptures below to bring vision and light to your life. See that the Kingdom of God is coming to a people that will be fit and prepared for that day. It is our calling, for King Jesus to rule and reign all over the earth through His people. As Micah 4:8 declares again, "*And thou, O tower of the flock, the strong hold of the daughter of Zion, unto thee shall it come, even the first dominion; **the kingdom shall come to the daughter of Jerusalem**.*" Will you be counted among this group?

I. Coming To The Kingdom

    A. Word definitions for "Kingdom"

        1. Hebrew – a rule, dominion, empire, realm, sovereign despot; it comes from a root that means – to reign, to ascend the throne, to set up a king, to induct into royalty

        2. Greek – royalty, rule or realm; it comes from a root that means – the foundation of a power, sovereign

    B. Scriptures Declaring God's Coming Kingdom

        1. Esther 4:13-14 – "*13Then Mordecai commanded to answer Esther, Think not with thyself that thou shalt escape in the king's house, more than all the Jews. 14For if thou altogether holdest thy peace at this time, then shall there enlargement and deliverance arise to the Jews from another place; but thou and thy father's house shall be destroyed: and who knoweth whether thou art come to the kingdom for such a time as this?*"

        2. Daniel 7:22-27 – "*22Until the Ancient of days came, and judgment was given to the saints of the most High; and the time came that the saints possessed the kingdom. 23Thus he said, The fourth beast shall be the fourth kingdom upon earth, which shall be diverse from all kingdoms, and shall devour the whole earth, and shall tread it down, and break it in pieces. 24And the ten horns out of this kingdom are ten kings that shall arise: and another shall rise after them; and he shall be diverse from the first, and he shall subdue three kings. 25And he shall speak great words against the most High, and shall wear out the saints of the most High, and think to change times and laws: and they shall be given into his hand until a time and times and the dividing of time. 26But the judgment shall sit, and they shall take away his dominion, to consume and to destroy it unto the end. 27And the kingdom and dominion, and the greatness of the kingdom under the whole heaven,*"

shall be given to the people of the saints of the most High, whose kingdom is an everlasting kingdom, and all dominions shall serve and obey him."

3. Obadiah 17-21 – "17But upon mount Zion shall be deliverance, and there shall be holiness; and the house of Jacob shall possess their possessions. 18And the house of Jacob shall be a fire, and the house of Joseph a flame, and the house of Esau for stubble, and they shall kindle in them, and devour them; and there shall not be any remaining of the house of Esau; for the Lord hath spoken it. 19And they of the south shall possess the mount of Esau; and they of the plain the Philistines: and they shall possess the fields of Ephraim, and the fields of Samaria: and Benjamin shall possess Gilead. 20And the captivity of this host of the children of Israel shall possess that of the Canaanites, even unto Zarephath; and the captivity of Jerusalem, which is in Sepharad, shall possess the cities of the south. 21And saviours shall come up on mount Zion to judge the mount of Esau; and the kingdom shall be the Lord's."

4. Ezekiel 16:13 – "Thus wast thou decked with gold and silver; and thy raiment was of fine linen, and silk, and broidered work; thou didst eat fine flour, and honey, and oil: and thou wast exceeding beautiful, and thou didst prosper into a kingdom."

5. Matthew 6:10 – "Thy kingdom come. Thy will be done in earth, as it is in heaven."

6. Matthew 6:33 – "But seek ye first the kingdom of God, and his righteousness; and all these things shall be added unto you."

7. Mark 4:11 – "And he said unto them, Unto you it is given to know the mystery of the kingdom of God: but unto them that are without, all these things are done in parables:"

8. Luke 8:1 – "And it came to pass afterward, that he went throughout every city and village, preaching and shewing the glad tidings of the kingdom of God: and the twelve were with him,"

9. Luke 9:1-6 – "1Then he called his twelve disciples together, and gave them power and authority over all devils, and to cure diseases. 2And he sent them to preach the kingdom of God, and to heal the sick. 3And he said unto them, Take nothing for your journey, neither staves, nor scrip, neither bread, neither money; neither have two coats apiece. 4And whatsoever house ye enter into, there abide, and thence depart. 5And whosoever will not receive you, when ye go out of that city, shake off the very dust from your feet for a testimony against them. 6And they departed, and went through the towns, preaching the gospel, and healing every where."

10. Luke 9:62 – "And Jesus said unto him, No man, having put his hand to the plough, and looking back, is fit for the kingdom of God."

11. Luke 13:18-22 – "18Then said he, Unto what is the kingdom of God like? and whereunto shall I resemble it? 19It is like a grain of mustard seed, which a man took, and cast into his garden; and it grew, and waxed a great tree; and the fowls of the air lodged in the branches of it. 20And again he said, Whereunto shall I liken the kingdom of God? 21It is like leaven, which a woman took and hid in three measures of meal, till the whole was leavened. 22And he went through the cities and villages, teaching, and journeying toward Jerusalem."

12. Luke 17:20-21 – "20And when he was demanded of the Pharisees, when the kingdom of God should come, he answered them and said, The kingdom of God cometh not with observation: 21Neither shall they say, Lo here! or, lo there! for, behold, the kingdom of God is within you."

13. Acts 14:22 – "Confirming the souls of the disciples, and exhorting them to continue in the faith, and that we must through much tribulation enter into the kingdom of God."

14. Romans 14:17 – "For the kingdom of God is not meat and drink; but righteousness, and peace, and joy in the Holy Ghost."

15. I Corinthians 4:20 – "For the kingdom of God is not in word, but in power."

16. I Corinthians 15:50 – "Now this I say, brethren, that flesh and blood cannot inherit the kingdom of God; neither doth corruption inherit incorruption."

17. I Thessalonians 2:12 – "That ye would walk worthy of God, who hath called you unto his kingdom and glory."

Chapter 8
How The Kingdom Of God Comes

As was said many times, the Kingdom of God is the reign of the Lord Jesus within a people. We will not see the kingdom flowing in the earth until Jesus is truly King within a people. So it is time now for a people to commit themselves to the vision of the Kingdom of God. God has to see a committed people, who have devoted themselves every hour of every day to Jesus, completely walking with Jesus. Then God will see that a people will be worthy of committing His power and authority. God is so ready and willing to pour out His Spirit and Kingdom on the earth.

Many people think that it is all just a mystery and we will never know until we get to heaven. However, Deuteronomy 29:29 tells us, "*The secret things belong unto the Lord our God: but those things which are revealed belong unto us and to our children forever.*" Moreover, I Corinthians 2:9-10 explains, "*Eye hath not seen, nor ear heard, neither have entered into the heart of man, the things which God hath prepared for them that love him. ¹⁰But God hath revealed them unto us by his Spirit: for the Spirit searcheth all things, yea, the deep things of God.*" God wants His Kingdom to come on earth and to a people, this will be revealed. I believe the day is coming that we will know when the Kingdom of God has come on earth as it is in heaven. In this lesson, we will look at this principle of knowing, scripturally, when the Kingdom of God has come on earth.

I. Scriptural Examples

    A. Matthew 12:22-28 – "*Then was brought unto him one possessed with a devil, blind, and dumb: and he healed him, insomuch that the blind and dumb both spake and saw. ²³And all the people were amazed, and said, Is not this the son of David? ...²⁸But if I cast out devils by the Spirit of God, then the kingdom of God is come unto you.*"

It is only when true miracles take place when the Kingdom of God is in effect. It is like the passage in I Kings 17:24 where the woman tells Elijah, after Elijah has healed her son, "*Now by this I know that thou art a man of God, and that the word of the Lord in thy mouth is truth.*" How did she know? She knew God was in the place because her son was healed.

    1. Other Translations:

"*But if it is by God's power that I am sending the evil spirits packing, then the kingdom of God is here for sure.*"
"*But if I by the Spirit of God, do cast out the demons, then come already unto you did the reign of God.*"

"But if I by the Spirit of God send out evil spirits, then the kingdom of God is come on you."
"But if I am casting out demons by the Spirit of God, then the kingdom of God has arrived among you."
"But if I use the power of God's Spirit to force out demons, then the kingdom of God has come to you."
"But if I cast out demons by the Spirit of God, then the kingdom of God has already overtaken you."
"But if it is by the power of the Spirit of God that I expel the demons, it is evident that he kingdom of God has come upon you."
"No it is not Beezebub, but God's Spirit, who gives me the power to drive out demons, which proves that the kingdom of God has already come upon you."
"But since by means of God's Spirit I am ejecting the demons, surely then the kingdom of God has come upon you unexpectedly."

2. How Does This Happen Scripturally?

   a. Exodus 19:3-6 – *"³And Moses went up unto God, and the Lord called unto him out of the mountain, saying, Thus shalt thou say to the house of Jacob, and tell the children of Israel; ⁴Ye have seen what I did unto the Egyptians, and how I bare you on eagles' wings, and brought you unto myself. ⁵Now therefore, if ye will obey my voice indeed, and keep my covenant, then ye shall be a peculiar treasure unto me above all people: for all the earth is mine: ⁶And ye shall be unto me a kingdom of priests, and an holy nation. These are the words which thou shalt speak unto the children of Israel."*

      1) A peculiar treasure – The first thing that God lets known in this passage is that God wants a people, a peculiar people for Himself. This is a revelation that our walk with God is not about us, but about God getting a people to advance His kingdom throughout the earth.
      2) A kingdom of priests – This peculiar people shall be people full of His anointing and authority, totally devoted to Him.

   b. Psalms 103:17-22 – *"¹⁷But the mercy of the Lord is from everlasting to everlasting upon them that fear him, and his righteousness unto children's children; ¹⁸To such as keep his covenant, and to those that remember his commandments to do them. ¹⁹The Lord hath prepared his throne in the heavens; and his kingdom ruleth over all. ²⁰Bless the Lord, ye his angels, that excel in strength, that do his commandments, hearkening unto the voice of his word. ²¹Bless ye the Lord, all ye his hosts; ye ministers of his, that do his pleasure. ²²Bless the Lord, all his works in all places of his dominion: bless the Lord, O my soul."*

We know the Kingdom of God has come where there is His dominion. His dominion is in places where there is a people who keep His covenant and do His pleasure. They not only say, they truly do; because, they have allowed King Jesus to reign and rule over all, over everything in their lives. His Kingdom moves in the earth where He has liberty to reign. When this is truly accomplished in a people, then His works, His Glory will manifest itself through them.

   c. Psalms 145:5-13 – *"I will speak of the glorious honour of thy majesty, and of thy wondrous works....¹⁰All thy works shall praise thee, O Lord; and thy saints shall bless thee. ¹¹They shall speak of the glory of thy kingdom, and talk of thy power; ¹²To make known to the sons of men his mighty acts, and the glorious majesty of his kingdom. ¹³Thy kingdom is an everlasting kingdom, and thy dominion endureth throughout all generations."*

When we lose ourselves to Jesus, we begin to talk about Him and His glory. When we get so caught up in Him and His glory, He can begin to manifest Himself and His power in the earth. It will take a people so dedicated and devoted to Him and not themselves; a people not interested in their own pursuits, but in His kingdom; a people who have died to themselves and their wants, a people who allow King Jesus to reign through them. So wherever they go, they can bring the Kingdom of God with them; because, it is in them.

We know the Kingdom of God has come when we see these greater works. Jesus promised that a people would do these greater works in John 14:12, "*Verily, verily, I say unto you, He that believeth on me, the works that I do shall he do also; and greater works than these shall he do; because I go unto my Father.*"

     d.   Ezekiel 16:8-14 – "*⁸Now when I passed by thee, and looked upon thee, behold, thy time was the time of love; and I spread my skirt over thee, and covered thy nakedness: yea, I sware unto thee, and entered into a covenant with thee, saith the Lord God, and thou becamest mine. ⁹Then washed I thee with water; yea, I throughly washed away thy blood from thee, and I anointed thee with oil. ¹⁰I clothed thee also with broidered work, and shod thee with badgers' skin, and I girded thee about with fine linen, and I covered thee with silk. ¹¹I decked thee also with ornaments, and I put bracelets upon thy hands, and a chain on thy neck. ¹²And I put a jewel on thy forehead, and earrings in thine ears, and a beautiful crown upon thine head. ¹³Thus wast thou decked with gold and silver; and thy raiment was of fine linen, and silk, and broidered work; thou didst eat fine flour, and honey, and oil: and thou wast exceeding beautiful, and thou didst prosper into a kingdom. ¹⁴And thy renown went forth among the heathen for thy beauty: for it was perfect through my comeliness, which I had put upon thee, saith the Lord God.*"

         1)   This passage speaks of those made ready to walk in His kingdom and do the mighty works because of their sanctification.

     e.   Daniel 4:25 – "*That they shall drive thee from men, and thy dwelling shall be with the beasts of the field, and they shall make thee to eat grass as oxen, and they shall wet thee with the dew of heaven, and seven times shall pass over thee, till thou know that the most High ruleth in the kingdom of men, and giveth it to whomsoever he will.*"

God will rule in men the ones He chooses.

     f.   Daniel 7:18, 22 – "*¹⁸But the saints of the most High shall take the kingdom, and possess the kingdom for ever, even for ever and ever. ²²Until the Ancient of days came, and judgment was given to the saints of the most High; and the time came that the saints possessed the kingdom.*"

The word "*ever*" means "an age." So forever, and ever and ever speak of the age of all ages. This is when Jesus sits down and turns everything back over to the Father so that God will be "*all in all*" (I Corinthians 15:28). That is when the age-lasting kingdom begins and there is no changing after that. The saints are going to possess this kingdom forever. They will possess the kingdom because the kingdom will have possessed them.

This is akin to Obadiah 17, which says that "*the house of Jacob shall possess their possessions.*" This does not speak of worldly possessions, but the true riches of God operating within the lives of His remnant. For 44 years I have been believing for healings, deliverances, salvation in people's lives to an unparalleled degree like the earth has never seen. I am believing to move in a prophetic realm without any hesitation, for the Holy Spirit to always operate freely. I believe that we are on the cusp of seeing all these things happen. I believe that there is going to be such a release coming for the gifts of the Spirit to be operating within the body of Christ, in those who are totally devoted to Jesus and His Kingdom.

     g.   Daniel 7:25-27 – "*²⁵And he shall speak great words against the most High, and shall wear out the saints of the most High, and think to change times and laws: and they shall be given into his hand until a time and times and the dividing of time. ²⁶But the judgment shall sit, and they shall take away his dominion, to consume and to destroy it unto the end. ²⁷And the kingdom and dominion, and the greatness of the kingdom under the whole heaven, shall be given to the people of the saints of the most High, whose kingdom is an everlasting kingdom, and all dominions shall serve and obey him."*

The phrase *"wear out"* in verse 25 speaks of the enemy attempting to wear out in a mental sense, to depress mentally God's people. However, despite all of the enemy's attempts, the Lord is going to give the kingdom to the saints of the Most High, who have allowed Him dominion in their lives.

> h. Micah 4:1-8 – *"But in the last days it shall come to pass, that the mountain of the house of the Lord shall be established in the top of the mountains, and it shall be exalted above the hills; and people shall flow unto it. ²And many nations shall come, and say, Come, and let us go up to the mountain of the Lord, and to the house of the God of Jacob; and he will teach us of his ways, and we will walk in his paths: for the law shall go forth of Zion, and the word of the Lord from Jerusalem. ³And he shall judge among many people, and rebuke strong nations afar off; and they shall beat their swords into plowshares, and their spears into pruninghooks: nation shall not lift up a sword against nation, neither shall they learn war any more. ⁴But they shall sit every man under his vine and under his fig tree; and none shall make them afraid: for the mouth of the Lord of hosts hath spoken it. ⁵For all people will walk every one in the name of his god, and we will walk in the name of the Lord our God for ever and ever. ⁶In that day, saith the Lord, will I assemble her that halteth, and I will gather her that is driven out, and her that I have afflicted; ⁷And I will make her that halted a remnant, and her that was cast far off a strong nation: and the Lord shall reign over them in mount Zion from henceforth, even for ever. ⁸And thou, O tower of the flock, the strong hold of the daughter of Zion, unto thee shall it come, even the first dominion; the kingdom shall come to the daughter of Jerusalem."*

The first thing to notice about this passage is that this passage is not talking about heaven, because there is not war going on in heaven. This is a prophetic passage about what is about to take place on the earth, where the Kingdom of God is going to be established in Zion, which is within a people. In other words, the kingdom shall be in operation through a people. They are going to utter laws and decrees from the kingdom while on earth.

Verse 5 brings out that during this time, everybody on earth will have made a decision whom they are going to serve. They will be walking in the name, the character of the god they had chosen. But His remnant will walk in the character of the Lord Jesus. A people will come forth who will exhibit the character of Jesus in the earth.

The remnant that makes up the Kingdom of God in the last days will be a broken, afflicted and humble people whom the Lord has gathered from every nation. When the Lord takes them, He is then going to reign in them. These afflicted people, by the grace of God, make it in. Just like in Luke 14:21, it says, *"Go out quickly into the streets and lanes of the city, and bring in hither the poor, and the maimed, and the halt, and the blind."* These were called because those who were bidden first made excuse with one consent and did not come. The halt, lame and broken are the only ones who will seem to respond to the call of God.

The tower of the flock is not only Jesus, but the remnant of God who have His image in their lives, the many-membered Jesus.

> i. Matthew 6:9-13 – *"⁹After this manner therefore pray ye: Our Father which art in heaven, Hallowed be thy name. ¹⁰Thy kingdom come. Thy will be done in earth, as it is in heaven. ¹¹Give us this day our daily bread. ¹²And forgive us our debts, as we forgive our debtors. ¹³And lead us not into temptation, but deliver us from evil: For thine is the kingdom, and the power, and the glory, for ever. Amen."*
>
> 1) Evil in Greek – Evil one

2) Power in Greek – dunamis – force, miraculous power
3) Glory in Greek – doxa – apparent dignity, honor; from a root that means to seem or think truthfully, be of reputation, seem good

This prayer has everything to do with the Kingdom of God. The first thing I want to point out is that prayer has everything to do with relationship. He is not the God a million miles away, He is our Father, our daddy.

The second thing about these verses is *"Hallowed be thy name."* Worship to God and to His name, or character, is vital. When you come into the presence of God and start talking to Him and about who He is, true communion in prayer takes place. He wants us to have a revelation of who He is.

Have we ever seen the Kingdom of God manifest itself on earth as it is in heaven? I do not think we have. Jesus said the Kingdom of God came while He was here on earth. However, Jesus has not had the dominion, the sovereignty or the reign within a people where heaven could literally be done in earth. We need to let God reign in our lives. The minute we let Him, everything changes. Can you image the Kingdom of Heaven manifesting itself in earth? There is no sickness in heaven. Nobody is weeping and tormented in heaven.

The next thing mentioned in the prayer is *"Thy will be done."* Remember when Jesus was in the garden of Gethsemane? He prayed earnestly three times for the cup to pass from Him. However, he surrendered and ultimately said, *"Thy will be done"* (Matthew 26:43). The ultimate surrender and breaking in our lives is when we submit to God's will. Our will, our flesh never wants to submit to God's will and is constantly trying to get the ascendancy. But we must put down all desires and the minute we surrender our souls to His will, then we can begin to see heaven manifest itself and flow through us. The more we submit to His will, the more we are changed. The more we are changed, the more we get to like the feeling of His glory flowing through us. The more we like the release of the glory from us, the more we understand that wherever we go now, heaven is becoming a reality. Every devil and principality must bow as God's kingdom manifests itself. Thus, His will becomes paramount in our lives, even though it might cost us everything, even our own lives. Therefore, when we die to our own flesh and will and His will lives through us, we will then have a real revelation. God will be able to give us anything. He will give you His secrets and the keys to His kingdom. He will give you His glory and power all because He knows that you belong to Him.

We should pray every day for His Kingdom to come and His will be done in the earth. When we speak of the earth, we should not just be thinking about the earth around us, but also in our earth, in our lives and bodies. Once the kingdom manifests in us, it will be released through us and we will truly see the deliverance and salvation throughout the earth.

j. Joel 2:1-11
k. Obadiah 17-21 – *"17But upon mount Zion shall be deliverance, and there shall be holiness; and the house of Jacob shall possess their possessions. 18And the house of Jacob shall be a fire, and the house of Joseph a flame, and the house of Esau for stubble, and they shall kindle in them, and devour them; and there shall not be any remaining of the house of Esau; for the Lord hath spoken it. 19And they of the south shall possess the mount of Esau; and they of the plain the Philistines: and they shall possess the fields of Ephraim, and the fields of Samaria: and Benjamin shall possess Gilead. 20And the captivity of this host of the children of Israel shall possess that of the Canaanites, even unto Zarephath; and the captivity of Jerusalem, which is in Sepharad, shall possess the cities of the south. 21And saviours shall come up on mount Zion to judge the mount of Esau; and the kingdom shall be the Lord's."*

Esau in this passage is a type of the flesh. The house of flesh is going to become stubble. Remember when Jacob and Esau were born, and what happened in Genesis 25:21-28? Esau was born first. The man of the flesh always is born first. But just as Esau was coming out, it says in Genesis 25:26, *"And after that came his brother out [Jacob], and his hand took hold on Esau's heel."* Spiritually speaking, I believe this means that at the birthing of the sons of God, they will have their hands on the heel of the man of the flesh. They will control the man of the flesh. Therefore, this passage in Obadiah tells us that there shall be holiness.

Moreover, this passage tells us that there is not going to be anything remaining of the house of Esau. God is going to burn up the flesh in our lives.

In verse 21 it says, "*and saviours shall come up on mount Zion.*" They shall come to mount Zion when the kingdom truly shall be the Lord's. This is a picture of the people of God when God has finished working in them, dealing with them, ministering to them and sanctifying them. When the Kingdom of God truly manifests itself within a people, sin and the flesh shall truly be done away with. God's people shall experience true holiness.

Also, this verse calls the remnant of God "*saviours*". We know that there is only one Savior of the World and His name is Jesus. However, I believe God's people will have a ministry like Jesus who will go about the earth doing the greater works and bringing salvation and deliverance, just like Joseph, who was called Zaphnathpaaneah by Pharoah, which name means, "savior of the world." Joseph was called to bring deliverance and bread to eat when the whole world was in famine. Therefore, in Zion, saviors will come up on mount Zion and the Kingdom of God will truly be the Lord's. Zion is not just a people, but a place in the glory of God where Jesus is enthroned.

B. When You See God's Power Being Released And People Getting Delivered, The Kingdom Has Come

1. Matthew 4:23-25 – "*23And Jesus went about all Galilee, teaching in their synagogues, and preaching the gospel of the kingdom, and healing all manner of sickness and all manner of disease among the people. 24And his fame went throughout all Syria: and they brought unto him all sick people that were taken with divers diseases and torments, and those which were possessed with devils, and those which were lunatick, and those that had the palsy; and he healed them. 25And there followed him great multitudes of people from Galilee, and from Decapolis, and from Jerusalem, and from Judaea, and from beyond Jordan.*"

When we see the power of God in action, which is the good news of the kingdom, the Kingdom of God has come. Jesus isn't just preaching about the kingdom, He is healing all manner of sicknesses and diseases. Can you image what is going to happen when it is not just one Jesus on the shores of Galilee, but a many-membered Jesus going throughout the earth doing the same works? When this happens, the Kingdom of God will be a reality.

2. Luke 8:1 – "*And it came to pass afterward, that he went throughout every city and village, preaching and shewing the glad tidings of the kingdom of God: and the twelve were with him.*"
3. Luke 17:20-21 – "*20And when he was demanded of the Pharisees, when the kingdom of God should come, he answered them and said, The kingdom of God cometh not with observation: 21Neither shall they say, Lo here! or, lo there! for, behold, the kingdom of God is within you.*"
4. Matthew 16:13-19 – "*13When Jesus came into the coasts of Caesarea Philippi, he asked his disciples, saying, Whom do men say that I the son of man am? 14And they said, Some say that thou art John the Baptist: some, Elias; and others, Jeremias, or one of the prophets. 15He saith unto them, But whom say ye that I am? 16And Simon Peter answered and said, Thou art the Christ, the Son of the living God. 17And Jesus answered and said unto him, Blessed art thou, Simon Barjona: for flesh and blood hath not revealed it unto thee, but my Father which is in heaven. 18And I say also unto thee, That thou art Peter, and upon this rock I will build my church; and the gates of hell shall not prevail against it. 19And I will give unto thee the keys of the kingdom of heaven: and whatsoever thou shalt bind on earth shall be bound in heaven: and whatsoever thou shalt loose on earth shall be loosed in heaven.*"

What was happening in this story? Something from heaven came to earth. In other words, revelation came and was revealed in the earth. In one instant, Peter received revelation from heaven. It is beyond the natural. It has nothing to do with intellect. It comes supernaturally and instantaneously. Revelation is like lightning.

This passage also says that Jesus is building His kingdom upon the rock. This rock is not Peter, but the rock of revelation that Peter just received about Jesus, the anointed one. Moreover, God is going to build His church on things coming from heaven into earth, things coming from the supernatural realm and finding their way into earthly existence.

This passage is also not telling us that the gates of hell are attacking and tormenting us. Rather, we are assailing the gates of hell and they will not be able to stand up against the onslaught of the church. What is it that the gates of hell will not be able to stand up against? They will not be able to stand up against revelation! Without revelation there is no building of the church and His kingdom! We need to be conduits of supernatural revelation that the enemy and his kingdom can never stand up against.

Finally, this passage says that the church is going to be given the keys of the kingdom of heaven. The keys to heavenly things are given to those who allow heaven to live in them. They will be given access and authority to His kingdom! This is like when it says it John 3:34 of Jesus, *"for God giveth not the Spirit by measure unto him."* Jesus had the fullness of God's Spirit operating in Him and through Him. Jesus healed everybody with whom He came in contact. When God's people get a hold of the keys of the Kingdom, all of heaven's resources will be available to them.

5. Matthew 20:20-28
6. Matthew 29:3-14 – *"...14And this gospel of the kingdom shall be preached in all the world for a witness unto all nations; and then shall the end come."*
7. Mark 4:11-13 – *"11And he said unto them, Unto you it is given to know the mystery of the kingdom of God: but unto them that are without, all these things are done in parables: 12That seeing they may see, and not perceive; and hearing they may hear, and not understand; lest at any time they should be converted, and their sins should be forgiven them. 13And he said unto them, Know ye not this parable? and how then will ye know all parables?"*

It is given to us to know the mysteries of the Kingdom of God. When we know His mysteries, then we can operate in it. The word *"mystery"* in this verse is the Greek word *musterion*, which means, "that which is known only to the initiated." You and I are not going to operate within the Kingdom of God unless we are initiated into the mysteries of the Kingdom of God. The reason many do not understand many things out of the Scriptures is for this simple reason. They are not initiated. The Bible says that in the last days, the books shall be opened. Revelation is open to those who give themselves to Jesus and the Scriptures. Just as knowledge is increasing naturally with things like the internet, spiritually there is a people hidden in the house of the Lord, who have been studying the Scriptures, pouring over them and giving themselves to the Word of God for years and years. God is letting the knowledge of His Glory just flow in and through them.

8. Mark 10:13-16 – *"13And they brought young children to him, that he should touch them: and his disciples rebuked those that brought them. 14But when Jesus saw it, he was much displeased, and said unto them, Suffer the little children to come unto me, and forbid them not: for of such is the kingdom of God. 15Verily I say unto you, Whosoever shall not receive the kingdom of God as a little child, he shall not enter therein. 16And he took them up in his arms, put his hands upon them, and blessed them."*
9. Luke 9:1-6, 10-11 – *"1Then he called his twelve disciples together, and gave them power and authority over all devils, and to cure diseases. 2And he sent them to preach the kingdom of God, and to heal the sick. 3And he said unto them, Take nothing for your journey, neither staves, nor scrip, neither bread, neither money; neither have two coats apiece. 4And whatsoever house ye enter into, there abide, and thence depart. 5And whosoever will not receive you, when ye go out of*

that city, shake off the very dust from your feet for a testimony against them. [6]And they departed, and went through the towns, preaching the gospel, and healing every where...[10]And the apostles, when they were returned, told him all that they had done. And he took them, and went aside privately into a desert place belonging to the city called Bethsaida. [11]And the people, when they knew it, followed him: and he received them, and spake unto them of the kingdom of God, and healed them that had need of healing."

a. Bethsaida – house of fish, house of provision. When Jesus spoke of the Kingdom of God, he also brought with it healing. Again, the Kingdom of God comes when healing and true miracles and deliverance come.

Chapter 9
The Story Of Esther Related To The Kingdom Of God

I believe that in this story in Esther, we find great revelation about the Kingdom of God and our purpose in the earth. So many people are hoodwinked into thinking that they are saved just to sit in a pew or fill a seat. They have a mentality that they are saved to be a deacon, a singer, a worship leader, pastor, etc. Therefore, their expectations of their life and purpose remains so low. What God wants from us, though, can be understood while looking at this passage in Esther. It will then be up to us to decide whether we will walk it out.

There is something strategic and specific that God has called us to and it is not a light thing. We are not just called to come to church and worship and enjoy the presence of God. We are not just called to bask when God's great glory falls. We are not just called to just preach or teach or even go to the nations. There is a job that is reserved for the sons of God that only they can accomplish. Just as in Abraham's day, before God would send His Son, in the likeness of sinful flesh to sacrifice Him, God needed to know that a man, a human being, was willing to do the exact same thing as He would. God looked at Abraham with Isaac bound on that altar with a knife over him, as Abraham was ready to plunge it into his son. God then said for Abraham to stop and said in Genesis 22:12, *"Now I know that thou fearest God, seeing thou hast not withheld thy son, thine only son from me."* God allowed all of that to take place. Many people have ridiculed this story. But they have no comprehension with what God was doing. He was looking for somebody who would be and act like Him.

What is about to take place in the earth is the most powerful revelation, the most powerful visitation that this earth has ever seen. Jesus' ministry was only 3 ½ years. That is an incomplete number. Seven is a complete number. So I believe there is yet another 3 ½ year ministry of Jesus to be accomplished on the earth before the last and second coming of the Lord.

As God has already defeated satan and threw him out of heaven by his death and resurrection, yet there is still something God must see in a people. There has to come forth a people. I John 3:8 says, *"For this purpose the Son of God was manifested, that he might destroy the works of the devil."* Jesus came for one reason and one reason alone: to die. It would just follow in suit, then, that the sons of God, those that are going to be like Him and follow in His footsteps, be willing to sacrifice their own lives to put an end to the reign of the devil. You and I have the opportunity to be a part of this company of saints.

I remember walking down the street as a newly saved Christian and looking up and thinking about how much the devil had destroyed my family, how my sisters' lives were destroyed. There are people I knew, whose lives were ripped apart because of the devil. The devil is our adversary and enemy. I remember saying to myself, "One day, if God will have mercy on me, I am going to pay the devil back for what he did to my family." I don't care about my life anymore. I have dealt with the things that I had to suffer. There is one thing in which I want to partake. Before the coming of the Lord where every eye shall see Him, I believe that there will be a man-child birthed out of a woman (the church) and that man-child will be caught up to heaven (as found in Revelation 12:5-11). Being caught up to God and to His throne means to be caught up to complete and total authority, power, revelation and relationship with God. As soon as that man-child is caught up, it says in Revelation 12:7, "*And there was war in heaven.*" Satan and his angels are cast out of heaven and down to the earth to be finally dealt with the second coming of the Lord. But the people, the agents, for bringing satan down from that heavenly place is the man-child. The man-child is the overcomers. As soon as they are caught up to God and to His throne, satan is cast down. I want to be in that company that brings him down. When satan is cast down, it then says in verse 10, "*Now is come salvation, and strength, and the kingdom of our God, and the power of his Christ.*" So when we talk about the Kingdom of God, we are talking about the spiritual kingdom that is within us, as Luke 17:20-21 says, "*The kingdom of God cometh not with observation... For, behold, the kingdom of God is within you.*" This kingdom will come to the earth when God's holy remnant are caught up to God and to His throne to bring down the reign of satan.

This story in Esther 3-6 is about God's bride, Esther being a type, who will be willing to sacrifice everything, even their own lives, to see the Kingdom come to God's people. I believe this story is a type of exactly what is happening right now in the earth. God is raising up a remnant of people who want to see the Kingdom come to the earth and who are willing to do anything to see it accomplished.

I. Esther 3:11-15, Esther 4:6-16 - "*³:¹³And the letters were sent by posts into all the king's provinces, to destroy, to kill, and to cause to perish, all Jews, both young and old, little children and women, in one day... ⁴:¹⁴(Mordecai speaking to Esther) If thou altogether holdest thy peace at this time, then shall there enlargement and deliverance arise to the Jews from another place; but thou and thy father's house shall be destroyed: and who knoweth whether thou art come to the kingdom for such a time as this? ¹⁵Then Esther bade them return Mordecai this answer, ¹⁶Go, gather together all the Jews that are present in Shushan, and fast ye for me, and neither eat nor drink three days, night or day: I also and my maidens will fast likewise; and so will I go in unto the king, which is not according to the law: and if I perish, I perish.*"

A. Important facts about this story

1. Hebrew for Haman – "alone, solitary, well disposed, a rioter, the rager, their tumult, magnificent;" Haman is a type of satan.

a. Haman was called an Agagite (Esther 3:1) - Agagite in Hebrew means – "flaming, to burn, warlike, lofty, I will overtop, I ravaged, I wasted, I burned." Again, a vivid picture of who satan is.

b. A descendent of the royal family of the Amalekites. The Amalekites were the most bitter enemy of God's people.

c. Haman's father's name was Hammedatha which means – "the opposer of justice or law."

d. Haman was angry because Mordecai would not bow to him (Esther 3:5).

In the story, Haman gets a decree passed to destroy all of the Jews because of Mordecai. This speaks to us that satan is against all of God's people today (New Jerusalem) and want to destroy us. This is seen also in the first coming of Jesus, when Herod slaughtered all of the babies two years old and under (Matthew 2:16). Likewise in Revelation 12:4 it says, "*The dragon stood before the woman which was ready to be delivered, for to devour her child as soon as it was born.*" I believe today satan wants to destroy all of those who have taken a stand and separated themselves from the world and are a witness in the earth today. Despite all of the enemy's plans, Revelation 12:11 says, "*And they overcame him by the blood of the Lamb, and by the word of their testimony; and they loved not their lives unto the death.*"

2. Hebrew for Mordecai – "little man, bruising, bitterly reduced, bitterness of my oppression." This is a type of Jesus in His humanity acting as our kinsman redeemer. The bitterness, the suffering that Jesus went through is seen in Mordecai.

3. King Ahasuerus in Hebrew – "king, mighty man, prince of the people, lion king." He is a type of God the Father. Why would God allow Haman (type of satan) to do the things he did? I believe because God needs to know that there is a Mordecai who will not bow! God needs to know that there is somebody somewhere that is not going to surrender to a prince of devils.

4. Esther in Hebrew – "star, she that is hidden;" She is a type of the bride, overcomers. God will have a people in the earth who are like Him and who have His character. There will be a Benjamin company (Benjamin means, "son of my right hand"), the bride, who will sit at the right hand of Jesus.

    a. Psalms 45:9 – *"Upon thy right hand did stand the queen in gold of Ophir."*
    b. Matthew 20:20-23 "[Jesus said] *But to sit on my right hand, and on my left, is not mine to give, but it shall be given to them for whom it is prepared of my Father."*

5. God the Father will allow satan in the last days another chance to win. He must be defeated by the overcomers to finalize his ultimate defeat.

    a. Abraham and Isaac, *"Now I know"* (Genesis 22:12) - Just as God had to know a man would be willing to sacrifice his son, He needs to know that an overcoming people are willing to lay down their lives to ensure the bringing in of the Kingdom of God (Revelation 12:5-11).

6. Esther 4:11 - *"All the king's servants, and the people of the king's provinces, do know, that whosoever, whether man or woman, shall come unto the king into the inner court, who is not called, there is one law of his to put him to death, except such to whom the king shall hold out the golden sceptre, that he may live: but I have not been called to come in unto the king these thirty days."*

This is Esther's response to Mordecai when Mordecai asks her to go in unto the king to petition for the lives of the people. Spiritually speaking, there are a lot of things to say about this passage. First of all, the bride is going to be called to the inner court, which speaks to us of the most holy place. At that moment, God is going to stretch out His golden scepter. As God does, what He is saying is, "I'm releasing to you my character." The bride will be given God's authority. But God's people are going to have to know that they are called and they will have to know how to go into the most holy place.

Moreover, they will have to go even though they weren't called for 30 days. Thirty in Scriptures is the number for preparation for ministry. Jesus was 30 when He began His public ministry. So was John the Baptist. In the priesthood, the Levites did not start their ministry until they were 30. These 30 days represent the preparation time the bride will go through before they are called to go through the final veil into the most holy place.

    a. Inner court – the most holy place
    b. Golden – God's nature and character
    c. Scepter – God's authority
       1) Genesis 49:10 – *"The scepter shall not depart from Judah, nor a lawgiver from between his feet, until Shiloh come."*
       2) The tribe of praise, the worshipping overcomers are going to have that scepter that God gave them.
    d. 30 days - preparation for ministry

B. Esther 4:13-14 - *"Then Mordecai commanded to answer Esther, Think not with thyself that thou shalt escape in the king's house, more than all the Jews. ¹⁴For if thou altogether holdest thy peace at this time, then shall there enlargement and deliverance arise to the Jews from another place; but thou and thy father's house shall be destroyed: and who knoweth whether thou art come to the kingdom for such a time as this?"*

First, Mordecai told Esther to not think that she will escape from this edict planned by Haman. What does this mean to us spiritually? That means to us that those people living in these last days who do not run after the Lord, who do not walk with the Lord, and who are not a part of this remnant are going to experience what the world will experience when judgment falls on the earth. You will not lose your salvation; but, you may lose your reward of brideship. What it means is that there will be weeping and gnashing of teeth. Who is weeping and gnashing of teeth? People who knew the Lord, who are in His kingdom, but decided not to follow on to know the Lord intimately (Luke 13:24-30; Matthew 7:21-23). How many people have no idea about the remnant? Are people really preparing themselves and getting ready for what is coming? We should not be fooled. It will take a great dying in God's people to see His Kingdom come.

If you and I do not decide to die to ourselves, then deliverance will arise from another place. God will find an Abraham. He will find a Job. He will find an Enoch, an Elijah or a Paul. He will find a people a take through the veil. God is giving His people here an opportunity to be a part of this glorious visitation. All of our lives are preparing for us to go into the most holy place.

Verse 14 tells us why we are called to His Kingdom right now. Brideship is not about walking around and showing everyone your beauty. The remnant, the overcomers will have a job to do. We are going to finish out the mystery of God. The calling is upon us to do it. This is a time when supernaturally a people's shoulders have been trained and built up to handle any kind of adversity, any kind of dealing, affliction and burden. Like Joseph, the bride will walk right out from under the burden; because, even though the devil did his best to keep him in prison, he will still come out as prime minister. We didn't come into the kingdom to tell each other how spiritual we are and just be queen like Esther. We must also be willing to lay down our lives and die to see the deliverance and the Kingdom come for God's people. What a selfless act God will require of His bride!

1. Other Translations of verse 14

    "who knows, maybe you were made Queen for just such a time"
    "who knoweth for a time like this thou has come to the kingdom?"
    "And who knows whether you have attained royalty for such a time as this?"
    "you came into your royal position precisely for such a time as this"
    "who can say but that God has brought you into the palace for just such a time as this"

2. Comparing Scriptures

    a. John 12:20-28 - *"24Verily, verily, I say unto you, Except a corn of wheat fall into the ground and die, it abideth alone: but if it die, it bringeth forth much fruit. 25He that loveth his life shall lose it; and he that hateth his life in this world shall keep it unto life eternal. 26If any man serve me, let him follow me; and where I am, there shall also my servant be: if any man serve me, him will my Father honour. 27Now is my soul troubled; and what shall I say? Father, save me from this hour: but for this cause came I unto this hour..."*

Jesus spoke these words in response to a group of Greeks who said to His disciples, *"We would see Jesus"* (John 12:21). This means to us that if the world will ever see the real Jesus through a people, they must die completely to themselves in order for Jesus to truly come forth within them.

Jesus in response to these Greeks also speaks of His own death. He tells them that the reason He came into this earth was to die. Jesus did not come for the healings, for the miracles, not the preaching and teaching in the temple, but for the hour of His death. Jesus' death was the most poignant, monumental hour of His life. Everything had led Him to this moment.

For the sons of God, this tells us that all of our lives are being prepared for one moment as well where we will show God that we are willing to sacrifice our own lives for the Kingdom's sake. We are going to let God know that there is a people on earth who are willing just like He was willing.

b. John 2:4 - *"Jesus saith unto her, Woman, what have I to do with thee? mine hour is not yet come."*

c. Dying To Self Scriptures:

1) II Samuel 14:14 - *"For we must needs die, and are as water spilt on the ground, which cannot be gathered up again; neither doth God respect any person: yet doth he devise means, that his banished be not expelled from him."*

2) Job 14:14-15 - *"14If a man die, shall he live again? all the days of my appointed time will I wait, till my change come. 15Thou shalt call, and I will answer thee: thou wilt have a desire to the work of thine hands."*

3) I Corinthians 15:31 - *"I protest by your rejoicing which I have in Christ Jesus our Lord, I die daily."*

4) Galatians 2:20 - *"I am crucified with Christ: nevertheless I live; yet not I, but Christ liveth in me: and the life which I now live in the flesh I live by the faith of the Son of God, who loved me, and gave himself for me."*

5) Psalms 138:8 - *"The Lord will perfect that which concerneth me: thy mercy, O Lord, endureth for ever: forsake not the works of thine own hands."*

d. Revelation 1:9 - *"I John, who also am your brother, and companion in tribulation, and in the kingdom and patience of Jesus Christ, was in the isle that is called Patmos, for the word of God, and for the testimony of Jesus Christ."* - Patmos - "my killing"

e. Romans 14:8 - *"For whether we live, we live unto the Lord; and whether we die, we die unto the Lord: whether we live therefore, or die, we are the Lord's."*

2. Kingdom in Hebrew - a dominion, realm or reign, royal empire

3. Kingdom in Greek - royalty, realm, place of rulership; it comes from a root that means - foundation of power, sovereign; another root - to walk, the foot.

C. Esther's and Our Resolve, *"Then Esther bade them return Mordecai this answer, 16Go, gather together all the Jews that are present in Shushan, and fast ye for me, neither eat nor drink three days, night or day: I also and my maidens will fast likewise; and so will I go in unto the king, which is not according to the law: and if I perish, I perish"* (Esther 4:15-16).

1. Other translations:

"if I die, I die"
"if death is to be my fate, then let it come"
"if I must die for doing it, I will die"
"I will go in to the king, against the Law, not being called, and expose myself to death and danger."
"even if I must die"

There must be something in us that was found in Esther that made her "a star." This is what makes the remnant who they are. They are willing to go the extra mile. They are willing to do the thing that nobody else will do. It is not some glorious thing that God asks Esther to do. It is something that nobody wants to do. The bride will be asked to be willing to offer up her life so the Kingdom of God can come forth in the earth.

We must be willing. When the bride goes in, Haman (type of satan) ultimately is defeated, being hung on the noose he created for God's people. What a deliverance will come when His Kingdom comes!

    2.   Perish in Hebrew - to lose oneself, to be undone, to have no way, to flee

D.   Kingdom Scriptures

    1.   Matthew 11:12 - *"And from the days of John the Baptist until now the kingdom of heaven suffereth violence, and the violent take it by force."*

    2.   Acts 14:22 - *"Confirming the souls of the disciples, and exhorting them to continue in the faith, and that we must through much tribulation enter into the kingdom of God."*

This Scripture tells us that we are not just given the Kingdom of God. We must enter into the Kingdom of God. This happens through much tribulation. There is really no other way in.

    3.   Luke 16:16 - *"The law and the prophets were until John: since that time the kingdom of God is preached, and every man presseth into it."* Presseth in Greek - to force, crowd oneself into. God is calling His people today to press into the Kingdom of God.

    4.   I Corinthians 4:20 - *"For the kingdom of God is not in word, but in power."*

    5.   II Thessalonians 1:5 - *"Which is a manifest token of the righteous judgment of God, that ye may be counted worthy of the kingdom of God, for which ye also suffer:"*

Chapter 10
Who Does Not Enter Into The Kingdom Of God

In this lesson we are going to look at the many passages relating to the Kingdom of God and those who were unable to enter into it. Remember, the Kingdom of God is the reign of King Jesus within the hearts of His people. Therefore it is important for us to look at those things that can keep us or hinder us from entering into the Kingdom of God.

I. Scriptures Declaring This

   A. Matthew 21:33-46 – "...*43Therefore say I unto you, The kingdom of God shall be taken from you, and given to a nation bringing forth the fruits thereof...*"

      1. First of all, this parable is speaking of the Jewish nation and how they stoned and killed the prophets, as well as, did not receive the Lord Jesus which led to his crucifixion. The Jewish nation even said in Matthew 27:25, "*His* [Jesus'] *blood be on us, and on our children.*" This brought upon them the curse that has lasted until this present day. They refused the Messiah. They were chosen by God, given the promises and the covenant. But ultimately they were stiff-necked and uncircumcised in heart and did always resist the Holy Ghost (Acts 7:51).

      2. I also believe this passage speaks not of the Jewish nation, but can speak of the church at large today, as well as leadership in the Body of Christ that does not receive Jesus or the anointing, resists Him and even stones those sent to them. There are more ways of stoning people than just killing them. We can stone people with our words as well. But when the Son comes and wants to manifest Himself in the midst of His people, they kill Him or get rid of Him.

      3. When the Son is manifested in this parable, the people's answer was this in verse 38, "*This is the heir; come, let us kill him, and let us seize on his inheritance.*" You cannot receive the inheritance that God wants you to have any other way unless you receive Jesus intimately. You cannot have the Kingdom of God unless the King is reigning and ruling in the midst. It is like the story in Luke 22:54 of Jesus being bound and led to the high priest's house. Jesus is in the house, but He is not free to rule and reign. He is bound and about to be crucified.

4. This parable says that Jesus is going to take the Kingdom of God away from them and is going to be given to a nation bringing forth fruit. It should have been the Jewish nation's greatest joy to receive the Messiah. They were waiting, saying they wanted to receive Him. But when He came, He was the stone that the builders rejected. But God made Him the head of the corner. Even today, Jesus is being rejected every time someone rejects the anointing, the manifest presence of God. The glory of God is God Himself. When you reject the glory, you are rejecting God. That is the spirit of antichrist. Therefore, even though this parable was dealing with Israel, I also believe this parable is dealing with leadership, those husbandmen who have been given positions of authority to cause God's vineyard to grow and to watch over it and protect it. It doesn't mean they lose their salvation. But it does mean that they will be unable to enter into the benefits of what the Kingdom of God represents, which is, God being all in all within a people.

5. It is interesting that when Jesus asked them in verse 40 what they think the Lord would do to those husbandmen. Out of their own mouths they say, *"He will miserably destroy those wicked men, and will let out his vineyard unto other husbandmen, which shall render him the fruits in their seasons"* (verse 41). Out of their own mouths they testify to their wickedness, even declaring that they hinder God's people from truly entering into what God wants for them.

6. Finally, in applying this passage to our own lives, let us not be ones who end up stoning those who are truly sent to us by God. Do we reject the truth that God may want to bring to us through some messenger? We find a tremendous truth that we find ourselves not attacking the message, but the messenger as well.

B. Mark 10:13-16 – "...*15Verily I say unto you, Whosoever shall not receive the kingdom of God as a little child, he shall not enter therein...*"

1. Mark 9:36-37 – "*36And he took a child, and set him in the midst of them: and when he had taken him in his arms, he said unto them, 37Whosoever shall receive one of such children in my name, receiveth me: and whosoever shall receive me, receiveth not me, but him that sent me.*"

    a. David said in Psalm 75:2, *"When I shall receive the congregation I will judge uprightly."* When you and I receive one another, we are not really receiving just that person, but the Lord Jesus in that person. Moreover, when I receive the Lord Jesus, I am also receiving God the Father who sent Him.

2. Greek for "child" – *paidion* – an infant of either sex, a half grown boy or girl, an immature Christian, little or young person; comes from a root, *pais*, that means a slave or servant, especially a minister to a king, and also a worshipper of God.

3. We can never enter into the things of the Kingdom of God here on earth without the attitude, humility and innocence of a child. Remember the story of the apostle John in the book of revelation. John, the great apostle, is at the end of his life on Patmos, which means "my killing". They had already tried to kill him once but could not. He is the only apostle left. So here is John on the island and Jesus gives him the revelation of Himself. And in doing so, Jesus tells John that he has to do something first. Jesus tells John in Revelation 10 that He is sending to John a messenger to him and John must humble himself and take the book from the messenger and eat it up. John was required by God to go humble himself and receive from that angel (messenger). John responded correctly in Revelation 10:9 by saying, *"Give me the little book."* That is the essence of the Kingdom of God. You have to receive the truths of the kingdom like a little child, an infant, even if the Lord has to speak a word of correction to us. We must respond to God just like a child would respond to his parents. A child does not question, but receives and believes what the parent is saying. Jesus also says in Matthew 11:29, *"Take my yoke upon*

you, and learn of me; for I am meek and lowly in heart: and ye shall find rest unto your souls." Jesus himself exemplified meekness and humility. Therefore, we should never get so big where we cannot receive or where we cannot be led. We must always approach God with a broken and a contrite heart, ready to receive and believe what He wants to say to us. We must give ownership of ourselves over to the Lord Jesus and forsake the arrogant and know-it-all attitudes. If we cannot receive as a little child, we will not enter into the Kingdom of God. We will still go to heaven, but we will not be in that company of people whom God lives and dwells among them and the earth sees as God's true representative.

C. Mark 10:17-27 – "...*²³And Jesus looked round about, and saith unto his disciples, How hardly shall they that have riches enter into the kingdom of God! ²⁴And the disciples were astonished at his words. But Jesus answereth again, and saith unto them, Children, how hard is it for them that trust in riches to enter into the kingdom of God! ²⁵It is easier for a camel to go through the eye of a needle, than for a rich man to enter into the kingdom of God... ²⁷And Jesus looking upon them saith, With men it is impossible, but not with God: for with God all things are possible."*

1. As we behold this story, we see something about this young man. First of all, nobody has kept all of the commandments from their youth up. But this young man obviously convinced himself that he has kept all the commandments according to the law. Jesus was saying, though, that the law was over now. You cannot offer up an animal anymore to cover your sins, because animal sacrifices does not get rid of it. The young man was still not free. How many people seem to have their life all together and everything in order? Then comes Jesus and asks for that one thing in their lives that they are lacking. Rather than receive His words, they bow out of the dealings of God. How do we respond when Jesus wants to point out the one thing in our lives that is lacking? Isn't it amazing that the finger of God can look at us in all of our so-called righteousness, thinking we are so pure and spotless, and point out the one thing that is truly lacking in our lives? The young man said to Jesus that he wanted to inherit eternal life. So when Jesus shows him how, all of the humility and seeking after God in the young man leaves.

2. After the young man told Jesus that he obeyed all of the commandments from his youth up, it says, *"Then Jesus beholding him loved him, and said unto him, One thing thou lackest..."* The word *"beholding"* in this verse means, "to discern clearly". Jesus discerned clearly and looked right through the young man. Seeing the pride, arrogance and self-righteousness in the young man, Jesus did not respond in anger. It says that Jesus beheld him and loved him. He saw right through him and loved him anyway. But he also saw what the young man needed, the one thing that was lacking that would make him fit for the Kingdom of God. The young man allowed his possessions to possess him. God does not have a problem with us having possessions, as long as they do not possess us.

3. We must be willing for Jesus to point out the one thing in our lives that is lacking. When this happens, we should not immediately start justifying and lying to ourselves. Everybody knows we are like that and we try to act like that is not the word of the Lord for our lives, when we know it is. The problem is we do not want to face the thing Jesus is pointing out. Sometimes it may take us a while to digest what God is trying to say to us, like the man in the parable in Matthew 21:29, who said, *"I will not: but afterward he repented, and went."* It took Jesus three times to bow to the will of the Father in the garden of Gethsemane. God knows we are flesh and it may take us some time to bow to what He is saying. But what matters is that we ultimately bow in the end. I believe the true test of the remnant is whether they are willing to bow and do what the Lord is saying to them.

4. The main problem in this story in relating to the Kingdom of God is how hard it is for people who trust in riches or who desire to be rich or want possessions to enter into the Kingdom of God. It could be one of the greatest things that hinders us from having all that God wants us to

have. Jesus said in Mark 10:24, *"How hard is it for them that trust in riches to enter into the kingdom of God!"*

a. II Kings 5:13-27 – *"...20But Gehazi, the servant of Elisha the man of God, said, Behold, my master hath spared Naaman this Syrian, in not receiving at his hands that which he brought: but, as the Lord liveth, I will run after him, and take somewhat of him...26And he said unto him, Went not mine heart with thee, when the man turned again from his chariot to meet thee? Is it a time to receive money, and to receive garments, and oliveyards, and vineyards, and sheep, and oxen, and menservants, and maidservants? 27The leprosy therefore of Naaman shall cleave unto thee, and unto thy seed for ever. And he went out from his presence a leper as white as snow."*

1) In this story Naaman, a Syrian, was healed of leprosy and he wanted to basically give an offering to Elisha for being healed, which Elisha refused to receive. First of all, you do not pay money to be healed by God. Healing is the gift of God. Jesus bore stripes on His back for our healing. Healing is part of our salvation. We do not have to give a special offering for an anointing to be healed.

2) Gehazi, the servant of Elisha, went back and received the money from Naaman after Elisha refused the money. Gehazi lied to Naaman as well as he lied to his master when he went back after taking the money from Naaman.

3) Elisha then told Gehazi that the leprosy of Naaman will cleave to him and his seed forever. This is an amazing truth. Everything we do does not just affect us, but everybody that is connected and is under our sphere of influenced is affected as well. When leadership does things that are not right, it also affects his seed as well.

4) The ministry isn't about money or receiving money. In John 10:12-13 Jesus calls those who are in the ministry for money hirelings. They will flee when trouble comes, *"because he is an hireling, and careth not for the sheep."*

5) Gehazi in Hebrew – Denier, valley of vision, the valley of sight

6) Other translations of verse 26:

"Tell me, is this a time to look after yourself, lining your pockets with gifts?"
"This isn't a time to take money, clothes, olives, etc."
"This is not the proper time to accept silver or to accept clothes..."
"How could you accept silver, clothes, olive orchards, vineyards..."
"So now thou hast received money, and received garments, to buy oliveyards, and vineyards...But the leprosy of Naaman shall also stick to thee and to thy seed forever."

b. Joshua 7:1-26 – *"1But the children of Israel committed a trespass in the accursed thing: for Achan, the son of Carmi, the son of Zabdi, the son of Zerah, of the tribe of Judah, took of the accursed thing: and the anger of the Lord was kindled against the children of Israel...11Israel hath sinned, and they have also transgressed my covenant which I commanded them: for they have even taken of the accursed thing, and have also stolen, and dissembled also, and they have put it even among their own stuff...21When I saw among the spoils a goodly Babylonish garment, and two hundred shekels of silver, and a wedge of gold of fifty shekels weight, then I coveted them, and took them; and, behold, they are hid in the earth in the midst of my tent, and the silver under it...26And they raised over him a great heap of stones unto this day. So the Lord turned from the fierceness of his anger. Wherefore the name of that place was called, The valley of Achor, unto this day."*

1) Tribe of Judah – praise
2) Zarhites in Hebrew – joy of parents, rising of light, shining
3) Zerah in Hebrew – rising of light
4) Zabdi in Hebrew – gift of Jehovah, Jehovah gave

5) Carmi in Hebrew – vinedresser, my vineyard, noble
6) Achan in Hebrew – serpent, vexation, trouble

Look how ungodliness can live in even a noble family line. Achan's whole family was destroyed. It didn't just cost him, but Israel and his whole family.

c. The Opposite Of This

1) Genesis 14:14-24 – "...*16And he brought back all the goods, and also brought again his brother Lot, and his goods, and the women also, and the people... 21And the king of Sodom said unto Abram, Give me the persons, and take the goods to thyself. 22And Abram said to the king of Sodom, I have lift up mine hand unto the Lord, the most high God, the possessor of heaven and earth, 23That I will not take from a thread even to a shoelatchet, and that I will not take any thing that is thine, lest thou shouldest say, I have made Abram rich: 24Save only that which the young men have eaten, and the portion of the men which went with me, Aner, Eshcol, and Mamre; let them take their portion.*"

Our response should be like Abraham's in these verses. It was not a time to receive money, but a time to help his brother out. Our emphasis in ministry should never be about money. I believe in today's charismatic world, we do not have enough teaching on when it is not a time to receive money. Of course God does not want us poor. However, I believe there is a line we can cross where we go from prosperity to excess. Personally, every time I go overseas to minister, I fill my pockets with money of that country so that during the time in the meetings when I minister to people, I give that money away. I want to tell those people that I did not come to their country to take from them; but, I came to give to them and bless them.

d. Proverbs 23:4 – "Labour not to be rich: cease from thine own wisdom."
e. Proverbs 28:20, 22 – "*A faithful man shall abound with blessings: but he that maketh haste to be rich shall not be innocent...22He that hasteth to be rich hath an evil eye, and considereth not that poverty shall come upon him.*"
f. Jeremiah 9:23 – "*Thus saith the Lord, Let not the wise man glory in his wisdom, neither let the mighty man glory in his might, let not the rich man glory in his riches:*"
g. Luke 6:24 – "*But woe unto you that are rich! for ye have received your consolation.*"
h. Luke 12:16-21 – "*16And he spake a parable unto them, saying, The ground of a certain rich man brought forth plentifully: 17And he thought within himself, saying, What shall I do, because I have no room where to bestow my fruits? 18And he said, This will I do: I will pull down my barns, and build greater; and there will I bestow all my fruits and my goods. 19And I will say to my soul, Soul, thou hast much goods laid up for many years; take thine ease, eat, drink, and be merry. 20But God said unto him, Thou fool, this night thy soul shall be required of thee: then whose shall those things be, which thou hast provided? 21So is he that layeth up treasure for himself, and is not rich toward God.*"
i. I Timothy 6:3-11 – "*...5Perverse disputings of men of corrupt minds, and destitute of the truth, supposing that gain is godliness: from such withdraw thyself. 6But godliness with contentment is great gain...9But they that will be rich fall into temptation and a snare, and into many foolish and hurtful lusts, which drown men in destruction and perdition. 10For the love of money is the root of all evil: which while some coveted after, they have erred from the faith, and pierced themselves through with many sorrows. 11But thou, O man of God, flee these things; and follow after righteousness, godliness, faith, love, patience, meekness.*"
j. 1 Timothy 6:17-19 – "*17Charge them that are rich in this world, that they be not highminded, nor trust in uncertain riches, but in the living God, who giveth us richly all things to enjoy; 18That they do good, that they be rich in good works, ready to distribute, willing to communicate; 19Laying up in store for themselves a good foundation against the time to come, that they may lay hold on eternal life.*"

k.   Revelation 3:14-19 – "*14And unto the angel of the church of the Laodiceans write; These things saith the Amen, the faithful and true witness, the beginning of the creation of God; 15I know thy works, that thou art neither cold nor hot: I would thou wert cold or hot. 16So then because thou art lukewarm, and neither cold nor hot, I will spue thee out of my mouth. 17Because thou sayest, I am rich, and increased with goods, and have need of nothing; and knowest not that thou art wretched, and miserable, and poor, and blind, and naked: 18I counsel thee to buy of me gold tried in the fire, that thou mayest be rich; and white raiment, that thou mayest be clothed, and that the shame of thy nakedness do not appear; and anoint thine eyes with eyesalve, that thou mayest see. 19As many as I love, I rebuke and chasten: be zealous therefore, and repent.*"

The Laodicean church seemingly had natural wealth; but, Jesus calls them the opposite. Jesus wants us to have true riches. True riches are not money or things. The true riches of God are His glory, revelation, intimacy with God, the presence of God. If you have the true riches, then God will take care of you.

1)   Laodicea in Greek – opinion of the people, ruled by the people, rule of the majority, democratic, the people's rights. We live in a theocracy, where God is king, and the man of God is in charge.

   a)   Acts 4:34-35 – "*34Neither was there any among them that lacked: for as many as were possessors of lands or houses sold them, and brought the prices of the things that were sold, 35And laid them down at the apostles' feet: and distribution was made unto every man according as he had need.*"
   b)   Numbers 27:16 – "*Let the Lord, the God of the spirits of all flesh, set a man over the congregation*"

l.   James 5:1-3 – "*1Go to now, ye rich men, weep and howl for your miseries that shall come upon you. 2Your riches are corrupted, and your garments are motheaten. 3Your gold and silver is cankered; and the rust of them shall be a witness against you, and shall eat your flesh as it were fire. Ye have heaped treasure together for the last days.*"
m.   Proverbs 11:28 – "*He that trusteth in his riches shall fall: but the righteous shall flourish as a branch.*"
n.   Psalms 49:6-13 – "*6They that trust in their wealth, and boast themselves in the multitude of their riches; 7None of them can by any means redeem his brother, nor give to God a ransom for him: 8(For the redemption of their soul is precious, and it ceaseth for ever:) 9That he should still live for ever, and not see corruption. 10For he seeth that wise men die, likewise the fool and the brutish person perish, and leave their wealth to others. 11Their inward thought is, that their houses shall continue for ever, and their dwelling places to all generations; they call their lands after their own names. 12Nevertheless man being in honour abideth not: he is like the beasts that perish. 13This their way is their folly: yet their posterity approve their sayings. Selah.*"
o.   Mark 4:7, 19   "*7And some fell among thorns, and the thorns grew up, and choked it, and it yielded no fruit...19And the cares of this world, and the deceitfulness of riches, and the lusts of other things entering in, choke the word, and it becometh unfruitful.*"

D.   I Corinthians 6:9-11 – "*Know ye not that the unrighteous shall not inherit the kingdom of God? Be not deceived: neither fornicators, nor idolaters, nor adulterers, nor effeminate, nor abusers of themselves with mankind, 10Nor thieves, nor covetous, nor drunkards, nor revilers, nor extortioners, shall inherit the kingdom of God. 11And such were some of you: but ye are washed, but ye are sanctified, but ye are justified in the name of the Lord Jesus, and by the Spirit of our God.*"

1.   We need to know first of all that for the born again believer, we have no danger of losing our

heavenly salvation. But to be able to walk in the Kingdom of God, that is, to have the Lord Jesus reigning sovereignly in every one of our lives, is another story. Remember the story of Esau, who sold his birthright for a bowl of lentils. How many sell their first born blessing of walking in the Kingdom of God for something of this earth. So the Kingdom of God is something you attain to, walked in.

2. Unrighteous in Greek – *adikos* – unjust, wicked, treacherous, wrong, heathen – It is interesting to note that Paul is writing to believers, not to unbelievers. Therefore, there are people walking unrighteously in the house of God.

    a. Psalms 71:4 – *"Deliver me, O my God, out of the hand of the wicked, out of the hand of the unrighteous and cruel man."* Have you ever met any Christians who are cruel? I certainly have. The meaning of unrightousness is doing wrong and cruel things. We must allow God to sanctify our adamic nature. Giving ourselves to unrighteous and holy things can keep us from walking in the Kingdom of God.

    b. Isaiah 55:6-8 – *"⁶Seek ye the Lord while he may be found, call ye upon him while he is near: ⁷Let the wicked forsake his way, and the unrighteous man his thoughts: and let him return unto the Lord, and he will have mercy upon him; and to our God, for he will abundantly pardon. ⁸For my thoughts are not your thoughts, neither are your ways my ways, saith the Lord."*

        1) We do not have to have unrighteous thoughts. We can allow the Holy Ghost and the Word of God to change us from the inside. We need to walk and live in the revelation that we have been made the righteousness of God in Christ Jesus. Proverbs 16:3 states, *"Commit thy works unto the Lord, and thy thoughts shall be established."* Moreover Philippians 4:8 exhorts us, *"...whatsoever things are true... honest... just... pure... think on these things."*

        2) Matthew 15:19-20 *"For out of the heart proceed evil thoughts, murders, adulteries, fornications, thefts, false witness, blasphemies: ²⁰These are the things which defile a man."* Unrighteousness does not come from the outside, but from within the heart of man. It originates from our carnal, adamic nature. What needs to happen is we need to be changed and sanctified from the inside out.

3. Fornicators in Greek – *pornos* – to sell sex, whoremonger, debauchery

    a. I Corinthians 5:9-13 – *"I wrote unto you in an epistle not to company with fornicators: ¹⁰Yet not altogether with the fornicators of this world, or with the covetous, or extortioners, or with idolaters; for then must ye needs go out of the world. ¹¹But now I have written unto you not to keep company, if any man that is called a brother be a fornicator, or covetous, or an idolater, or a railer, or a drunkard, or an extortioner; with such an one no not to eat. ¹²For what have I to do to judge them also that are without? do not ye judge them that are within? ¹³But them that are without God judgeth. Therefore put away from among yourselves that wicked person."*

        1) There are fornicators in the body of Christ, where sex means more to them than the Holy Ghost. We must allow the Lord to deliver us from lust.
        2) James 1:14-16 – *"But every man is tempted, when he is drawn away of his own lust, and enticed. ¹⁵Then when lust hath conceived, it bringeth forth sin: and sin, when it is finished, bringeth forth death. ¹⁶Do not err, my beloved brethren."* I believe that there is a conception period before we decide to sin. We must not decide to give in to our baser inclinations. We must allow the Holy Ghost to help us overcome.

b. Hebrews 12:14-17 – *"Follow peace with all men, and holiness, without which no man shall see the Lord: ¹⁵Looking diligently lest any man fail of the grace of God; lest any root of bitterness springing up trouble you, and thereby many be defiled; ¹⁶Lest there be any fornicator, or profane person, as Esau, who for one morsel of meat sold his birthright. ¹⁷For ye know how that afterward, when he would have inherited the blessing, he was rejected: for he found no place of repentance, though he sought it carefully with tears."*

    1) This does not mean that Esau did not make it into heaven. If you follow the life of Esau, he actually received his brother Jacob later in life and they ended up with a restored relationship. However, what Esau lost was his first born blessing, not his relationship with God.

c. I Corinthians 10:8 – *"Neither let us commit fornication, as some of them committed, and fell in one day three and twenty thousand."*

4. Idolaters in Greek – *eidololatres* – image or idol worshipper, servant of an image, worship of a heathen god. An idol does not necessarily have to be an image of stone. An idol is anything we worship. It could be a relationship, a job or anything we place before the Lord Jesus. Jesus should be first before everything else in our lives. Remember it says in Isaiah 6:1, *"In the year that king Uzziah died I saw also the Lord, sitting upon a throne, high and lifted up..."* This tells me that king Uzziah kept Isaiah from seeing the Lord high and lifted up. Anything that keeps you from seeing Jesus high and lifted up needs to be dumped from our lives. Exodus 20:1 states, *"Thou shalt have no other gods before me."*

a. I Corinthians 10:5-7 – *"But with many of them God was not well pleased: for they were overthrown in the wilderness. ⁶Now these things were our examples, to the intent we should not lust after evil things, as they also lusted. ⁷Neither be ye idolaters, as were some of them; as it is written, The people sat down to eat and drink, and rose up to play."*

b. Leviticus 19:4 – *"Turn ye not unto idols, nor make to yourselves molten gods: I am the Lord your God."*

c. Leviticus 26:1 – *"Ye shall make you no idols nor graven image, neither rear you up a standing image, neither shall ye set up any image of stone in your land, to bow down unto it: for I am the Lord your God."*

d. II Chronicles 15:8-15 – *"And when Asa heard these words, and the prophecy of Oded the prophet, he took courage, and put away the abominable idols out of all the land of Judah and Benjamin, and out of the cities which he had taken from mount Ephraim, and renewed the altar of the Lord, that was before the porch of the Lord...¹²And they entered into a covenant to seek the Lord God of their fathers with all their heart and with all their soul; ¹³That whosoever would not seek the Lord God of Israel should be put to death, whether small or great, whether man or woman. ¹⁴And they sware unto the Lord with a loud voice, and with shouting, and with trumpets, and with cornets. ¹⁵And all Judah rejoiced at the oath: for they had sworn with all their heart, and sought him with their whole desire; and he was found of them: and the Lord gave them rest round about."*

e. Psalms 106:34-42 – *"They did not destroy the nations, concerning whom the Lord commanded them: ³⁵But were mingled among the heathen, and learned their works. ³⁶And they served their idols: which were a snare unto them. ³⁷Yea, they sacrificed their sons and their daughters unto devils, ³⁸And shed innocent blood, even the blood of their sons and of their daughters, whom they sacrificed unto the idols of Canaan: and the land was polluted with blood. ³⁹Thus were they defiled with their own works, and went a whoring with their own inventions. ⁴⁰Therefore was the wrath of the Lord kindled against his people, insomuch that he abhorred his own inheritance. ⁴¹And he gave them into the hand of the heathen; and they that hated them ruled over them. ⁴²Their enemies also oppressed them, and they were brought into subjection under their hand."*

f. Isaiah 2:8, 18 – *"Their land also is full of idols; they worship the work of their own hands, that which their own fingers have made...¹⁸And the idols he shall utterly abolish."*

g. Hosea 14:5-9 – *"...Ephraim shall say, What have I to do any more with idols? I have heard him, and observed him: I am like a green fir tree. From me is thy fruit found. ⁹Who is wise, and he shall understand these things? prudent, and he shall know them? for the ways of the Lord are right, and the just shall walk in them: but the transgressors shall fall therein."*

5. Adulterers in Greek – *moichos* – an illicit lover, apostate. We need to be faithful to our spouse and not let sin run rampant in our lives. We live in a day where we see so much adultery in the body of Christ.

    a. James 4:4 – *"Ye adulterers and adulteresses, know ye not that the friendship of the world is enmity with God? whosoever therefore will be a friend of the world is the enemy of God."*

    b. Hebrews 13:4-6 – *"Marriage is honourable in all, and the bed undefiled: but whoremongers and adulterers God will judge. ⁵Let your conversation be without covetousness; and be content with such things as ye have: for he hath said, I will never leave thee, nor forsake thee. ⁶So that we may boldly say, The Lord is my helper, and I will not fear what man shall do unto me."*

    c. Leviticus 20:10 – *"And the man that committeth adultery with another man's wife, even he that committeth adultery with his neighbour's wife, the adulterer and the adulteress shall surely be put to death."*

    d. Job 24:15 – *"The eye also of the adulterer waiteth for the twilight, saying, No eye shall see me: and disguiseth his face."*

    e. Exodus 20:14 – *"Thou shalt not commit adultery."*

    f. Proverbs 6:32-33 – *"But whoso committeth adultery with a woman lacketh understanding: he that doeth it destroyeth his own soul. ³³A wound and dishonour shall he get; and his reproach shall not be wiped away."*

    g. Matthew 5:27-28 – *"Ye have heard that it was said by them of old time, Thou shalt not commit adultery: ²⁸But I say unto you, That whosoever looketh on a woman to lust after her hath committed adultery with her already in his heart."*

    h. Proverbs 6:26-29 – *"For by means of a whorish woman a man is brought to a piece of bread: and the adulteress will hunt for the precious life. ²⁷Can a man take fire in his bosom, and his clothes not be burned? ²⁸Can one go upon hot coals, and his feet not be burned? ²⁹So he that goeth in to his neighbour's wife; whosoever toucheth her shall not be innocent."* When we commit adultery, our clothes are burned. This means that everything that we gained in God, our inheritance, is destroyed when you commit adultery. Is there anything worse than seeing betrayal and a marriage fall apart.

    i. John 8:1-12 – Woman caught in adultery. In the Old Testament, when someone committed adultery, they were stoned. But look at how Jesus dealt with the situation. He had mercy upon the woman. He brought mercy and truth to her life and said in verse 11, *"Neither do I condemn thee: go, and sin no more."*

6. Effeminate in Greek – "perverts and homosexuals, soft, wears fine clothing"

    a. Romans 1:21-32 – *"Because that, when they knew God, they glorified him not as God, neither were thankful; but became vain in their imaginations, and their foolish heart was darkened. ²² Professing themselves to be wise, they became fools, ²³And changed the glory of the uncorruptible God into an image made like to corruptible man, and to birds, and fourfooted beasts, and creeping things. ²⁴Wherefore God also gave them up to uncleanness through the lusts of their own hearts, to dishonor their own bodies between themselves: ²⁵Who changed the truth of God into a lie, and worshipped and served the creature more than the Creator, who is blessed for ever. ²⁶For this cause God gave them up unto vile affections: for even their women did change the natural use into that which is against nature: ²⁷And likewise also the men, leaving the natural use of the woman, burned in their lust one toward another; men with men working that which is unseemly, and receiving in themselves that recompense of their error which was meet."*

1) When you say God is like you and you bring Him down to your level, you are changing the incorruptible God to a corruptible man. Verse 27 is obviously speaking of lesbian women and homosexual men. It is vile. God turns you over to it because you are so full of lust and you don't want to retain God in your knowledge. You end up worshipping the creature more than the creator.

b. Leviticus 18:22 – *"Thou shalt not lie with mankind, as with womankind: it is abomination."*

1) It is very clear that homosexuality is an abomination to God. This doesn't mean we do not love homosexuals. We love the sinner, but hate the sin. However, we must be willing to make a stand for the truth. We are in a world today where anything goes. And if we say anything against the effeminate, homosexual lifestyle, we are ostracized, told we are not a person of decency and tolerance. The Scriptures are clear, though, that God doesn't have a tolerance for it. It is an abomination. Despite that, God loves everybody, no matter what our sins may be. I can honestly say that homosexuality is probably one of the hardest sins to overcome.

7. Thieves in Greek – *kleptes* – a stealer or robber
8. Covetous in Greek – *pleonektes* – desiring more, eager for gain, defrauder
   a. Psalms 10:3 – *"For the wicked boasteth of his heart's desire, and blesseth the covetous, whom the Lord abhorreth."*
   b. II Timothy 3:1-5 – *"³This know also, that in the last days perilous times shall come. ²For men shall be lovers of their own selves, covetous, boasters, proud, blasphemers, disobedient to parents, unthankful, unholy, ³Without natural affection, trucebreakers, false accusers, incontinent, fierce, despisers of those that are good, ⁴Traitors, heady, highminded, lovers of pleasures more than lovers of God; ⁵Having a form of godliness, but denying the power thereof: from such turn away."*
   c. Ephesians 5:5-7 – *"⁵For this ye know, that no whoremonger, nor unclean person, nor covetous man, who is an idolater, hath any inheritance in the kingdom of Christ and of God. ⁶Let no man deceive you with vain words: for because of these things cometh the wrath of God upon the children of disobedience. ⁷Be not ye therefore partakers with them."*
   d. II Peter 2:9-22 – *"...¹⁴Having eyes full of adultery, and that cannot cease from sin; beguiling unstable souls: an heart they have exercised with covetous practices; cursed children: ¹⁵Which have forsaken the right way, and are gone astray, following the way of Balaam the son of Bosor, who loved the wages of unrighteousness..."*
   e. Proverbs 15:27 – *"He that is greedy of gain troubleth his own house; but he that hateth gifts shall live."*
   f. Proverbs 1:19 *"So are the ways of every one that is greedy of gain; which taketh away the life of the owners thereof."*
   g. I Timothy 6:2-8 – *"...³If any man teach otherwise, and consent not to wholesome words, even the words of our Lord Jesus Christ, and to the doctrine which is according to godliness; ⁴He is proud, knowing nothing, but doting about questions and strifes of words, whereof cometh envy, strife, railings, evil surmisings, ⁵Perverse disputings of men of corrupt minds, and destitute of the truth, **supposing that gain is godliness**: from such withdraw thyself. ⁶But godliness with contentment is great gain. ⁷For we brought nothing into this world, and it is certain we can carry nothing out. ⁸And having food and raiment let us be therewith content."*
   h. Hebrews 13:5 – *"Let your conversation be without covetousness; and be content with such things as ye have: for he hath said, I will never leave thee, nor forsake thee."*

    i.   Exodus 18:19-23 – "...²¹*Moreover thou shalt provide out of all the people able men, such as fear God, men of truth, hating covetousness; and place such over them, to be rulers of thousands, and rulers of hundreds, rulers of fifties, and rulers of tens...*"

    j.   Psalms 119:35-38 – "³⁵*Make me to go in the path of thy commandments; for therein do I delight. ³⁶Incline my heart unto thy testimonies, and not to covetousness. ³⁷Turn away mine eyes from beholding vanity; and quicken thou me in thy way. ³⁸Stablish thy word unto thy servant, who is devoted to thy fear.*"

    k.   Luke 12:15 – "*And he said unto them, Take heed, and beware of covetousness: for a man's life consisteth not in the abundance of the things which he possesseth.*"

    l.   Ephesians 5:1-3 – "¹*Be ye therefore followers of God, as dear children; ²And walk in love, as Christ also hath loved us, and hath given himself for us an offering and a sacrifice to God for a sweetsmelling savour. ³But fornication, and all uncleanness, or covetousness, let it not be once named among you, as becometh saints;*"

9.   Drunkards in Greek – *methusos* – tipsy, a sot; from a root that means to drink to intoxication

10. Revilers in Greek – *loidoros* – mischief, abusive, railer

11. Extortioners in Greek – *harpazo* – to seize in various ways, to take by force

E.   I Corinthians 15:47-54 - "*Now this I say, brethren, that flesh and blood cannot inherit the kingdom of God; neither doth corruption inherit incorruption.*"

1.   It is obvious from this verse that flesh and blood is the hindering force that keeps us from inheriting the Kingdom of God. It is important to see that we have the choice in our lives to either walk in the bad moral influences of our flesh, our baser inclinations, or to live by the Spirit of God that is within us. We have been born into this world in sin. But in Christ Jesus, we have escaped the corruption that is in the world. We have been delivered out of it and must choose to now walk in it. The Kingdom of God, the sovereign rule of King Jesus in our lives, does not take place when we choose the things of the flesh rather than the things of the kingdom. Corruption, the flesh and all the things this world has to offer can keep us from entering into His glorious kingdom. We must choose Him every day of our lives.

2.   Other Translations:

"*Flesh and blood cannot have a part in the Kingdom of God. Something that will ruin cannot have a part in something that never ruins.*"
"*Flesh and blood cannot possess the kingdom of God; neither shall corruption possess incorruption*", "*neither does corruption inherit incorruptibility.*"
"*What is made of flesh and blood cannot share in God's Kingdom, and what is mortal cannot possess immortality.*"

3.   Word Definitions:

    a.   Incorruption in Greek, <u>*aphthrsia*</u> – unending existence, unending genuiness and sincerity, undecaying in essence or continuance.

    b.   Corruption in Greek, *phthora* – decay, ruin, be destroyed or perish; it comes from a root, *phtheiro* – to pine or waste, shrivel or wither by any process; it happens by bad moral influences that deprave and cause to decay and ruin; to defile or destroy self.

4. Corruption in Scriptures:

    a.   Isaiah 38:17-20 – "¹⁷*Behold, for peace I had great bitterness: but thou hast in love to my soul delivered it from the pit of corruption: for thou hast cast all my sins behind thy back. ¹⁸For the grave cannot praise thee, death can not celebrate thee: they that go down into the pit*" *cannot hope for thy truth. [19]The living, the living, he shall praise thee, as I do this day: the father to the children shall make known thy truth. [20]The Lord was ready to save me: therefore we will sing my songs to the stringed instruments all the days of our life in the house of the Lord."*

b. Romans 8:18-23 – *"[20]For the creature was made subject to vanity, not willingly, but by reason of him who hath subjected the same in hope, [21]Because the creature itself also shall be delivered from the bondage of corruption into the glorious liberty of the children of God."*

   1) God allowed us to be subject to vanity. He put us in a world of corruption, of disease and of tribulation. However, He did it with the hope that we would receive Him and come out of it to receive a kingdom that cannot be removed. When we were born into the earth we were born with corruptible seed. When we were born again, we were born with incorruptible seed.

   2) Corruption is bondage. Liberty is glorious!

c. Galatians 6:7-8 – *"[7]Be not deceived; God is not mocked: for whatsoever a man soweth, that shall he also reap. [8]For he that soweth to his flesh shall of the flesh reap corruption; but he that soweth to the Spirit shall of the Spirit reap life everlasting."*

d. II Peter 1:1-4 – *"Simon Peter, a servant and an apostle of Jesus Christ, to them that have obtained like precious faith with us through the righteousness of God and our Saviour Jesus Christ: [2]Grace and peace be multiplied unto you through the knowledge of God and of Jesus our Lord. [3]According as his divine power hath given unto us all things that pertain unto life and godliness, through the knowledge of him that hath called us to glory and virtue: [4]Whereby are given unto us exceeding great and precious promises: that by these ye might be partakers of the divine nature, having escaped the corruption that is in the world through lust."*

   1) These precious promises that allow us to escape corruption of our fleshy human desires and be a partaker of the divine nature is the Word of God. His divine nature wants to live in and through us. Every day we have the choice to allow that nature to become a part of us! That is why it is so important to give ourselves to the Word of God everyday of our lives.

   2) Other Translations of verse 4:

"By means of these He has bestowed upon us His precious and exceedingly great promises, so that through them you may escape by flight from the moral decay, rottenness and corruption that is in the world because of covetous, lust and greed, and become sharers, partakers of the divine nature."

"We were also given absolutely terrific promises to pass on to you; your tickets to participation in the life of God, after you turned your back on a world corrupted by lust."

"And because of his glory and excellence, he has given us great and precious promises. These are promises that enable you to share His divine nature and escape the world's corruption caused by human desires."

"And by that same mighty power He has given us all the other rich and wonderful blessings He promised; for instance, the promise to save us from the lust and rottenness all around us, and to give us His own character."

"caused by evil desires", "because of sinful desires"

"that you might come to share in God's nature and escape the corruption which evil desires have brought into the world."

"Through these He gave us very great and precious promises, with these gifts you share in being like God, and the world will not ruin you with it's evil desires."

"So that by them we may have our part in God's being, and be made free from the destruction which is in the world, through the desires of the flesh."
"He has granted us his precious and wondrous promises in order that through them you may one and all, become sharers in the very nature of God, having completely escaped the corruption which exists in the earthly cravings."
"you may escape from the destructive lust that is in the world, and may come to share the divine nature."

e. II Peter 2:9-22 – *"The Lord knoweth how to deliver the godly out of temptations, and to reserve the unjust unto the day of judgment to be punished: 10But chiefly them that walk after the flesh in the lust of uncleanness, and despise government. Presumptuous are they, selfwilled, they are not afraid to speak evil of dignities... 12But these, as natural brute beasts, made to be taken and destroyed, speak evil of the things that they understand not; and shall utterly perish in their own corruption...19While they promise them liberty, they themselves are the servants of corruption: for of whom a man is overcome, of the same is he brought in bondage."*

1) I believe this passage is not speaking of the world, but people within the church who are giving themselves over to the flesh and to corruption.

f. John 3:6 – *"That which is born of the flesh is flesh; and that which is born of the Spirit is spirit."*

g. I John 2:15-20 – *"15Love not the world, neither the things that are in the world. If any man love the world, the love of the Father is not in him. 16For all that is in the world, the lust of the flesh, and the lust of the eyes, and the pride of life, is not of the Father, but is of the world. 17And the world passeth away, and the lust thereof: but he that doeth the will of God abideth for ever. 18Little children, it is the last time: and as ye have heard that antichrist shall come, even now are there many antichrists; whereby we know that it is the last time. 19They went out from us, but they were not of us; for if they had been of us, they would no doubt have continued with us: but they went out, that they might be made manifest that they were not all of us. 20But ye have an unction from the Holy One, and ye know all things."*

1) Verse 15 does not say that God doesn't love those who love the world. Rather it means that the love of God is not operating in the person's life. It means the Father has not been put first in his/her life.

h. Matthew 26:41 – *"Watch and pray, that ye enter not into temptation: the spirit indeed is willing, but the flesh is weak."*

i. Romans 6:15-21 – *"15What then? shall we sin, because we are not under the law, but under grace? God forbid. 16Know ye not, that to whom ye yield yourselves servants to obey, his servants ye are to whom ye obey; whether of sin unto death, or of obedience unto righteousness? 17But God be thanked, that ye were the servants of sin, but ye have obeyed from the heart that form of doctrine which was delivered you. 18Being then made free from sin, ye became the servants of righteousness. 19I speak after the manner of men because of the infirmity of your flesh: for as ye have yielded your members servants to uncleanness and to iniquity unto iniquity; even so now yield your members servants to righteousness unto holiness. 20For when ye were the servants of sin, ye were free from righteousness. 21What fruit had ye then in those things whereof ye are now ashamed? for the end of those things is death."*

j. Romans 7:4-25, Romans 8:1-16

k. I Corinthians 1:26-31 – *"26For ye see your calling, brethren, how that not many wise men after the flesh, not many mighty, not many noble, are called: 27But God hath chosen the foolish things of the world to confound the wise; and God hath chosen the weak things of the* *world to confound the things which are mighty; ²⁸And base things of the world, and things which are despised, hath God chosen, yea, and things which are not, to bring to nought things that are: ²⁹That no flesh should glory in his presence. ³⁰But of him are ye in Christ Jesus, who of God is made unto us wisdom, and righteousness, and sanctification, and redemption: ³¹That, according as it is written, He that glorieth, let him glory in the Lord." (Jeremiah 9:23)*

l. II Corinthians 4:11-18 – *"¹¹For we which live are alway delivered unto death for Jesus' sake, that the life also of Jesus might be made manifest in our mortal flesh. ¹²So then death worketh in us, but life in you. ¹³We having the same spirit of faith, according as it is written, I believed, and therefore have I spoken; we also believe, and therefore speak; ¹⁴Knowing that he which raised up the Lord Jesus shall raise up us also by Jesus, and shall present us with you. ¹⁵For all things are for your sakes, that the abundant grace might through the thanksgiving of many redound to the glory of God. ¹⁶For which cause we faint not; but though our outward man perish, yet the inward man is renewed day by day. ¹⁷For our light affliction, which is but for a moment, worketh for us a far more exceeding and eternal weight of glory; ¹⁸While we look not at the things which are seen, but at the things which are not seen: for the things which are seen are temporal; but the things which are not seen are eternal."*

m. II Corinthians 7:1 – *"Having therefore these promises, dearly beloved, let us cleanse ourselves from all filthiness of the flesh and spirit, perfecting holiness in the fear of God."*

n. II Corinthians 10:3-6 – *"³For though we walk in the flesh, we do not war after the flesh: ⁴(For the weapons of our warfare are not carnal, but mighty through God to the pulling down of strong holds;) ⁵Casting down imaginations, and every high thing that exalteth itself against the knowledge of God, and bringing into captivity every thought to the obedience of Christ; ⁶And having in a readiness to revenge all disobedience, when your obedience is fulfilled."*

o. Galatians 2:17-21 – *"¹⁷But if, while we seek to be justified by Christ, we ourselves also are found sinners, is therefore Christ the minister of sin? God forbid. ¹⁸For if I build again the things which I destroyed, I make myself a transgressor. ¹⁹For I through the law am dead to the law, that I might live unto God. ²⁰I am crucified with Christ: nevertheless I live; yet not I, but Christ liveth in me: and the life which I now live in the flesh I live by the faith of the Son of God, who loved me, and gave himself for me. ²¹I do not frustrate the grace of God: for if righteousness come by the law, then Christ is dead in vain."*

p. Galatians 3:1-3 – *"¹O foolish Galatians, who hath bewitched you, that ye should not obey the truth, before whose eyes Jesus Christ hath been evidently set forth, crucified among you? ²This only would I learn of you, Received ye the Spirit by the works of the law, or by the hearing of faith? ³Are ye so foolish? having begun in the Spirit, are ye now made perfect by the flesh?"*

q. Galatians 5:13-25 – *"¹³For, brethren, ye have been called unto liberty; only use not liberty for an occasion to the flesh, but by love serve one another..."*

r. Ephesians 2:1-15

s. Philippians 3:3   *"For we are the circumcision, which worship God in the spirit, and rejoice in Christ Jesus, and have no confidence in the flesh."*

    1) We have made our choice. We are not going back anymore to the flesh. We have no confidence in anything this world has to offer us! We worship Him in Spirit and in truth.

t. I Peter 4:1 – *"Forasmuch then as Christ hath suffered for us in the flesh, arm yourselves likewise with the same mind: for he that hath suffered in the flesh hath ceased from sin."*

    1) When you suffer in the flesh enough for your sin, the time will come when you will not want to do that anymore and you will cease from sin. You cannot walk a double life, or have a double heart and a double mind. Eventually you make a choice that you do not want to live that way anymore. Lightning is not going to strike and we stop sinning. It is a choice we make to honor the Lord Jesus.

u. Luke 16:14-16 – "*¹⁴And the Pharisees also, who were covetous, heard all these things: and they derided him. ¹⁵And he said unto them, Ye are they which justify yourselves before men; but God knoweth your hearts: for that which is highly esteemed among men is abomination in the sight of God. ¹⁶The law and the prophets were until John: since that time the kingdom of God is preached, and every man presseth into it.*"

1) The Pharisees, who were covetous, derided Jesus. They came against the nature of God within Him. What Jesus was carrying within Him was more precious than anything that this world has to offer and they were reproaching Him for it.

2) God knows everyone's heart and the Pharisees were those who loved the praises of men more than the praises of God. This is the furthest thing from the Kingdom of God.

3) There is a place for pressing into the kingdom. There is a place for violent praise and worship, violent interecession. There is a place where we speak to our souls to not bow the knee to anything other than the Lord Jesus and His kingdom.

Chapter 11
Looking Back Makes Us Unfit For The Kingdom Of God

We are moving into a day where the Kingdom of God is the central message of the body of Christ. The remnant, the bride, those that are devoted to the Lord, who hear His voice, are running after Him with all their hearts. Jesus is becoming the Lord of lords and King of kings in their lives. *"As He is, so are we in this world"* (I John 4:17). The Kingdom of God is about Jesus becoming who He fully is within His people, where we are beginning to experience heaven on earth and heaven in our earth.

However, in this lesson we want to look at a principle of looking back in the Scriptures. As we will see, looking back can make us unfit for the Kingdom of God. There are people, places, things, and experiences in which we have not let go. Until we let them go from our lives, we will stay in bondage to those things and keep looking back. Like Samson, in Judges 16:21, *"But the Philistines... bound him with fetters of brass; and he did grind in the prison house."* In other words, we will be just going around in circles, in bondage and never going on in God.

Looking back can keep us from entering into the Kingdom of God. This does not mean that someone who looks back will not go to heaven. It does mean, though, that it can keep someone from participating in the Kingdom of God, which is a revelation of Jesus within a people on the earth. Therefore, we must be pressing on into the Kingdom and not looking back.

I.   Looking Back Makes Us Unfit For The Kingdom Of God

A.   Luke 9:57-62 – *"⁵⁷And it came to pass, that, as they went in the way, a certain man said unto him, Lord, I will follow thee whithersoever thou goest. ⁵⁸And Jesus said unto him, Foxes have holes, and birds of the air have nests; but the Son of man hath not where to lay his head. ⁵⁹And he said unto another, Follow me. But he said, Lord, suffer me first to go and bury my father. ⁶⁰Jesus said unto him, Let the dead bury their dead: but go thou and preach the kingdom of God. ⁶¹And another also said, Lord, I will follow thee; but let me first go bid them farewell, which are at home at my house. ⁶²And Jesus said unto him, No man, having put his hand to the plough, and looking back, is fit for the kingdom of God."*

When we make statements like, "Lord, I'll go wherever you want me to go," it is easier said than done. You can say it; but, the reality is as Jesus said, *"Foxes have holes, and birds of the air have nests; but the Son of man hath not where to lay his head."* (Luke 9:58) In other words, when you decide to follow Jesus, you have no guarantee of a permanent place. You do not have a guarantee of luxuries and all the things that we are taught in this word of faith, charismatic world that we live in. The true son of God really does not know where he is going to end up, because he works for somebody else. His life is lived to another.

Secondly, is the principle of familial ties. "Let me first go bury my father." Families can be the biggest hindrance in our walk with God. Jesus said, "Let the dead bury their dead. You need to be concerned about following me." That is a hard word, but it is still the truth. Once somebody is dead, they are dead.

He goes on to say, "Let me first go bid them farewell, which are at my house." Friends, the people that we love, are the second thing that keeps us from the things of God. Relationships that we have had try to prevail upon us, put pressure on us, to keep us from pressing into the kingdom. Though people may never tell you to not press in, by their actions and by the way they live their lives, they will try to keep you from pressing into God.

We must disassociate ourselves from the people and the things of our past. It may be a church you have been going to or people in whom you know you are not supposed to be involved. Holding on to these things and looking back keeps you from your future in God. It is like the story in Mark 8:22-26, when those who cared about a certain blind man brought him to Jesus, who then took him by the hand and led him <u>out of the town</u> to heal him. The reason he did this is because that man could never receive his healing around his family and those people who sincerely loved him. Sometimes, you have to get out from where you are to receive from God. Because without realizing it, the unbelief (lack of faith) of all those other people in our lives can hinder us and make us unfit for use in the kingdom of God. Ultimately, each and every one of us must personally decide, "I have to go on." Nobody can make that decision but you. We must not look back and be willing to let these things go from our lives.

1. Word definitions:

   a. Fit in Greek – *euthetos* – well placed, appropriate, able. This tells me that if you are looking back, you will not be appropriate, well-placed or able to walk in the Kingdom of God.
   b. Looking back in Greek – to take heed of what is past, regard, behold, to look at, to keep in sight. How many people are constantly reminded in their soulish realm of some past thing, person, experience or dealing? When you take heed of and regard and look constantly at your past, it can keep you from going on. If you always live in what has been, it will keep you from further triumphs in God.

2. Other translations of verse 62:

"No one who puts his hand to the plow and looks back to the things behind is fit for the kingdom of God."
"Jesus said, No procrastination. No backward looks. You can't put God's kingdom off till tomorrow. Seize the day."
"...is of no use in the kingdom."
"...is good enough for the kingdom."
"...looks behind him..."
"...is fit for the reign of God."
"...is fit for service in the kingdom of God."
"Anyone who lets himself be distracted from the work I plan for him is not fit for the kingdom of God."
"No one who puts his hand to the plow and keeps looking back is fit to service the kingdom of God."
"...and looking back to the things he left behind, is fit..."
"...Anyone who starts to plow and then keeps looking back is of no use for the kingdom of God."

Again, this does not mean that we will not go to heaven; but, we will not enjoy and participate in the Kingdom of God, which is the revelation of God in a people on the earth.

B. Companion Scriptures

1. Luke 17:26-37 – "...*30Even thus shall it be in the day when the Son of man is revealed. 31In that day, he which shall be upon the housetop, and his stuff in the house, let him not come down to take it away: and he that is in the field, let him likewise <u>not return back</u>. 32<u>Remember Lot's wife.</u> 33Whosoever shall seek to save his life shall lose it; and whosoever shall lose his life shall preserve it...*"

What does it mean when it says "*in the day when the Son of man is revealed?*" Many people believe it just speaks of the second coming of Jesus. However, I believe it speaks of when the Son of man, Jesus, is revealed in a people. The son of man is revealed when sonship takes place, when the son of God comes forth in His own sons and daughters and it is no longer they that live; but, Jesus that lives fully within them (Galatians 2:20-21). This earth is going to see a true revelation of Jesus again, not in heaven but in the earth. Jesus has already sat down in heaven at the right hand of the Father. Everything that He is going to ever do now until He splits the sky at the last trumpet, He is going to do in a people. So the earth is waiting for the "*manifestation of the sons of God*" (Romans 8:19). One translation says that the whole earth is "*waiting on tip toes for the manifestation of the sons of God.*" When the sons of God are manifested, then *the* Son of God will reveal Himself and manifest Himself them.

The housetop speaks of a place of revelation in God. If you are on a housetop, do not go down for your stuff in the house. Do not become preoccupied with things that will remove you from your place in God.

Likewise, if we are in the field, we should not return. The field speaks of the world as well as our place in the kingdom as well as the ministry. We do not need to go back. Once we have made the decision that we are going on in God, we should not question that decision and return from it.

Finally we are told to remember Lot's wife. Lot's wife looked back on Sodom, looked back on things that still held her heart. When she did, she became a pillar of salt, forever preserved and unable to go on anymore in God. When Jesus is to be revealed within a people, looking back can keep us from having Jesus manifested within us and revealed.

a. Other translations of verse 33:

"*If you grasp and cling to life on your own terms, you'll lose it, but if you let that life go, you'll get life on God's terms.*"
"*Whosoever aims at preserving his own life will lose it, but whosoever loses his life will stay alive.*"
"*...those who give up their lives will save them.*"
"*...anyone who makes it his object to keep his own life safe, will lose it.*"
"*...whoever tries to make his life secure will lose it.*"

b. Word definitions in Greek:

1) Save – to protect, keep whole, deliver
2) Life – *psuche* – the soul, carnal, adamic man
3) Lose – to destroy fully, to cause to die or perish
4) Preserve – to rescue, to be saved from death

Most people live in their *psuche*, or in their soulish life. This is akin to Adam eating from the tree of the knowledge of good and evil. This was how man fell. We originally were called to eat from the Tree of Life, which is Jesus. We need to live by the witness of His Spirit and not in the realm of the soul any longer. Like Abraham, when the Lord told him to go and leave all He ever knew, He went. Hebrews 11:8 says, "*By faith Abraham, when he was called to go out into a place which he should after receive for an inheritance, obeyed; and he went out, not knowing whither he went.*" However, when we begin to think and reason in our minds, we are allowing our soulish man to get in the way. Romans 8:7 says, *"Because the carnal mind is enmity against God."* We are not to live there. We are not to be controlled by our thoughts, our emotions and feelings. This verse tells us that living by our soulish man can make us lose out on entering into His life and kingdom. Therefore, we must lose, destroy fully, to cause to die or perish, that soulish man. We must put it to death by the Spirit of God and by the Word of God. When John was on the Isle of Patmos (which means "my killing"), he got the revelation of Jesus. What did he kill? He put to death His soulish, carnal life.

2. Isaiah 43:18-21 – *"¹⁸Remember ye not the former things, neither consider the things of old. ¹⁹Behold, I will do a new thing; now it shall spring forth; shall ye not know it? I will even make a way in the wilderness, and rivers in the desert..."*

    a. Word definitions in Hebrew:

        1) Remember – to keep in mind (so as to be recognized), to make mention of, to still think on
        2) Not – never, no, nothing worth it, something different rather than that
        3) Former – first in place, time, or rank; things of old time, that were before, things in the past. From a root – the head easily shaken by these things.

We do not need to keep things in our past first in our lives. Jesus needs to be first. Also, the head (our souls) can be easily shaken by things of our past. None of these things should move us because we should not live in the realm of the soul any longer. Galatians 5:16 says, *"Walk in the Spirit, and ye shall not fulfill the lust of the flesh."* We need to live in the Spirit. Proverbs 20:27, *"The spirit of man is the candle of the Lord."* Our spirit man is the place where God can speak to us at any moment. But when we get over into the soulish realm, we start thinking and regretting and can be easily shaken up.

        4) Things – same as former
        5) Consider – to separate or distinguish mentally, look well to, to think, cause to understand, view
        6) Old – they that went before. From a root – to project oneself backwards, precede, disappoint, prevent.

        Disappointments can easily cause us to look back and regret our past. We must forget about those things and move on.

    b. Other translations:

"Forget about what's happened, don't keep going over old history. Be alert, be present. I'm about to do something brand new. It's bursting out! Don't you see it?"
"But forget all that; it is nothing compared to what I am going to do."
"Do not dwell on the past."
"Do not call to mind the former things. Or ponder things of the past."
"Do not cling to the events of the past."
"Stop dwelling on past events and brooding over times gone by."
"The Lord says, Forget what happened before, and do not think about the past."
"Pay no attention to things of old."
"Give no thought to the things which are past, let the early things go out of your minds."
"Don't dwell on what happened long ago."

3. Genesis 19:15-26 – *"¹⁵And when the morning arose, then the angels hastened Lot, saying, Arise, take thy wife, and thy two daughters, which are here; lest thou be consumed in the iniquity of the city. ¹⁶And while he lingered, the men laid hold upon his hand, and upon the hand of his wife, and upon the hand of his two daughters; the Lord being merciful unto him: and they brought him*

forth, and set him without the city. 17And it came to pass, when they had brought them forth abroad, that he said, Escape for thy life; <u>look not behind thee</u>, neither stay thou in all the plain; escape to the mountain, lest thou be consumed...24Then the Lord rained upon Sodom and upon Gomorrah brimstone and fire from the Lord out of heaven; 25And he overthrew those cities, and all the plain, and all the inhabitants of the cities, and that which grew upon the ground. 26But his wife <u>looked back</u> from behind him, and she became a pillar of salt."

First of all, II Peter 2:7-8 says that God, *"delivered just Lot, vexed with the filthy conversation of the wicked: 8(For that righteous man dwelling among them, in seeing and hearing, vexed his righteous soul from day to day with their unlawful deeds;)"* God, in His mercy, delivered Lot simply because he was related to Abraham. Just because he was in the family, God sent angels to take him out of that situation. Wherever our children or family members are today, God will deliver them, even if they are in homosexual Sodom and Gomorrah, simply because you and I are pressing toward the mark.

It says that Lot lingered around. Sin had a hold on him and his righteous soul was vexed every day. There was something about the place that still appealed to him, even though he knew he should not be there. Why do we stay in places when we know the witness of the Spirit tells us to leave? In this story, the angels had to literally grab him and take him out of the house. He did not even know that his life was hanging in the balance. Again Luke 17:33 states, *"Whosoever shall seek to save his life shall lose it; and whosoever shall lose his life shall preserve it."*

They were told to not look back and escape for their lives. However, Lot's wife looked back and she became a pillar of salt. She was forever preserved in that state and could never go on with God. Another example is Jacob's wife, Rachel, who it says in Genesis 35:18 that she died in the way to Ephrath (Bethlehem). Why did Rachel die on the way? I believe it was because she had idols in her life. Remember, Genesis 31:32 says that Rachel stole and hid her father's idols with her when she ran away with Jacob. Rachel could not make it to where God had called her because she would not let go of the idols out of her life. Keeping idols in our lives can keep us from Kingdom of God.

    a.   Word definitions:

        1)   Behind in Hebrew –from a root – to loiter, to procrastinate, to be late, to be slack, stay there
        2)   Pillar in Hebrew – something stationary, a statue; from a root – to make to stand

When you keep looking back and you allow things behind you to rule you and control you, you will be frozen in that place. Hebrews 10:38 states, *"If any man draw back, my soul shall have no pleasure in him."* Going on with God is a progression. It is forward and onward and upward. There is no standing still in God. We must remember this principle of Lot's wife and go on with God no matter what, even if it costs us relationships, friends, family, lands, possessions, etc. Jesus said in Matthew 19:20, *"And everyone that hath forsaken houses, or brethren, or sisters, or father, or mother, or wife, or children, or lands, for my name's sake, shall receive an hundredfold, and shall inherit everlasting life."*

    4.   Philippians 3:12-13 – *"Not as though I had already attained, either were already perfect: but I follow after, if that I may apprehend that for which also I am apprehended of Christ Jesus. 13Brethren, I count not myself to have apprehended: but this one thing I do, forgetting those things which are behind, and reaching forth unto those things which are before,"*

Did you know that we were apprehended by Christ Jesus for a reason? We just did not get saved. God chose us and apprehended us for a divine purpose in the Kingdom of God. In light of that, Paul is saying that there is one thing that he now does. He forgets the things that are behind him and is reaching forth unto the things which are before. We are not to look back. We should lengthen our stride and run straight towards the goal of the high calling of God in Christ Jesus.

    a.   Word definitions:

        1)   Forgetting in Greek – to lose out of mind, to neglect
        2)   Behind in Greek – of direction, to the back. From a root – from the rear (as a secure aspect), at the back (as of a position of time)

    b.   Other translations:

"I've got my eye on the goal where God is beckoning us onward, to Jesus. I'm off and running, and I'm not turning back."
"Forgetting the past and straining toward what lies ahead."
"Instead, I am single minded, Forgetting those things that are behind, and reaching out for the things ahead."
"...letting go of the things which are past..."
"This is what I do; I don't look back, I lengthen my stride and I run straight toward the goal."
"In fact, I am completely forgetting the things that are behind, and am stretching forward."

    D.   Corresponding Biblical Passages

       1.   II Kings 7:3-11 – *"...³Why sit we here until we die?..."*

This is the story of the four lepers standing by the gates in Samaria during the great famine when the Syrian army was besieging the city. The four lepers were not wanted in the city of Samaria because they were lepers. But outside the city was the Syrian army. So the lepers didn't know what to do and said to each other, *"Why sit here until we die?"* Therefore they decided to go on with God and fall into the hands of the Syrians in the jeopardy of their lives. These lepers were not looking back. They did not care about their lives. They stepped out in faith and God wrought through them the deliverance of the whole city.

       2.   Job 11:13-19 – *"¹³If thou prepare thine heart, and stretch out thine hands toward him; ¹⁴If iniquity be in thine hand, put it far away, and let not wickedness dwell in thy tabernacles. ¹⁵For then shalt thou lift up thy face without spot; yea, thou shalt be stedfast, and shalt not fear: ¹⁶Because thou shalt forget thy misery, and remember it as waters that pass away..."*
       3.   Isaiah 54:1-5 – *"...⁴Fear not; for thou shalt not be ashamed: neither be thou confounded; for thou shalt not be put to shame: for thou shalt forget the shame of thy youth, and shalt not remember the reproach of thy widowhood any more."*
       4.   Revelation 21:4 – *"⁴And God shall wipe away all tears from their eyes; and there shall be no more death, neither sorrow, nor crying, neither shall there be any more pain: for the former things are passed away."*

       5.   Mark 5:2-9, 18 – *"²And when he was come out of the ship, immediately there met him out of the tombs a man with an unclean spirit, ³Who had his dwelling among the tombs...⁵And always, night and day, he was in the mountains, and in the tombs, crying, and cutting himself with stones..."*

          a.   Tombs in Greek – a remembrance

       6.   I Kings 18:21 – *"And Elijah came unto all the people, and said, <u>How long halt ye between two opinions?</u> if the Lord be God, follow him: but if Baal, then follow him. And the people answered him not a word."*
       7.   Ecclesiastes 1:11 – *"There is no remembrance of former things; neither shall there be any remembrance of things that are to come with those that shall come after."*
       8.   Acts 14:22 – *"Confirming the souls of the disciples, and exhorting them to continue in the faith, and that we must through much tribulation enter into the kingdom of God."*

9. Luke 21:36 – *"Watch ye therefore, and pray always, that ye may be accounted worthy to escape all these things that shall come to pass, and to stand before the Son of man."*
10. Matthew 26:46 – *"Rise, let us be going..."*
11. Matthew 4:18-20 – *"¹⁸And Jesus, walking by the sea of Galilee, saw two brethren, Simon called Peter, and Andrew his brother, casting a net into the sea: for they were fishers. ¹⁹And he saith unto them, Follow me, and I will make you fishers of men. ²⁰And they straightway left their nets, and followed him."* – They left the former things behind them.
11. Deuteronomy 2:3 – *"Ye have compassed this mountain long enough: turn you northward."*

Chapter 12
A Kingdom Which Cannot Be Moved

In this lesson we want to look specifically at the principle that the Kingdom of God cannot be moved. The people of God are the Israel of God, made up of born-again believers, who have received Jesus into their hearts. They are the city of the living God, the new Jerusalem, the church of the firstborn. This is who God is dealing with in the earth today. Natural Israel's kingdom was removed. The new Kingdom is made up of the sons of the living God, with Jesus reigning as King. This is a Kingdom which will never be removed. As believers, before we can enter into the Kingdom of God, we must allow God to shake everything in our lives that can be shaken. To enter the kingdom that cannot be moved, everything in our lives needs to be dealt with by God, where there is nothing of the world, flesh or devil living within us. None of these things must have a hold in our souls any longer. Then God will truly be King. We need to start thinking like kingdom people and take on a corporate mentality where as a body, we are moving together into the things of God. And in this chapter, we want to look specifically at the fact that the Kingdom of God that is coming is a kingdom which cannot be moved, where God is going to shake everything that can be shaken, so only those things that cannot be shaken may remain.

I.   Hebrews 12:18-29

    A.   Hebrews 12:28 – *"Wherefore we receiving a kingdom which cannot be moved, let us have grace, whereby we may serve God acceptably with reverence and godly fear:"*

    B.   The Context Of This Passage (verse 18-29)

The day is coming when we shall actually see Him for who He is. As Israel saw God in the natural realm, we will see Him in the spirit realm. We shall see Him just as they saw Him, in all of His glory. In Exodus 19, God came down in all of His glory in a smoke. There were voices, lightning, thunders and trumpets sounding. Most importantly, they saw a God of fire that frightened them so much that they refused to go near Him and pleaded with Moses to go alone to talk to God for them. But for us today, that cannot be our response to God. We have got to find the ability to hear God for ourselves. We are going to have to stand in front of a God that is full of an awesome and a glorious fire. Everything that cannot abide, that fire will be burned. As Paul says in I Corinthians 3:13, *"Every man's work shall be made manifest: for it shall be revealed by fire; and the fire shall try every man's work of what sort it is."* The fire of God comes to every one of our lives to try us, to prove us and test us.

1. Verses 18-20 – "*18For ye are not come unto the mount that might be touched, and that burned with fire, nor unto blackness, and darkness, and tempest, 19And the sound of a trumpet, and the voice of words; which voice they that heard intreated that the word should not be spoken to them any more: 20(For they could not endure that which was commanded, And if so much as a beast touch the mountain, it shall be stoned, or thrust through with a dart:"*

   a. Paul was referring to Exodus 19:9-24 in this passage (see below). We have not come to the same thing that Israel has come. We are not a partaker of the old covenant and the law. We are new covenant people. Jesus is the revelation of all that God is doing. As John 1:17 says, "*For the law was given by Moses, but grace and truth came by Jesus Christ.*" They could not endure what was commanded because it was the law. But by His grace, we can now approach His holy presence.

   I personally have been in some mighty moves and visitations of God. I have had sacred experiences and have actually been to heaven once and I can tell you this: I have trembled in His presence, but I have never been afraid of God. There is a difference in fearing God (having an awesome respect and reverence) and fearing that your life is going to be taken from you. The Israelites were afraid of God. When they saw Him, they did not want to get near. But for believers today, we ought to have a desire to be caught up to God and to His throne. We do not have to be like those Israelites anymore, who were afraid of God. We have come to mount Zion.

   b. Exodus 19:9-24 – "*…12And thou shalt set bounds unto the people round about, saying, Take heed to yourselves, that ye go not up into the mount, or touch the border of it: whosoever toucheth the mount shall be surely put to death: 13There shall not an hand touch it, but he shall surely be stoned, or shot through; whether it be beast or man, it shall not live: when the trumpet soundeth long, they shall come up to the mount…22And let the priests also, which come near to the Lord, sanctify themselves, lest the Lord break forth upon them. 23And Moses said unto the Lord, The people cannot come up to mount Sinai: for thou chargedst us, saying, Set bounds about the mount, and sanctify it. 24And the Lord said unto him, Away, get thee down, and thou shalt come up, thou, and Aaron with thee: but let not the priests and the people break through to come up unto the Lord, lest he break forth upon them.*"

   c. Exodus 20:18-21 – "*18And all the people saw the thunderings, and the lightnings, and the noise of the trumpet, and the mountain smoking: and when the people saw it, they removed, and stood afar off. 19And they said unto Moses, Speak thou with us, and we will hear: but let not God speak with us, lest we die. 20And Moses said unto the people, Fear not: for God is come to prove you, and that his fear may be before your faces, that ye sin not. 21And the people stood afar off, and Moses drew near unto the thick darkness where God was.*"

2. Verses 22-24 – "*22But ye are come unto mount Sion, and unto the city of the living God, the heavenly Jerusalem, and to an innumerable company of angels, 23To the general assembly and church of the firstborn, which are written in heaven, and to God the Judge of all, and to the spirits of just men made perfect, 24And to Jesus the mediator of the new covenant, and to the blood of sprinkling, that speaketh better things than that of Abel.*"

   a. These verses are speaking of born again believers who have now come to mount Zion, the city of the living God, the heavenly Jerusalem. Forget the earthly Jerusalem. It is all about the heavenly Jerusalem now. Remember Jesus said in John 4:21,23:
   "*Jesus saith unto her, Woman, believe me, the hour cometh, when ye shall neither in this mountain, nor yet at Jerusalem, worship the Father… 23But the hour cometh, and now is, when the true worshippers shall worship the Father in spirit and in truth…*"

Zion is not a place in the natural anymore, but a place in the spirit realm, where God is enthroned upon the hearts of a devoted, worshipping people.

1) Psalms 50:2 – *"Out of Zion, the perfection of beauty, God hath shined."* (Psalms 81:1- *"Thou that dwellest between the cherubims, shine forth."*)

When we begin to worship and honor God, the glory comes. The angels then come and worship with us. All of a sudden, then, God can come down with His train and His throne and be seated upon the hearts of His people; because, He knows He is really loved there. This is when God's people experience the manifest presence of God. How many churches does the manifest presence of God come?

b. Did you know that the church is a place with an innumerable company of angels? When we enthrone God with our worship, angels are all around us and the spirit realm is much greater than the natural world we can touch and feel.

1) Psalms 68:17-19 – *"[17]The chariots of God are twenty thousand, even thousands of angels: the Lord is among them, as in Sinai, in the holy place. [18]Thou hast ascended on high, thou hast led captivity captive: thou hast received gifts for men; yea, for the rebellious also, that the Lord God might dwell among them. [19]Blessed be the Lord, who daily loadeth us with benefits, even the God of our salvation. Selah."*

a) This verse says twenty thousand, even thousands of angels! This is what we have come to because the resurrection of Jesus brought captivity captive. He took us to a new place. He broke through, so now we can break through as well?

c. It is the church of the firstborn. The firstborn in Scriptures was always the blessed one who received the special inheritance. The firstborn is not just one person anymore, it is a people now. Everyone who is born again now has a right to be the firstborn.

d. Jesus is the mediator of the New Covenant. The New Covenant has with it, its great blessings, mercy, grace, and love; and, the fact that we can now know God intimately. It is a new day. A covenant based on "better promises." It is an everlasting kingdom that cannot be moved.

1) Hebrews 10:16-23 – *"[16]This is the covenant that I will make with them after those days, saith the Lord, I will put my laws into their hearts, and in their minds will I write them; [17]And their sins and iniquities will I remember no more. [18]Now where remission of these is, there is no more offering for sin. [19]Having therefore, brethren, boldness to enter into the holiest by the blood of Jesus, [20]By a new and living way, which he hath consecrated for us, through the veil, that is to say, his flesh; [21]And having an high priest over the house of God; [22]Let us draw near with a true heart in full assurance of faith, having our hearts sprinkled from an evil conscience, and our bodies washed with pure water. [23]Let us hold fast the profession of our faith without wavering; (for he is faithful that promised;)"*

2) Hebrews 9 – whole chapter

3) Hebrews 10:1-4 – *"[1]For the law having a shadow of good things to come, and not the very image of the things, can never with those sacrifices which they offered year by year continually make the comers thereunto perfect. [2]For then would they not have ceased to be offered? because that the worshippers once purged should have had no more conscience of sins. [3]But in those sacrifices there is a remembrance again made of sins*

every year. ⁴For it is not possible that the blood of bulls and of goats should take away sins."

    4)   Galatians 3:16-29

    5)   Galatians 4:19-31 – Bondwoman and freewoman - *"²⁶But Jerusalem which is above is free, which is the mother of us all."* – The heavenly Jerusalem is free. We walk with God out of love and not out of fear.   We do not have to walk around anymore condemned and guilt-ridden.

3.   Verse 25 – *"See that ye refuse not him that speaketh. For if they escaped not who refused him that spake on earth, much more shall not we escape, if we turn away from him that speaketh from heaven."*

    a.   We cannot refuse to hear this great message of grace. The Law and the Old Covenant have made way for the New. We are not to go back to the Old.

    b.   The Hebrew Christians needed to hear this.

    c.   For if they received no escape from that monstrous Law, how can we escape if we neglect His merciful grace?

4.   Verses 26-27 – *"²⁶Whose voice then shook the earth: but now he hath promised, saying, Yet once more I shake not the earth only, but also heaven. ²⁷And this word, Yet once more, signifieth the removing of those things that are shaken, as of things that are made, that those things which cannot be shaken may remain."*

    a.   As His voice then shook the earth, He will shake not only our earth (flesh); but, also the heavens, to finish His great plan.

    b.   Shake in Hebrew – *ra`ash* – to undulate, make afraid, make to tremble through fear, earthquake, uproar, vibration.

    c.   Shake in Greek – *seio* – to rock or vibrate sideways or to and fro, to agitate, to throw into a tremor (of fear or concern), to move or quake.

When God begins to shake us, we get concerned and afraid because He is about to take or remove from our lives something we might love. God wants to get to the things within our heart and soul that He wants to deal with Jesus said in John 12:25, *"He that loveth his life shall lose it; and he that hateth his life in this world shall keep it unto life eternal."* The only way to find life is to find the life of Jesus in our soul. Paul echoes this in Galatians 2:20, *"I am crucified with Christ: nevertheless I live; yet not I, but Christ liveth in me."* We have to be willing to give up everything and truly walk this out. When we do, heaven will begin to invade our earth to prepare us to go into the glory of God. We cannot go into that glory as we are. God has to shake everything that can be shaken. God is after the secret things within our hearts. It is like an earthquake. An earthquake brings up things from under the earth. The earth starts shaking and vibrating where the rocks begin to move, which then expose the hidden areas of the earth. God can then get to those things in our lives that He wants to deal with. We must be open to His shaking in our lives so that we can enter the kingdom that cannot be moved.

    d.   The things that have been made or created have been shaken and removed.

        1)   The Law
        2)   Man's Fleshly Kingdoms
        3)   Rebellion
        4)   Man's Sin And Flesh (Soulish Desires)
        5)   Our Enemies

    e.   God Has Removed And Shaken These Things

1) Psalms 46:6 – *"The heathen raged, the kingdoms were moved: he uttered his voice, the earth melted."*
2) Psalms 18:3-17 – *"...⁷Then the earth shook and trembled; the foundations also of the hills moved and were shaken, because he was wroth..."*
3) Psalms 2
4) Psalms 77:15-20 – *"...¹⁸The voice of thy thunder was in the heaven: the lightnings lightened the world: the earth trembled and shook..."*
5) Psalms 68:4-11 – *"...⁸The earth shook, the heavens also dropped at the presence of God: even Sinai itself was moved at the presence of God, the God of Israel..."*

f. God is not only bringing a shaking to believers individually; but, there is also coming a shaking to the whole earth.

1) Haggai 2:6-9, 18-23 – *"⁶For thus saith the Lord of hosts; Yet once, it is a little while, and I will shake the heavens, and the earth, and the sea, and the dry land; ⁷And I will shake all nations, and the desire of all nations shall come: and I will fill this house with glory, saith the Lord of hosts. ⁸The silver is mine, and the gold is mine, saith the Lord of hosts. ⁹The glory of this latter house shall be greater than of the former, saith the Lord of hosts: and in this place will I give peace, saith the Lord of hosts...¹⁸Consider now from this day and upward, from the four and twentieth day of the ninth month, even from the day that the foundation of the Lord's temple was laid, consider it. ¹⁹Is the seed yet in the barn? yea, as yet the vine, and the fig tree, and the pomegranate, and the olive tree, hath not brought forth: from this day will I bless you. ²⁰And again the word of the Lord came unto Haggai in the four and twentieth day of the month, saying, ²¹Speak to Zerubbabel, governor of Judah, saying, I will shake the heavens and the earth; ²²And I will overthrow the throne of kingdoms, and I will destroy the strength of the kingdoms of the heathen; and I will overthrow the chariots, and those that ride in them; and the horses and their riders shall come down, every one by the sword of his brother. ²³In that day, saith the Lord of hosts, will I take thee, O Zerubbabel, my servant, the son of Shealtiel, saith the Lord, and will make thee as a signet: for I have chosen thee, saith the Lord of hosts."*

   a) God is going to shake each one of us until our only desire is Jesus, who is the desire of all nations.
   b) God is going to shake His house so that He can fill His house, His church, with the glory of God.
   c) God is about to overthrow all of the thrones of the kingdoms of earth, which is satan's seat. Satan will be cast out of the second heaven and all of the nations are going to experience great upheaval.

2) Joel 3:11-21 – *"Assemble yourselves, and come, all ye heathen, and gather yourselves together round about: thither cause thy mighty ones to come down, O Lord. ¹²Let the heathen be wakened, and come up to the valley of Jehoshaphat: for there will I sit to judge all the heathen round about. ¹³Put ye in the sickle, for the harvest is ripe: come, get you down; for the press is full, the fats overflow; for their wickedness is great. ¹⁴Multitudes, multitudes in the valley of decision: for the day of the Lord is near in the valley of decision. ¹⁵The sun and the moon shall be darkened, and the stars shall withdraw their shining. ¹⁶The Lord also shall roar out of Zion, and utter his voice from Jerusalem; and the heavens and the earth shall shake: but the Lord will be the hope of his people, and the strength of the children of Israel. ¹⁷So shall ye know that I am the Lord your God dwelling in Zion, my holy mountain: then shall Jerusalem be holy, and there shall no strangers pass through her any more. ¹⁸And it shall come to pass in that day, that the mountains shall drop down new wine, and the hills shall flow with milk, and all the rivers of Judah shall flow with waters, and a fountain shall come forth of the*

house of the Lord, and shall water the valley of Shittim...²⁰But Judah shall dwell for ever, and Jerusalem from generation to generation. ²¹For I will cleanse their blood that I have not cleansed: for the Lord dwelleth in Zion."

a) The first place Jesus is coming to and through is a people. Jesus is coming back within His people. He is going to come completely in them. The in-dwelling presence of the Lord is going to fill a people full. As it does, they are going to roar the judgments of God in the earth.

b) When the Lord roars out of Zion, a great shaking will take place in heaven and earth. A true manifestation of God's power and deliverance will take place.

c) God's people will truly be holy and full of the image and glory of God.

3) Isaiah 2:2-22 – "...⁶*Therefore thou hast forsaken thy people the house of Jacob, because they be replenished from the east, and are soothsayers like the Philistines, and they please themselves in the children of strangers...¹⁹And they shall go into the holes of the rocks, and into the caves of the earth, for fear of the Lord, and for the glory of his majesty, when he ariseth to shake terribly the earth. ²⁰In that day a man shall cast his idols of silver, and his idols of gold, which they made each one for himself to worship, to the moles and to the bats; ²¹To go into the clefts of the rocks, and into the tops of the ragged rocks, for fear of the Lord, and for the glory of his majesty, when he ariseth to shake terribly the earth...*"

a) Replenished (verse 6) in Hebrew – influenced

4) Isaiah 13:9-13 – "...¹³*Therefore I will shake the heavens, and the earth shall remove out of her place, in the wrath of the Lord of hosts, and in the day of his fierce anger.*"

5) Isaiah 52:1-15

6) Zechariah 2:7-13 – "⁷*Deliver thyself, O Zion, that dwellest with the daughter of Babylon. ⁸For thus saith the Lord of hosts; After the glory hath he sent me unto the nations which spoiled you: for he that toucheth you toucheth the apple of his eye. ⁹For, behold, I will shake mine hand upon them, and they shall be a spoil to their servants: and ye shall know that the Lord of hosts hath sent me. ¹⁰Sing and rejoice, O daughter of Zion: for, lo, I come, and I will dwell in the midst of thee, saith the Lord. ¹¹And many nations shall be joined to the Lord in that day, and shall be my people: and I will dwell in the midst of thee, and thou shalt know that the Lord of hosts hath sent me unto thee. ¹²And the Lord shall inherit Judah his portion in the holy land, and shall choose Jerusalem again. ¹³Be silent, O all flesh, before the Lord: for he is raised up out of his holy habitation.*"

7) II Peter 3:8-14 – "...¹⁰*But the day of the Lord will come as a thief in the night; in the which the heavens shall pass away with a great noise, and the elements shall melt with fervent heat, the earth also and the works that are therein shall be burned up. ¹¹Seeing then that all these things shall be dissolved, what manner of persons ought ye to be in all holy conversation and godliness, ¹²Looking for and hasting unto the coming of the day of God, wherein the heavens being on fire shall be dissolved, and the elements shall melt with fervent heat? ¹³Nevertheless we, according to his promise, look for new heavens and a new earth, wherein dwelleth righteousness. ¹⁴Wherefore, beloved, seeing that ye look for such things, be diligent that ye may be found of him in peace, without spot, and blameless.*"

8) Matthew 24:1-51 – "¹*And Jesus went out, and departed from the temple: and his disciples came to him for to shew him the buildings of the temple. ²And Jesus said unto them, See ye not all these things? Verily I say unto you, There shall not be left here one stone upon another, that shall not be thrown down. ³And as he sat upon the mount of Olives, the disciples came unto him privately, saying, Tell us, when shall these things be? and what shall be the sign of thy coming, and of the end of the world?...²⁹Immediately*

after the tribulation of those days shall the sun be darkened, and the moon shall not give her light, and the stars shall fall from heaven, and the powers of the heavens shall be shaken:...[45]Who then is a faithful and wise servant, whom his lord hath made ruler over his household, to give them meat in due season? [46]Blessed is that servant, whom his lord when he cometh shall find so doing...[51]And shall cut him asunder, and appoint him his portion with the hypocrites: there shall be weeping and gnashing of teeth."

When looking at this passage, I feel it is important to understand how this passage relates to our lives as believers as well as how it relates to the Kingdom of God. In verse 2 of this Scripture, Jesus was prophesying that 70 years later, Solomon's Temple will be thrown down and destroyed. History tells us that this was exactly what happened. So, the first things Jesus tells the disciples was that Jerusalem was finished. Then the disciples asked Jesus on Mount Olives three specific questions: 1) When shall these things be? 2) What shall be the sign of your coming? and 3) When is the end of the world? Then in the remaining verses in Matthew 24, Jesus answers all three of these questions; but, He doesn't answer them the way in which we want them. He doesn't speak of things chronologically. He speaks of these three things in a way that we can understand them in a corporate sense as well as in a personal sense. He speaks of what God is not only going to do in the earth, but in our lives personally.

I believe verses 3-26 speak of the first question, *"When shall these things be?"* Verses 27-35 answer the question, *"What shall be the sign of your coming?"* and verses 36-51 answer the final question, *"When is the end of the world?"*

    a)   When shall these things be? – verses 4-26

        (1)   When Jesus begins speaking, He is not speaking of the destruction of natural Jerusalem anymore (He already mentioned that in verse 2). He is speaking of things that are coming in the future.

        (2)   Verse 5 – *"For many shall come in my name, saying, I am Christ; and shall deceive many."* Deception comes when someone comes proclaiming Jesus is the Christ, the anointed one, and still brings deception.

        (3)   Wars and rumors of wars – We are exhorted to not be troubled, but recognize that we are in the last times.

        (4)   Verse 7– *"For nation shall rise against nation, and kingdom against kingdom."*

Once the Kingdom of God comes into fullness, where God brings His people into the fullness of His glory, there is going to be an all-out battle against the kingdom of darkness. An example of this is seen in Jeremiah 12:5, *"How shalt thou do in the swelling of the Jordan?"* The swelling of the Jordan always happens at harvest time. When the waters of Jordan swell, the waters overflow and drive all of the beasts surrounding it inland toward the city. So, before the waters of Jordan hit the people (the swelling of the Jordan being a type of the last great move of God), the first thing they must face will be the beasts rushing towards them. Paul said in I Corinthians 15:32, *"I have fought with beasts at Ephesus."* He wasn't fighting with natural animals. He was fighting with demon spirits. I believe the beasts we are going to face in these end times will be demons.

Luke 17:26 says, *"And as it was in the days of Noe, so shall it be also in the days of the Son of man."* What was happening in Noah's day? In Noah's day, Genesis 6:4 says, *"There were giants in the earth in those days."* I do not believe we will be fighting with natural giants, but spiritual giants; people filled with the devil. The number 666 is not just one person, but a nephilim spirit (the Hebrew word in Genesis 6:4 for *"giants"* is the word nephilim), which is the anti-Christ spirit. Six is the number for man and satan. Take the revelation to its fullness and you get 666, which is the fullness of man and the fullness of satan combined together, working together. That is the kingdom of darkness that will arise against the Kingdom of God in the last days. But thanks be unto God, there will be some David's in the Kingdom of God who will be able to deal with the Goliaths of the earth. The people of the Kingdom of God will arise, fight and overcome the kingdom of darkness; and, the Lord will roar out of Zion.

(5) There shall be famines, and pestilences, and earthquakes in divers places

    (a) Revelation 6 (Zechariah 6) – Four horses of the Apocalypse – war, famine, poverty, death and economic crisis. All these things are going to take place shortly and many of these things are already taking place.

    (b) These are also the seals that are being opened in Revelation 6. I believe the white horse in Revelation 6:2 is the sons of God. Revelation 6:2 says, *"And I saw, and behold a white horse: and he that sat on him had a bow; and a crown was given unto him: and he went forth conquering, and to conquer."* The color white in Scriptures always speaks of innocence and purity. There is nothing evil spoken of against this white horse. Therefore, I believe that the first seal being opened in Revelation 6:1-2 is the release of the sons of God. They are going forth to conquer. Before the other seals are opened up, God looses the sons of God in the earth.

(6) Verse 9 – God's people are going to be hated and persecuted throughout the earth for His name's sake (for His character's sake), simply because of their love for Jesus.

    (a) Psalms 2:1-4 – *"Why do the heathen rage, and the people imagine a vain thing? ²The kings of the earth set themselves, and the rulers take counsel together, against the Lord, and against his anointed, saying, ³Let us break their bands asunder, and cast away their cords from us. ⁴He that sitteth in the heavens shall laugh: the Lord shall have them in derision."* – The anointed do not just speak of Jesus; but, against the anointed people of God. We are encouraged to not let our hearts be troubled. God is in control of what is happening in the earth.

(7) Verses 10-11 – Many shall be offended and betray and hate one another. This will happen within the church as well. We must be willing to suffer reproach for His name's sake.

(8) Verse 12 – The love of many shall wax cold. I believe we see this today in the priesthood and leadership as well. Why should the people walk with God when the men and women of God over them are not walking intimately with the Lord? This will cause the love of the people to wax cold as well.

(9) Verse 14 – The Gospel of the Kingdom shall be preached in all the world. The Gospel is the good news. People always say we need to preach the Gospel. But it is not just the Gospel. It is the Gospel of the Kingdom. It is the good news of the reign of King Jesus within a people and must be preached in all the world.

(10) Verse 15

    (a) Daniel 11:28 – *"Then shall he return into his land with great riches; and his heart shall be against the holy covenant; and he shall do exploits, and return to his own land. ²⁹At the time appointed he shall return, and come toward the south; but it shall not be as the former, or as the latter. ³⁰For the ships of Chittim shall come against him: therefore he shall be grieved, and return, and have indignation against the holy covenant: so shall he do; he shall even return, and have intelligence with them that forsake the holy covenant. ³¹And arms shall stand on his part, and they shall pollute the sanctuary of strength, and shall take away the daily sacrifice, and they shall place the abomination that maketh desolate. ³²And such as do wickedly against the covenant shall he corrupt by flatteries: but the people that do know their God shall be strong, and do exploits."*

I have stopped trying to figure out who the anti-Christ is. When I read the Bible, I try to read it without preconceived ideas and with an open heart, knowing that it speaks personally to my life. I believe that these Scriptures speak of the king of all anti-Christ spirits, which is satan himself.

The altar of strength in verse 31 speaks of the altar of God, which is the manifest presence of God. Moreover, when it speaks of the taking away of the daily sacrifice, I do not believe that it speaks of taking away the sacrificing of animals anymore. Many people believe this passage speaks of a natural rebuilt temple in Jerusalem where daily sacrifices under the Mosaic law are again taking place. That will never happen again because Jesus is the sacrifice of God. He is the lamb slain from the foundation of the world. The sacrifice of all sacrifices has already taken place. God will not reinstitute sacrifices. So the sacrifices that are spoken of here are different sacrifices. They are personal sacrifices offered up by the people of God. As New Testament believers, we are to offer daily sacrifices ourselves, as Hebrews 13:15 states, *"By him therefore let us offer the sacrifice of praise to God continually, that is the fruit of our lips giving thanks to his name."* So satan is wanting to take away our daily sacrifice, our praying without ceasing, our personal time we spend with Jesus. As Christians, we are the ones who have the covenant with God. Satan is coming against us who have the covenant.

What is the abomination of desolation? I believe it is when satan (evil) stands in the most holy place. Spiritually, this means that when the people of God allow idols to sit upon the throne of their hearts and life. Satan is going to induce us with flatteries, use intelligences, to find out what our weaknesses are. Then, he is going to exploit them and do his best to try to live in us. And many people will let him live. The only beast that I am concerned about is myself, my flesh, my adamic nature that can allow satan to come and live within.

But the good news is that *"the people that do know their God shall be strong, and do exploits."* This means that those Christians who know their God intimately will not have the abomination of desolation. They shall be strong and do exploits.

> (11) Verse 19 – I used to think that when it says woe unto those that are giving suck to babies, it was talking naturally. But, I believe it speaks of spiritual children.
> (12) Verse 20 – Winter can speak of the hard places and times in our lives.
> (13) Verse 23 – We do not have to go travel somewhere else to find the Christ. The Kingdom of God is within us.

> b) What shall be the sign of your coming? – Verses 27-35

> (1) Verses 27-28 – Jesus begins this part of His discourse and tells us that the coming of the Lord is going to be like revelation (lightning flashing). I believe the eagles gathered together are the sons of God (the overcomers) coming together. These eagles are going to be gathered at the carcase (when we die to ourselves), gathered as a body together. They are going to be centered around the Lord Jesus. Jesus is going to appear to His sons. The sons are going to arise, be caught up unto God and to His throne (Revelation 12:5).

(2) Verse 29 – After the sons of God are caught up to God's throne (verse 28) immediately there is great tribulation and the powers of heaven are going to be shaken. This is seen in Revelation 12:5-17. Immediately after the man-child is caught up to God and to His throne, satan is kicked out of the second heaven and coming to the earth, never to be in charge of the second heavens ever again.

When it speaks of the sun, moon and stars, I believe Jesus is speaking to us spiritually. Stars can speak of angels, which make up *"principalities, against powers, against the rulers of the darkness of this world, against spiritual wickedness in high places"* (Ephesians 6:12). These principalities are going to be shaken.

(3) Verses 30-31 – What do clouds speak of? Hebrews 12:1 declares there is a *"cloud of witnesses."* Clouds can speak of people. Once the sons of God are loosed in the earth, it will be glorious and the earth will have never seen the likeness of them. It will be no longer themselves living anymore, but Christ, His glory and power, living and radiating through them. Therefore, Jesus coming in the clouds of heaven is simply Jesus returning within a people of great power and glory.

Angels, in verse 31, is just another word for "messenger." Trumpets always speak of a prophetic proclamation. The sons of God are going to be sent out with a prophetic message to the whole world. This is akin to Ezekiel 37 in the vision of the valley of dry bones. In Ezekiel's vision, the spirit of prophesy comes and prophesies over the dead bones and the bones come together, into an exceeding great army. So it is going to take a prophetic trumpet blasting throughout the earth, preaching the gospel of the Kingdom, prophesying the coming of the Lord and the release of the glory in His people. These messengers will actually live it and show it to the earth. Then God's people are going to come from every corner of the earth.

When this happens, millions of people will come to Jesus and church as we know it will be over. I believe the passage in Ephesians 4 will be fulfilled, where it says:

"And he gave some, apostles; and some, prophets; and some, evangelists; and some, pastors, and some teachers... 13Till we all come in the unity of the faith, and of the knowledge of the Son of God, unto a perfect man, unto the measure of the stature of the fullness of Christ..." (Ephesians 4:11-15)

There will be a true representation of Jesus on the earth, manifesting itself within a people. When they minister and prophesy at that time, like will beget like. A man or woman will always minister who they are. But when there will be a people who no longer live, and Christ fully lives within them, they will have a glorious ministry. These pioneering group of men and women are going to break through first. When they stand and minister the Word of God, they will speak the living Word of God, pure and undiluted. When their seed is sown throughout the earth, it can bring forth fruit quickly in a person's life, 100-fold. This will happen simply because that man or woman who sowed the seed had a 100-fold, Jesus-filled life.

(4) Verse 32-35 – When Jesus says in verse 34, *"This generation shall not pass, till all these things be fulfilled,"* He was not talking about the generation in which He was currently living. He was speaking of the last day generation of saints who will be living when all of these things are taking place. So, when we see these things happening, we can know that that generation is not going to pass before all of these things be fulfilled.

c) When is the end of the world? – Verses 36-51

(1) Verse 36 – People who tell you that they know the exact day of the coming of the Lord are not telling the truth; because, it clearly says no one knows that day or hour.

(2) Verses 37-38 – We are definitely living in days like Noah's day. Are not people living lives of sin, free to do whatever they want? Man is reaching its fullness. But while man was eating, drinking and being merry, Noah was building an ark. People must have mocked him when they told him that it will never rain; because, they had never seen it before. Then, suddenly, water began to drop from the heavens which then flooded the earth. The same water that judged the earth is the glory of God that lifted the ark above judgment and placed it upon a mountain.

(3) Verses 42-51 – Jesus ends His discourse giving a parable of the faithful and wise steward, once again asking us who is going to be the ones whom Jesus will make ruler over all His goods. The ones who will rule and reign with Jesus are those who are faithful.

I believe that the portion that is assigned to those who were not faithful, where there will be weeping and gnashing of teeth, is not hell. I believe this outer darkness is simply those who will have to remain on the earth during the great tribulation, which will be their portion with the unbelievers. I believe it is the 3½ years where God will judge the earth for its wickedness.

9) Daniel 2:31-45 – Many people will try to tell you which specific nations these images represent. I believe what is important is that the great image is an evil one, an anti-Christ spirit. It is similar to Nebuchadnezzar's image in Daniel 3.

Verse 34 says, *"Thou sawest till that a stone was cut out without hands, which smote the image upon his feet that were of iron and clay, and brake them to pieces."* I believe the stone here that smites the image is the Kingdom of God. The stone smote the image upon his feet, which speaks of this image's ability to walk and propogate his evil will be stopped.

Verse 35 continues, *"Then was the iron the clay, the brass, the silver, and the gold, broken to pieces together, and became like the chaff of the summer threshingfloors; and the wind carried them away, that no place was found for them: and the stone that smote the image became a great mountain, and filled the whole earth."* After the stone deals with the propagation of this evil, all of these images, the brass, iron, silver and gold get dealt with and destroyed all at once. The wind in this Scripture is a type of the Holy Ghost. I believe the stone that becomes a great mountain and fills the whole earth are the sons of God. We are the stone that is cut out of the mountain that is going to bring down that image of satan, whatever it is. It is just like David defeating Goliath. The great giant that caused the whole earth to tremble came down by a stone. All we need is the name of Jesus, which causes every knee to bow. These sons of God will bow the knee completely to Jesus and will bring down satan's image in the earth.

C. Other translations of Hebrews 12:28

"Let us therefore, receiving a kingdom that is firm and stable and cannot be shaken..."
"Do you see what we've got? An unshakable kingdom..."
"If then we have a kingdom which will never be moved..."
"Since we have a kingdom that nothing can destroy..."

D. Definition of "cannot be moved" in Greek – *asaleutos* – unshaken, immovable, cannot be moved

E. Scriptures Declaring This Kingdom Cannot Be Moved

1. No Matter What The Enemy Tries, It Will Not Work

    a. Matthew 16:17-19 – "*17And Jesus answered and said unto him, Blessed art thou, Simon Barjona: for flesh and blood hath not revealed it unto thee, but my Father which is in heaven. 18And I say also unto thee, That thou art Peter, and upon this rock I will build my church; and the gates of hell shall not prevail against it. 19And I will give unto thee the keys of the kingdom of heaven: and whatsoever thou shalt bind on earth shall be bound in heaven: and whatsoever thou shalt loose on earth shall be loosed in heaven.*"

        1) Prevail in Greek – to overpower; from two root words:

            a) *kata* – down
            b) *ischuo* – to have or exercise force, to be of strength, to avail

        2) Other translations of verse 18:

"*...and the gates of Hades, the powers of the infernal region, shall not overpower it, or be strong to its detriment or hold out against it.*"
"*...a church so expansive with energy that not the gates of hell will be able to keep it out.*"
"*...and all the powers of hell will not conquer it.*"
"*...and the power of death will not be able to defeat it.*"
"*...and the doers of hell will not overcome it.*"
"*...and the might of Hades shall not triumph over it.*"
"*...the councils of the unseen shall not overpower it.*"

        3) The rock that Jesus is building His house upon is not Peter, but upon the rock of revelation that Jesus is the Christ. Moreover, Jesus is the one who builds the church. Psalms 127:1 states, "*Except the Lord build the house, they labour in vain that build it.*"
        4) This Scripture is not written in the sense that the church is withstanding the assault of the enemy. Rather, the church is assaulting the enemy himself.
        5) The Kingdom of God is a kingdom which cannot be stopped. When we are walking in His kingdom and Jesus is truly Lord of our lives, we will not only conquer the things in our own lives; we will also conquer the enemy in other people's lives.

    b. I Samuel 2:9-10 – "*9He will keep the feet of his saints, and the wicked shall be silent in darkness; for by strength shall no man prevail. 10The adversaries of the Lord shall be broken to pieces; out of heaven shall he thunder upon them: the Lord shall judge the ends of the earth; and he shall give strength unto his king, and exalt the horn of his anointed.*"

        1) We have a God who will watch out for us, not only in protecting and keeping us, but in the revelation that no enemy will prevail against us.

    c. Isaiah 54:17 – "*No weapon that is formed against thee shall prosper; and every tongue that shall rise against thee in judgment thou shalt condemn. This is the heritage of the servants of the Lord, and their righteousness is of me, saith the Lord.*"
    d. Exodus 23:22 – "*But if thou shalt indeed obey his voice, and do all that I speak; then I will be an enemy unto thine enemies, and an adversary unto thine adversaries.*"

        1) All we have to do is obey His voice and He will be an enemy to our enemies.

e. Philippians 1:28 – *"And in nothing terrified by your adversaries: which is to them an evident token of perdition, but to you of salvation, and that of God."*

    1) Other translations:

"And do not for a moment be frightened or intimidated in any thing by your opponents and adversaries, for such constancy and fearlessness will be a clear sign and proof and seal to them of their impending destruction."
"...not flinching or dodging in the slightest before the opposition. Your courage and unity will show them what they're up against: defeat for them, victory for you..."
"Don't be intimidated in any way be your enemies. This will be a sign to them that they are going to be destroyed, but that you are going to be saved, even by God Himself."
"...fearlessly no matter what your enemies may do. They will see this as a sign of their downfall..."
"...in no way alarmed by your opponents, which is a sign of destruction for them..."
"Having no fear of those who are against you..."
"Never for a moment quail before your antagonists..."
"Don't be afraid of your enemies; always be courageous, and this will prove to them that they will lose and you will win, because it is God who gives you the victory."
"And do not be terrified in even one thing by those who are entrenched in their opposition against you, which failure on your part to be frightened is an indication of such a nature as to present clear evidence to them of their utter destruction, also clear evidence of your salvation, and this evidence from God."

    2) Greek for terrified – *pturo* – to frighten. From a root – *ptoeo* – the idea of causing to fall, or to scare or cause to fly away

    3) Greek for nothing – *medeis* – not even one man, woman, or thing; none at all

    4) The day is coming when we will say of the enemy, as it says in Isaiah 14:16-17, *"They that see thee shall narrowly look upon thee, and consider thee, saying Is this the man that made the earth to tremble, that did shake kingdoms; [17]That made the world as a wilderness, and destroyed the cities thereof; that opened not the house of his prisoners."*

    5) When the enemy attacks us and we are overwhelmed, the Lord will raise up a shield round about us.

        a) Isaiah 59:19 – *"When the enemy shall come in, like a flood the Spirit of the Lord shall lift up a standard against him."*

        b) Zechariah 2:5 – *"For I, saith the Lord, will be unto her a wall of fire round about, and will be the glory in the midst of her."*

        c) Psalms 3:1-3 – *"[3]But thou, O Lord, art a shield for me; my glory, and the lifter up of my head."*

    6) Many times satan will try to go through our lives, as Luke 22:31 states, *"And the Lord said, Simon, Simon behold, Satan hath desired to have you, that he may sift you as wheat."* The enemy will try to go through our lives with a fine-toothed comb to find areas of fear and concern that he can exploit. But when he finds that we are not terrified of him, we will begin to overcome.

f. Revelation 12:10-11 – *"[10]And I heard a loud voice saying in heaven, Now is come salvation, and strength, and the kingdom of our God, and the power of his Christ: for the accuser of our brethren is cast down, which accused them before our God day and night. [11]And they overcame him by the blood of the Lamb, and by the word of their testimony; and they loved not their lives unto the death."*

    1) Romans 16:20 – *"And the God of peace shall bruise Satan under your feet shortly. The grace of our Lord Jesus Christ be with you. Amen."*

2) Luke 10:19 – "*Behold, I give unto you power to tread on serpents and scorpions, and over all the power of the enemy: and nothing shall by any means hurt you.*"

3) Isaiah 29:7-8 – "*⁷And the multitude of all the nations that fight against Ariel, even all that fight against her and her munition, and that distress her, shall be as a dream of a night vision. ⁸It shall even be as when an hungry man dreameth, and, behold, he eateth; but he awaketh, and his soul is empty: or as when a thirsty man dreameth, and, behold, he drinketh; but he awaketh, and, behold, he is faint, and his soul hath appetite: so shall the multitude of all the nations be, that fight against mount Zion.*"

4) The kingdoms of this world are being shaken and will one day come under the dominion of the Kingdom of God. Revelation 11:15 states, "*The kingdoms of this world are become the kingdoms of our Lord, and of his Christ; and he shall reign for ever and ever.*" The term, "*his Christ*", refers not only to Jesus, but to the sons of God as well.

5) The enemy is always out to accuse us, but as II Corinthians 2:11 states, "*We are not ignorant of his devices.*"

6) The sons of God will overcome the enemy by the blood of the Lamb, their testimony and will even overcome their fear of death.

g. I John 4:4 – "*Ye are of God, little children, and have overcome them: because greater is he that is in you, than he that is in the world.*"

1) Other translations:

"*...because He who lives in you is mightier.*"
"*...for the Spirit in you is far stronger than anything in the world.*"
"*...because the Spirit, who is in you, is greater than the devil, who is in the world.*"
"*...because the Spirit who is in you is more powerful than the spirit in those who belong to the world.*"

2) Greater in Greek – larger or more, literally or figuratively – The Holy Spirit within us is larger and more than the spirit of anti-Christ and more than anything in which the people of this world can come up. Jesus is the greater one within us!

a) II Kings 6:16-17, "*Fear not: for they that be with us are more than they that be with them. ¹⁷And Elisha prayed, and said, Lord, I pray thee, open his eyes, that he may see. And the Lord opened the eyes of the young man; and he saw: and, behold, the mountain was full of horses and chariots of fire round about Elisha.*"

h. Romans 8:35-39 – "*³⁵Who shall separate us from the love of Christ? shall tribulation, or distress, or persecution, or famine, or nakedness, or peril, or sword? ³⁶As it is written, For thy sake we are killed all the day long; we are accounted as sheep for the slaughter. ³⁷Nay, in all these things we are more than conquerors through him that loved us. ³⁸For I am persuaded, that neither death, nor life, nor angels, nor principalities, nor powers, nor things present, nor things to come, ³⁹Nor height, nor depth, nor any other creature, shall be able to separate us from the love of God, which is in Christ Jesus our Lord.*"

1) Greek for separate – to put space between – satan is always trying to put space between God and His people. The enemy tries to put space between through tribulation, afflictions, famine, sword, nakedness, distress, peril and sword. God's covenant is with Jesus and Jesus lives within His people.

2) Greek for conquerors – to vanquish beyond, gain a decisive victory, more than conquer – We are more than conquerors through Him who dwells within us.

i. Luke 6:46-49 – "*⁴⁶And why call ye me, Lord, Lord, and do not the things which I say? ⁴⁷Whosoever cometh to me, and heareth my sayings, and doeth them, I will shew you to whom he is like: ⁴⁸He is like a man which built an house, and digged deep, and laid the foundation on a rock: and when the flood arose, the stream beat vehemently upon that house, and could not shake it: for it was founded upon a rock. ⁴⁹But he that heareth, and doeth not, is like a man that without a foundation built an house upon the earth; against which the stream did beat vehemently, and immediately it fell; and the ruin of that house was great.*"

1) The foundation of our lives is the revelation that Jesus Christ is the anointed one and that He is the King of His Kingdom. The foundation is also having a foundation of His Word laid up in our lives (Hebrews 6:1-3).

j. There Are More With Us Than The Enemy

1) II Chronicles 32:7-8 – "*⁷Be strong and courageous, be not afraid nor dismayed for the king of Assyria, nor for all the multitude that is with him: for there be more with us than with him: ⁸With him is an arm of flesh; but with us is the Lord our God to help us, and to fight our battles. And the people rested themselves upon the words of Hezekiah king of Judah.*"

2) II Kings 6:12-17 – "*¹²And one of his servants said, None, my lord, O king: but Elisha, the prophet that is in Israel, telleth the king of Israel the words that thou speakest in thy bedchamber. ¹³And he said, Go and spy where he is, that I may send and fetch him. And it was told him, saying, Behold, he is in Dothan. ¹⁴Therefore sent he thither horses, and chariots, and a great host: and they came by night, and compassed the city about. ¹⁵And when the servant of the man of God was risen early, and gone forth, behold, an host compassed the city both with horses and chariots. And his servant said unto him, Alas, my master! how shall we do? ¹⁶And he answered, Fear not: for they that be with us are more than they that be with them. ¹⁷And Elisha prayed, and said, Lord, I pray thee, open his eyes, that he may see. And the Lord opened the eyes of the young man; and he saw: and, behold, the mountain was full of horses and chariots of fire round about Elisha.*"

k. II Corinthians 2:14 – "*Now thanks be unto God, which always causeth us to triumph in Christ, and maketh manifest the savour of his knowledge by us in every place.*"

l. I Corinthians 15:57 – "*But thanks be to God, which giveth us the victory through our Lord Jesus Christ.*"

m. Psalms 60:12 – "*Through God we shall do valiantly: for he it is that shall tread down our enemies.*"

n. Isaiah 11:13 – "*The envy also of Ephraim shall depart, and the adversaries of Judah shall be cut off: Ephraim shall not envy Judah, and Judah shall not vex Ephraim.*"

II. The God Who Fights For Us

I absolutely love this feature of God's character because it is comforting to know that when I am in trouble, He fights for me. If more of us realized this, it would give us a lot more peace and confidence. There is great security in knowing that when we are fighting against our enemies, we are not alone. That the Creator of the universe cares enough to fight for me, and loves me enough to do it, is overwhelming.

Satan, our adversary, and all other enemies will now no longer be able to declare or trick us. Because we know that the sovereign God of the universe is backing us with all of heaven's resources, we know we will ultimately triumph. Let this lesson and these Scriptures sink deep into our hearts, and a quiet confidence and assurance will arise in us. Then we can become the warriors in God's army that He has called us to be. If we receive this principle and take it to heart, we will never be the same again!

A.   The Lord fights for us.

1.   Exodus 14:9-25 – "*...for the Lord fighteth for them...*"
2.   Joshua 6:16 – "*...shout for the Lord hath given you the city...*"
3.   Joshua 10:14 – "*...the Lord fought for Israel...*"
4.   Joshua 23:3-10 – "*...the Lord your God He it is that fighteth for you...*"
5.   Proverbs 21:31 – "*The horse is prepared against the day of the battle: but safety is of the Lord.*"
6.   Exodus 14:14 – "*The Lord shall fight for you and ye shall hold your peace.*"
7.   Deuteronomy 1:30 – "*The Lord your God which goeth before you, he shall fight for you...*"
8.   Deuteronomy 3:22 – "*Ye shall not fear them, for the Lord your God he shall fight for you...*"
9.   II Chronicles 20:29 – "*Be not afraid nor dismayed by reason of this great multitude; for the battle is not yours but God's.*"
10.   Deuteronomy 20:2-5 – "*Hear O Israel, ye approach this day unto battle against your enemies, let not your hearts faint, fear not, and do not tremble neither be ye terrified because of them; For the Lord your God is he that goeth with you, to fight for you against your enemies to save you.*"
11.   Nehemiah 4:15-21 – "*15And it came to pass, when our enemies heard that it was known unto us, and God had brought their counsel to nought, that we returned all of us to the wall, every one unto his work. 16And it came to pass from that time forth, that the half of my servants wrought in the work, and the other half of them held both the spears, the shields, and the bows, and the habergeons; and the rulers were behind all the house of Judah. 17They which builded on the wall, and they that bare burdens, with those that laded, every one with one of his hands wrought in the work, and with the other hand held a weapon. 18For the builders, every one had his sword girded by his side, and so builded. And he that sounded the trumpet was by me. 19And I said unto the nobles, and to the rulers, and to the rest of the people, The work is great and large, and we are separated upon the wall, one far from another. 20In what place therefore ye hear the sound of the trumpet, resort ye thither unto us: our God shall fight for us. 21So we laboured in the work: and half of them held the spears from the rising of the morning till the stars appeared.*"

   a.   Rebuilding the wall
   b.   Half the people labored
   c.   Half the people stood ready with weapons

12.   Isaiah 31:4-5 – "*...so shall the LORD of hosts come down to fight for mount Zion, and for the hill thereof. 5As birds flying, so will the LORD of hosts defend Jerusalem; defending also he will deliver it; and passing over he will preserve it.*"
13.   Zechariah 14:3 – "*Then shall the Lord go forth, and fight against these nations, as when he fought in the day of battle.*"
14.   Psalm 60:12 – "*Through God we shall do valiantly: for he it is that shall tread down our enemies.*" (Psalm 108:13)
15.   Isaiah 42:13 – "*The Lord shall go forth as a mighty man, he shall stir up jealously like a man of war: He shall cry, yea, roar; he shall prevail against his enemies.*"
16.   II Corinthians 2:14 – "*Now thanks be unto God which always causeth us to triumph in Christ...*"
17.   I Corinthians 15:57 – "*But thanks be to God, which giveth us the victory through our Lord Jesus Christ.*"

What a great comfort to know we have the greatest power in the universe on our side. God and us are an unbeatable team. Amen!

III.   The Battle Is The Lord's

A.   Scriptures

1. II Chronicles 32:7-8 – "*7Be strong and courageous, be not afraid nor dismayed for the king of Assyria, nor for all the multitude that is with him: for there be more with us than with him: 8With him is an arm of flesh; but with us is the LORD our God to help us, and to fight our battles. And the people rested themselves upon the words of Hezekiah king of Judah.*"

2. Deuteronomy 20:1-4 – "*1When thou goest out to battle against thine enemies, and seest horses, and chariots, and a people more than thou, be not afraid of them: for the LORD thy God is with thee, which brought thee up out of the land of Egypt. 2And it shall be, when ye are come nigh unto the battle, that the priest shall approach and speak unto the people, 3And shall say unto them, Hear, O Israel, ye approach this day unto battle against your enemies: let not your hearts faint, fear not, and do not tremble, neither be ye terrified because of them; 4For the LORD your God is he that goeth with you, to fight for you against your enemies, to save you.*"

3, I Chronicles 14:13-17 – "*13And the Philistines yet again spread themselves abroad in the valley. 14Therefore David inquired again of God; and God said unto him, Go not up after them; turn away from them, and come upon them over against the mulberry trees. 15And it shall be, when thou shalt hear a sound of going in the tops of the mulberry trees, that then thou shalt go out to battle: for God is gone forth before thee to smite the host of the Philistines. 16David therefore did as God commanded him: and they smote the host of the Philistines from Gibeon even to Gazer. 17And the fame of David went out into all lands; and the LORD brought the fear of him upon all nations.*"

4. II Chronicles 20:14-25

5. Psalms 24:8 – "*Who is this King of glory? The LORD strong and mighty, the LORD mighty in battle.*"

6. Psalms 140:7 – "*O GOD the Lord, the strength of my salvation, thou hast covered my head in the day of battle.*"

7. Isaiah 13:1-6 – Day of the Lord against Babylon

8. Zechariah 10:1-7 – Time of the latter rain

IV. Our Trust Is In Him To Get Us The Victory – If all we had was ourselves, is it any wonder why we would doubt? Our trust is not in ourselves, but in God, to get us the victory.

A. Scriptural Examples

1. Psalm 20:7-9 – "*...some trust in chariots and some in horses but we will remember the name of the Lord our God.*"

2. I Samuel 17:45-47 – "*...but I come to thee in the name of the Lord of Hosts, the God of the armies of Israel, whom thou hast defied. This day will the Lord deliver thee into mine hand, and I will smite thee, and take thine head from thee... that all the earth may know that there is a God in Israel. And all this assembly shall know that the Lord saveth not with sword and spear; for the battle is the Lord's and he will give you into my hand.*"

3. Psalm 60:11-12 – "*Give us help from trouble, for vain is the help of man. Through God we shall do valiantly...*"

4. Psalm 146:3 – "*Put not your trust in princes nor the son of man in whom there is no help.*"

5. Proverbs 21:31 – "*The horse is prepared against the day of battle, but safety is of the Lord.*"

6. Joshua 10:8 – "*Fear them not; for I delivered them into thine hand.*"

7. I Samuel 2:1 – "*My mouth is enlarged over mine enemies; because I rejoice in thy salvation.*"

8. Psalm 41:11 – "*I know that thou favorest me, because mine enemy doth not triumph over me.*"

9. Micah 5:9,10 – "*Thine hand shall be lifted up upon thine adversaries and all thine enemies shall be cut off... I will cut off...*"

10. John 16:33 – "*Be of good cheer, I have overcome the world.*"

11. I John 5:4 – "*Whatsoever is born of God overcometh the world.*"

12. Revelation 12:11 – "*They overcame him by the blood of the Lamb...*"

13. Exodus 15:1 – "*I will sing unto the Lord, for he hath triumphed gloriously: the horse and his rider he hath thrown into the sea.*"

14. Exodus 15:6 – *"Thy right hand O Lord is become glorious in power: thy right hand, O Lord, hath dashed in pieces the enemy."*
15. Mark 16:20 – *"...the Lord working with them and confirming the Word with signs following..."*
16. Nehemiah 2:20 – *"...the God of heaven, he will prosper us..."*
17. Revelation 3:10 – *"...I will also keep thee from the hour of temptation..."*
18. II Peter 2:9 – *"The Lord knoweth how to deliver the godly out of temptation..."*
19. Acts 26:18 – *"To open their eyes, and to turn them from darkness to light, and from the power of Satan unto God, that they may receive..."*
20. Psalms 98:1 – *"O sing unto the LORD a new song; for he hath done marvellous things: his right hand, and his holy arm, hath gotten him the victory."*
21. Isaiah 25:7-9 – *"⁷And he will destroy in this mountain the face of the covering cast over all people, and the vail that is spread over all nations. ⁸He will swallow up death in victory; and the Lord GOD will wipe away tears from off all faces; and the rebuke of his people shall he take away from off all the earth: for the LORD hath spoken it. ⁹And it shall be said in that day, Lo, this is our God; we have waited for him, and he will save us: this is the LORD; we have waited for him, we will be glad and rejoice in his salvation."*
22. Matthew 12:17-21 – *"¹⁷That it might be fulfilled which was spoken by Esaias the prophet, saying, ¹⁸Behold my servant, whom I have chosen; my beloved, in whom my soul is well pleased: I will put my spirit upon him, and he shall shew judgment to the Gentiles. ¹⁹He shall not strive, nor cry; neither shall any man hear his voice in the streets. ²⁰A bruised reed shall he not break, and smoking flax shall he not quench, till he send forth judgment unto victory. ²¹And in his name shall the Gentiles trust."*
23. I Corinthians 15:57 – *"But thanks be to God, which giveth us the victory through our Lord Jesus Christ."*

V. God Will Help Us Against Our Adversaries

A. Scriptures

1. Hebrews 10:27 – *"...fiery indignation, which shall devour the adversaries."*
2. II Samuel 4:9 – *"...As the Lord liveth, who hath redeemed my soul out of all adversity"*
3. Proverbs 17:17 – *"A friend loveth at all times, and a brother is born for adversity."*
4. Psalms 31:7 – *"...thou hast known my soul in adversities"*
5. Nahum 1:2 – *"...the Lord will take vengeance on his adversaries, and he reserveth wrath for his enemies."*
6. Isaiah 59:18 – *"According to their deeds, accordingly he will repay, fury to his adversaries..."*
7. Nehemiah 4:11, 14-20
8. 1 Samuel 2:10 – *"The adversaries of the LORD shall be broken to pieces..."*
9. Deuteronomy 32:43 – *"Rejoice, O ye nations, with his people: for he will avenge the blood of his servants, and will render vengeance to his adversaries..."*
10. 1 Samuel 10:19 – *"And ye have this day rejected your God, who himself saved you out of all your adversities and your tribulations..."*
11. Isaiah 50:8-9 – *"He is near that justifieth me; who will contend with me? let us stand together: who is mine adversary? let him come near to me. Behold, the Lord GOD will help me..."*
12. Jeremiah 46:10 – *"For this is the day of the Lord GOD of hosts, a day of vengeance, that he may avenge him of his adversaries..."*
13. Jeremiah 30:16 – *"Therefore all they that devour thee shall be devoured; and all thine adversaries, every one of them, shall go into captivity..."*
14. Exodus 23:22 – *"But if thou shalt indeed obey his voice, and do all that I speak; then I will be an enemy unto thine enemies, and an adversary unto thine adversaries."*
15. Isaiah 64:2 – *"...to make thy name known to thine adversaries, that the nations may tremble at thy presence!"*

16. Isaiah 11:13 – *"The envy also of Ephraim shall depart, and the adversaries of Judah shall be cut off..."*

From the above Scriptures, we can rest assured that at some point God will stand with us against our enemies. In truth, they become His enemy; and, then His judgment comes. Sometimes it is hard to be patient as Ecclesiastes says, *"Because sentence against an evil work is not executed speedily, therefore the heart of the sons of men is fully set in them to do evil. Though a sinner do evil an hundred times, and his days be prolonged...But it shall not be well with the wicked..."* (Ecclesiastes 8:11-13). But as we wait in faith and a right heart, the Lord will come bringing His judgment, bringing His vengeance, and repaying our adversaries.

VI. **None Of These Things Move Me** – Acts 20:17-24 – *"¹⁷And from Miletus he sent to Ephesus, and called the elders of the church. ¹⁸And when they were come to him, he said unto them, Ye know, from the first day that I came into Asia, after what manner I have been with you at all seasons, ¹⁹Serving the Lord with all humility of mind, and with many tears, and temptations, which befell me by the lying in wait of the Jews: ²⁰And how I kept back nothing that was profitable unto you, but have shewed you, and have taught you publickly, and from house to house, ²¹Testifying both to the Jews, and also to the Greeks, repentance toward God, and faith toward our Lord Jesus Christ. ²²And now, behold, I go bound in the spirit unto Jerusalem, not knowing the things that shall befall me there: ²³Save that the Holy Ghost witnesseth in every city, saying that bonds and afflictions abide me. ²⁴But <u>none of these things move me,</u> neither count I my life dear unto myself, so that I might finish my course with joy, and the ministry, which I have received of the Lord Jesus, to testify the gospel of the grace of God."*

We have to get to the place like what Psalms 112:7 states, *"He shall not be afraid of evil tidings: his heart is fixed, trusting in the Lord."* When we hear bad tidings or an evil report, we do not get moved from our place of faith in Him. The enemy is always out to put space between us and the Lord as well as to frustrate our purpose in God. The enemy also wants to get us upset, out of the realm of the spirit and into the realm of the soul, where we lose our peace. Then, once we are in the flesh, the enemy has us and we will make mistakes, which we wouldn't have made if we had stayed in the spirit. As Ecclesiastes 10:8 says, *"Whoso breaketh an hedge, a serpent shall bite him."* But if we stay under the divine hedge; then, the Lord will be a wall of fire round about us.

A. What things (vs. 23)? Bonds and afflictions

1. Word Definitions

a. "Afflictions" in the Greek, *thlipsis* – pressure, anguish, persecution, trouble, tribulation, burdens; it comes from the root word, *thlibo* – to crowd, to narrow, to cause to suffer; this word in the King James is also translated – tribulation, anguish, persecution, trouble, burdened

b. "Bonds" in the Greek, *desmos* – a bond or shackle or chain, an impediment for disability, to be bound like a prisoner.

c. "Move" in the Greek, *poieo* – to make or cause someone to do something, to cause to waiver, to disturb, incite, or agitate

B. Other translations of verses 23-24:

"...hard times and prison ahead, but that matters little..."
"...chains and tribulation await me, but I take no account of these things..."
"...troubles and jail await me. I don't care about my own life..."
"...I fear none of these things..."
"...even the sacrifice of my life, I count as nothing..."
"...these things don't count..."
"...but I make account of none of these..."

VII. Companion Scriptures About Not Being Moved

A. I Thessalonians 3:3-4 – "*³That no man should be moved by these afflictions: for yourselves know that we are appointed thereunto. ⁴For verily, when we were with you, we told you before that we should suffer tribulation; even as it came to pass, and ye know.*" – "moved" in the Greek – *saino* – to shade or disturb; it comes from a root – *seio* – to rock or vibrate, to throw in to fear or concern, to agitate, to cause to tremble, to shake sideways or to and fro. We should never be moved by afflictions or by the dealings of God.

Afflictions and trouble arise from four places in our lives. They come from the devil, our own mistakes, the dealings of God, or life itself. If we can determine where our afflictions are coming from; then, we can deal with them accordingly. If it were coming from the devil, we can bind him and cast him out. If our mistakes are bringing trouble, then we can repent and go on with God. We will reap what we sow; but, the Lord will eventually turn the situation on our behalf. If it were just life itself, we learn how to deal with them and pass through them, as John 16:33 states, "*In the world ye shall have tribulation: but be of good cheer; I have overcome the world.*" Finally, if God were doing something in our lives, there is nothing we can do but bow our hearts and allow Him to do His work quickly within us, as Mark 4:17 states, "*affliction or persecution ariseth for the word's sake.*" Instead of allowing them to move us, let us rest in the revelation of Romans 8:18, "*For I reckon that the sufferings of this present time are not worthy to be compared with the glory which shall be revealed in us.*" Moreover II Corinthians 4:17 states, "*For our light affliction, which is but for a moment, worketh for us a far more exceeding and eternal weight of glory.*"

B. Matthew 7:13-14 – "*¹³Enter ye in at the strait gate: for wide is the gate, and broad is the way, that leadeth to destruction, and many there be which go in thereat: ¹⁴Because strait is the gate, and narrow is the way, which leadeth unto life, and few there be that find it.*" The word "*narrow*" is the same Greek word as afflictions in Acts 20:24.

C. II Thessalonians 2:2 – "*That ye be not soon shaken in mind, or be troubled, neither by spirit, nor by word, nor by letter as from us, as that the day of Christ is at hand.*"

VIII. Scriptural Ways The Kingdom Of God Prevents Us From Being Moved

A. 12 Scriptural ways – 12 in Scripture is the number for divine government.

1. **The Word of God**, Isaiah 54:11-14 – "*¹¹O thou afflicted, tossed with tempest, and not comforted, behold, I will lay <u>thy stones</u> with fair colours, and lay <u>thy foundations</u> with sapphires. ¹²And I will make thy windows of agates, and thy gates of carbuncles, and all thy borders of pleasant stones. ¹³And all thy children shall be <u>taught of the Lord</u>; and great shall be the peace of thy children. ¹⁴In righteousness shalt thou be established: thou shalt be far from oppression; for thou shalt not fear: and from terror; for it shall not come near thee.*"

2. **Being planted in a local church**, II Samuel 7:10 – "*Moreover I will appoint a place for my people Israel, and will plant them, that they may dwell in a place of their own, and <u>move no more</u>; neither shall the children of wickedness afflict them any more, as beforetime,*"

    Being planted in God's place means it is a place of our own. There will be peace in our lives and the enemy cannot afflict us as he did previously. We can then begin to stop being tossed to and fro in our lives and become planted and grow in all that God has for our lives.

3. **Dying to self**, II Corinthians 4:7-12 – "*⁷But we have this treasure in earthen vessels, that the excellency of the power may be of God, and not of us. ⁸We are troubled on every side, <u>yet not</u>*

distressed; we are perplexed, <u>but not in despair</u>; ⁹Persecuted, <u>but not forsaken</u>; cast down, <u>but not destroyed</u>; ¹⁰Always bearing about in the body the dying of the Lord Jesus, that the life also of Jesus might be made manifest in our body. ¹¹For we which live are alway delivered unto death for Jesus' sake, that the life also of Jesus might be made manifest in our mortal flesh. ¹²So then death worketh in us, but life in you."

4. **The sovereignty of God**, Psalms 121 – *"¹I will lift up mine eyes unto the hills, from whence cometh my help. ²My help cometh from the Lord, which made heaven and earth. ³<u>He will not suffer thy foot to be moved</u>: he that keepeth thee will not slumber. ⁴Behold, he that keepeth Israel shall neither slumber nor sleep. ⁵<u>The Lord is thy keeper</u>: the Lord is thy shade upon thy right hand. ⁶The sun shall not smite thee by day, nor the moon by night. ⁷<u>The Lord shall preserve thee from all evil</u>: he shall preserve thy soul. ⁸The Lord shall preserve thy going out and thy coming in from this time forth, and even for evermore."*

5. **Worship**, Psalms 66:8-9 – *"⁸O bless our God, ye people, and make the voice of his praise to be heard: ⁹Which <u>holdeth our soul in life</u>, and <u>suffereth not our feet to be moved</u>."*

    If we are a steady and true worshipper, having a lifestyle of worshipping God where we can enter into His presence at any given moment in our lives, God will not allow us to be moved.

6. **The Holy Ghost river inside of us**, Psalms 46:4-5 – *"⁴There is a river, the streams whereof shall make glad the city of God, the holy place of the tabernacles of the most High. ⁵<u>God is in the midst of her; she shall not be moved</u>: God shall help her, and that right early."*

    Jesus said in John 7:38, *"He that believeth on me, as the scripture hath said, out of his belly shall flow rivers of living water."* If we allow the river of God within us to flow out of us (and the best way to do that is to pray in tongues), then we shall not be moved, because we are in a constant place of the glory. Jude 20 states, *"But ye, beloved, building up yourselves on your most holy faith, praying in the Holy Ghost."*

7. **Waiting upon the Lord**, Psalms 62:1-2, 5-6 – *"¹Truly my soul waiteth upon God: from him cometh my salvation. ²He only is my rock and my salvation; he is my defence; <u>I shall not be greatly moved</u>…⁵My soul, wait thou only upon God; for my expectation is from him. ⁶He only is my rock and my salvation: he is my defence; I shall not be moved."*

8. **Continuing on in the Lord**, Colossians 1:23 – *"If ye continue in the faith grounded and settled, and be not moved away from the hope of the gospel, which ye have heard, and which was preached to every creature which is under heaven; whereof I Paul am made a minister;"*

    How many people walk with the Lord for a time, but fall away when afflictions, trials and testings came into their lives? The floods came, the dealings came and they did not allow a foundation to be laid in their lives. Therefore, there was nothing to hold them when the afflictions came. When the floods beat vehemently against them, their house fell. However, Jesus said in John 8:31, *"If ye continue in my word, then are ye my disciples indeed; ³²And ye shall know the truth, and the truth shall make you free."*

    When we are a part of the Kingdom of God and allow Jesus to become more and more the King in our lives, there is like a mighty fortress built up within us. If we just keep on and continue in Him, eventually we break through and come out of those hard seasons of our lives and we find we are not moved easily away from Him. God builds within us true discipline.

9. **The principle of giving**, Psalms 112:5-9 – *"⁵A good man <u>sheweth favour, and lendeth</u>: he will guide his affairs with discretion. ⁶<u>Surely he shall not be moved for ever</u>: the righteous shall be in*

everlasting remembrance. ⁷He shall not be afraid of evil tidings: his heart is fixed, trusting in the Lord. ⁸His heart is established, he shall not be afraid, until he see his desire upon his enemies. ⁹He hath dispersed, he hath given to the poor; his righteousness endureth for ever; his horn shall be exalted with honour."

10. **Staying in the manifest presence of God**, Psalms 16:8 – *"I have <u>set the Lord always before me</u>: because he is at my right hand, <u>I shall not be moved</u>."*

11. **Ways listed in Psalms 15** – *"¹Lord, who shall abide in thy tabernacle? who shall dwell in thy holy hill? ²He that walketh uprightly, and worketh righteousness, and speaketh the truth in his heart. ³He that backbiteth not with his tongue, nor doeth evil to his neighbour, nor taketh up a reproach against his neighbour. ⁴In whose eyes a vile person is contemned; but he honoureth them that fear the Lord. He that sweareth to his own hurt, and changeth not. ⁵He that putteth not out his money to usury, nor taketh reward against the innocent. <u>He that doeth these things shall never be moved</u>."*

    a. Walks uprightly
    b. Works righteousness
    c. Speaks the truth in their heart
    d. Does not backbite with their tongue
    e. Does not do evil to your neighbor
    f. In whose eyes a vile person is contemned
    g. Honoreth them that fear the Lord
    h. Sweareth to his own hurt and changeth not
    i. Putteth not out his money to usury
    j. Does not take reward against the innocent

12. **Submitting to the fivefold ministry**, Ephesians 4:11-16 – *"¹¹And he gave some, apostles; and some, prophets; and some, evangelists; and some, pastors and teachers; ¹²For the perfecting of the saints, for the work of the ministry, for the edifying of the body of Christ: ¹³Till we all come in the unity of the faith, and of the knowledge of the Son of God, unto a perfect man, unto the measure of the stature of the fulness of Christ: ¹⁴<u>That we henceforth be no more children, tossed to and fro, and carried about with every wind of doctrine</u>, by the sleight of men, and cunning craftiness, whereby they lie in wait to deceive; ¹⁵But speaking the truth in love, may grow up into him in all things, which is the head, even Christ: ¹⁶From whom the whole body fitly joined together and compacted by that which every joint supplieth, according to the effectual working in the measure of every part, maketh increase of the body unto the edifying of itself in love."*

Once we achieve verse 13, which says, *"till we all come in the unity of the faith, and of the knowledge of the Son of God, unto a perfect man, unto the measure of the stature of the fullness of Christ,"* we won't be tossed to and fro anymore, not being moved any longer. In order to get to that place, we need to be under the five-fold ministry. If we are, then we are being perfected for the ministry, we are being edified, we are being brought into that place of being a perfect man, which will keep us from being moved.

Chapter 13

Eden – The Kingdom Of God On Earth

I believe there is something within all of us that cries out for communion with God himself. There is nothing in this life that can compare with that manifest presence of God as it interacts with our human spirits. It is the most beautiful and wonderful interaction. I would like to look at the Garden of Eden and how that it is a type of the Kingdom of God here on earth. Also, it is a type of what we have to look forward to in the future.

All of the things that can give us pleasure in this life, I believe, has been perverted by satan. I believe God wants His people to experience pleasure in their lives. Psalms 36:8 states, "*Thou shalt make them drink of the river of thy pleasures.*" The Hebrew word for "*pleasures*" is a physical word. It is the same word, translated "*Eden*" in other places. Therefore this word and the revelation of Eden is not just a spiritual word, but a physical one as well. I believe that as we step through that veil into glory, we are going to experience not only spiritual sensations, but physical sensations. No feeling in this life is going to compare with the absolute pure physical feelings when Eden is restored. I am actually looking forward to heaven, not only spiritually, but emotionally and physically as well.

In the beginning was a garden named Eden, which was also called paradise. What do you think about when you think of paradise? The actual word for pleasure means "to live voluptuously." Satan has deceived us. He has made us to think that everything good is evil. He perverted the things that God originally created to be a blessing to us.

In this lesson we are going to look at these tremendous parallels between Eden and the Kingdom of God on earth.

I.   Parallels Between Eden And The Kingdom Of God

   A.   Examples

      1.   In the original Eden, there was a serpent and through his cunning and deceit man was cast out.

         a.   Genesis 3

b. Proverbs 30:18-19 – "...*¹⁹the way of a serpent upon a rock...*" – This is how the devil preys upon our flesh. The rock here speaks of our fleshly, carnal nature and the serpent here speaks of the devil.

c. Ecclesiastes 10:8 – "*He that diggeth a pit shall fall into it; and whoso breaketh an hedge, a serpent shall bite him.*"

d. II Corinthians 11:3 – "*But I fear, lest by any means, as the serpent beguiled Eve through his subtilty, so your minds should be corrupted from the simplicity that is in Christ.*"

e. We, right now, face an enemy that is cunning, subtle and deceitful. However, when the Kingdom of God comes in all of its fullness, and the people of that kingdom has the Lord Jesus reigning King and sovereign in their lives, then they will no longer have to deal with the devil anymore. There will be no more serpent or his cunning and deceitfulness. The devil will have been cast out; because, a people will have overcome the world, flesh and the devil.

   1) John 14:30 – "*Hereafter I will not talk much with you: for the prince of this world cometh, and hath nothing in me.*"

      a) Satan is the god of this world, or in the Greek it should be translated "age" (II Corinthians 4:4). An age has an end! Satan is only given a time period that he is allowed to have any kind of dominion.

         (1) We are no longer of the world (John 15:19, John 17:14-16).

      b) Other translation: "*...he has nothing in common with me...*"

      c) Just as the enemy had nothing in common with Jesus, I believe a people, who will be conformed to the image of Jesus, will also have this reality in their lives as well. Satan will be under their feet. He will not find anything in them anymore because they have allowed the dealings of God, the Word of God and the Holy Spirit to completely purge and cleanse them (Isaiah 4:3-4).

      d) Luke 22:31 – "*³¹And the Lord said, Simon, Simon, behold, Satan hath desired to have you, that he may sift you as wheat: ³²But I have prayed for thee, that thy faith fail not: and when thou art converted, strengthen thy brethren.*"

         (1) Satan sifts through our lives until he finds the things in which he can tempt us. He watches what we say and how we act. So he knows the ways to try to get us. We must not be ignorant of his devices (II Corinthians 2:11).

   2) John 12:31-32 – "*³¹Now is the judgment of this world: now shall the prince of this world be cast out. ³²And I, if I be lifted up from the earth, will draw all men unto me.*"

      a) Satan is the prince of this world. We are in the world, but we are not of the world. We are seated with Christ in heavenly places (Ephesians 2:6).

      b) As we lift up Jesus in our own lives, we are drawn up with him and to him. Judgment comes to our own lives, to the earth, the flesh, the parts that the devil has a hold of in our lives, and it is cast out of us.

      c) Micah 4:8 "*And thou, O tower of the flock, the strong hold of the daughter of Zion, unto thee shall it come, even the first dominion; the kingdom shall come to the daughter of Jerusalem.*" I believe the first dominion spoken of here is Eden, paradise restored. A people will have back what satan took from them before the fall. All those in the Kingdom of God will have that dominion operating within their lives and satan will have nothing to do with them anymore.

3)   Isaiah 27:1 – *"In that day the Lord with his sore and great and strong sword shall punish leviathan the piercing serpent, even leviathan that crooked serpent; and he shall slay the dragon that is in the sea."* *"In that day"* speaks of the day of the Lord when the sons of God are to be revealed.

4)   Revelation 12:5-11 – *"⁵And she brought forth a man child, who was to rule all nations with a rod of iron: and her child was caught up unto God, and to his throne. ⁶And the woman fled into the wilderness, where sha hath a place prepared of God, that they should feed her there a thousand two hundred and three score days. ⁷And there was war in heaven: Michael and his angels fought against the dragon; and the dragon fought and his angels, ⁸And prevailed not; neither was their place found any more in heaven. ⁹And the great dragon was cast out, that old serpent, called the Devil, and Satan, which deceiveth the whole world: he was cast out into the earth, and his angels were cast out with him. ¹⁰And I heard a loud voice saying in heaven, Now is come salvation, and strength, and the kingdom of our God, and the power of his Christ: for the accuser of our brethren is cast down, which accused them before our God day and night. ¹¹And they overcame him by the blood of the Lamb, and by the word of their testimony; and they loved not their lives unto the death."*

    a)   The woman is the 60-fold aspect of the church. She gives birth to the man-child.

    b)   Being caught up to God and to His throne can speak of being caught up physically;
       and, it can speak of being caught up spiritually to authority.

    c)   Once the man-child is caught up, the woman goes into the wilderness, which speaks spiritually of the dealings of God. I believe that if we go through wilderness experiences now and allow God to deal with us now; then, we will not have to go through wilderness experiences then. Therefore, this woman speaks of the 60-fold church who has not paid that final price of going on with God and must now be dealt with.   God will give this woman a chance during the last 3 ½ year tribulation, away from satan, to be perfected and purified.

    d)   Satan is now ruling in the second heavens. But when the sons of God are caught up to God and to His throne; then, war breaks out in heaven and satan is cast out, because the sons of God are beginning to rule and reign in the place where satan once had dominion. Then verse 10 becomes a reality, *"Now is come salvation and strength, and the kingdom of our God, and the power of his Christ: for the accuser of our brethren is cast down."* I believe that man-child is going to join with the angelic host and literally dethrone satan from the second heaven. Satan will then be thrown to the earth. That is why there is going to be such horror and tribulation during those last 3 ½ years.

    e)   Once satan is cast down, there will be no more darkness ruling the universe. When the Kingdom of God comes and the *dunamis*, the miracle power and force of the anointed (which speaks of Jesus and his sons), is released in the earth, then satan loses. This is unlike the Garden of Eden, where Adam submitted himself to the serpent. Therefore, instead of Adam (man) being kicked out of the garden, when the Kingdom of God comes, satan will be the one cast out now. We will then be restored to our original place of dominion.

2.   In the Garden of Eden there were two trees: the tree of life and the tree of the knowledge of good and evil.

    a.   In the Kingdom of God that is to come, there is only one tree, Jesus, the true tree of life.

b. Kingdom people will have dealt with their souls, where the knowledge of good and evil reigns. This is a people who have been changed from their own soulish realm into the image of Christ Jesus. When this people are conformed into the image of Christ, they are no longer eating of the knowledge of good and evil, but only partaking from the tree of life.

1) Galatians 2:20 – *"I am crucified with Christ: nevertheless I live; yet not I, but Christ liveth in me: and the life which I now live in the flesh I live by the faith of the Son of God, who loved me, and gave himself for me."*

2) II Corinthians 3:18 – *"But we all, with open face beholding as in a glass the glory of the Lord, are changed into the same image from glory to glory, even as by the Spirit of the Lord."*

3) Romans 8:29 – *"For whom he did foreknow, he also did predestinate to be conformed to the image of his Son, that he might be the firstborn among many brethren."*

4) Ephesians 3:19 – *"And to know the love of Christ, which passeth knowledge, that ye might be filled with all the fulness of God."*

Jesus had all the fullness of God bodily; and, we are to be <u>like him</u>. If we are like Him, then we will have the same exact thing. It does not mean we will be Jesus; but, we will be like him. We will walk as a king and priest on the earth.

5) Ephesians 4:11-13 – *"[11]And he gave some, apostles; and some, prophets; and some, evangelists; and some, pastors and teachers; [12]For the perfecting of the saints, for the work of the ministry, for the edifying of the body of Christ: [13]Till we all come in the unity of the faith, and of the knowledge of the Son of God, <u>unto a perfect man, unto the measure of the stature of the fulness of Christ</u>:"*

That means every part of you redounds with the Lord Jesus. As Revelation 2:7 states, *"To him that overcometh will I give to eat of the tree of life, which is in the midst of the paradise of God."*

6) Luke 9:23-24 – *"[23]And he said to them all, If any man will come after me, let him deny himself, and take up his cross daily, and follow me. [24]For whosoever will save his life shall lose it: but whosoever will lose his life for my sake, the same shall save it."* – Greek word for *"life"* is *psuche*, which means our soulish, carnal life.

7) John 12:23-26 – *"[23]And Jesus answered them, saying, The hour is come, that the Son of man should be glorified. [24]Verily, verily, I say unto you, Except a corn of wheat fall into the ground and die, it abideth alone: but if it die, it bringeth forth much fruit. [25]He that loveth his life shall lose it; and he that hateth his life in this world shall keep it unto life eternal. [26]If any man serve me, let him follow me; and where I am, there shall also my servant be: if any man serve me, him will my Father honour."*

c. When the Kingdom of God comes, there will be no more eating from the tree of the knowledge of good and evil. People who cannot make decisions in their lives are tormented by the knowledge of good and evil. However, we are supposed to live by the tree of life and not by the knowledge of good and evil. For example, when we make decisions in our lives, many of us will make a list of all the good things about that decision and all the bad things about that decision. Then, we make our decision accordingly. But, that is still eating from the knowledge of good and evil. The knowledge of good can be just as bad as the knowledge of evil because the knowledge of good may not be the knowledge of God. The knowledge of God supersedes the knowledge of good. Therefore, we are to live by the tree of life, by His Spirit, as Romans 8:14 states, *"For as many as are led by the Spirit of God, they are the sons of God."* Living by the tree of life is living in the Kingdom of God.

3. In the first Eden man was on trial. He had to choose.

    a. In the Kingdom of God, man has already made his choice, choosing Jesus and communion with God. When man will enter into the Kingdom of God, man will be purified and perfected. He has chosen Jesus, period.

4. In Eden, life was a garden where man lived in the manifest presence of God. They were not sick, depressed, poor, lonely, nor did they fear death. God was everything to them (before the fall).

    a. It will be the same again for those who enter into the Kingdom of God. They will not be sick anymore, depressed, poor, lonely. They will conquer their fear of death because death will no longer have dominion over them. God will be their all-in-all; because, He will be their sovereign Lord.

II. God Is Returning Us To Eden By Bringing The Kingdom Of God To Our Earth

A. Word Definitions

1. *Eden* in Hebrew – pleasure, delight, delicate. From a root – to be soft or pleasant, to live voluptuously, to delight oneself.

    a. Voluptuously means – living in luxury, pleasure, sensuous enjoyment – Derived from a root word that means the gratification of the senses. This means we are to be gratified by God, in the original way God intended for us. The glory so far outweighs everything in this natural life. Imagine what it is going to be like when we step into Eden. The word "Eden" is also translated "paradise" and "pleasure." No more sadness, no more worry and fear any longer, when we enter into Eden. God will restore paradise in our lives.

2. *Paradise* in Greek – a park, a place of happiness

    a. II Corinthians 12:3-4 – "*3And I knew such a man, (whether in the body, or out of the body, I cannot tell: God knoweth;) 4How that he was <u>caught up into paradise</u>, and heard unspeakable words, which it is not lawful for a man to utter.*"

        Paul actually went to paradise and heard things he could not talk about or describe here on earth. He experienced things that we are going to experience one day.

    b. Revelation 2:7 – "*He that hath an ear, let him hear what the Spirit saith unto the churches; To him that overcometh will I give to eat of the tree of life, which is in the midst of the <u>paradise</u> of God.*"

B. The Remnant Will Return To Eden Via The Kingdom Of God

1. Matthew 6:10 – "*Thy kingdom come. Thy will be done in earth, as it is in heaven.*"

    Nobody is suffering in heaven.

2. I John 4:17 – "*Herein is our love made perfect, that we may have boldness in the day of judgment: because <u>as he is, so are we in this world</u>.*"

3. I John 3:2-3 – *"²Beloved, now are we the sons of God, and it doth not yet appear what we shall be: but we know that, when he shall appear, <u>we shall be like him; for we shall see him as he is</u>. ³And every man that hath this hope in him purifieth himself, even as he is pure."*

We are going to be able to enjoy what is going on in heaven without any earthly hindrances whatsoever.

C. The Actual Return Back To Eden Scripturally

1. Isaiah 51:3 – *"For the Lord shall comfort Zion: he will comfort all her waste places; and he will make her wilderness like Eden, and her desert like the garden of the Lord; joy and gladness shall be found therein, thanksgiving, and the voice of melody."*

We do not like to talk about our waste places, the desolate places in our soul. Everybody has them. What we need is His grace, the divine influence upon the heart. As we continue to walk with the Lord, study his word, worship him, give ourselves to him, not listen to the naysayers, not hang around those who do not really press in, He will make her wilderness like Eden and her desert like the garden of the Lord. In your life, instead of depression and sadness, there will be joy and gladness!

2. Joel 2:1-11 – *"...²A day of darkness and of gloominess, a day of clouds and of thick darkness, as the morning spread upon the mountains: a great people and a strong; there hath not been ever the like, neither shall be any more after it, even to the years of many generations. ³A fire devoureth before them; and behind them a flame burneth: the land is as the garden of Eden before them, and behind them a desolate wilderness; yea, and nothing shall escape them..."*

When everything else is dark and awful, there is going to be a people of whom the earth has never seen the likeness. It is like Eden before them. Everywhere they go, they are going to bring that dominion, that first dominion, delight, the paradise of God. When they walk into a room, the room changes. They bring with them paradise.

We have to get used to living in Eden. Once you have been in the glory, and you have been immersed and bathed in it, there is nothing that can compare to it. It is paradise. And if you spend time with Him, and give yourself to Him, and He knows your heart, and you know His heart, and that relationship becomes so interwoven, life changes for you. And then you begin to change other people's lives by your very presence. Because the kingdom of God is within you; and, wherever you go, you take the kingdom.

3. Ezekiel 36:33-36 – *"³³Thus saith the Lord God; In the day that I shall have cleansed you from all your iniquities I will also cause you to dwell in the cities, and the wastes shall be builded. ³⁴And the desolate land shall be tilled, whereas it lay desolate in the sight of all that passed by. ³⁵And they shall say, This land that was desolate is become like the garden of Eden; and the waste and desolate and ruined cities are become fenced, and are inhabited. ³⁶Then the heathen that are left round about you shall know that I the Lord build the ruined places, and plant that that was desolate: I the Lord have spoken it, and I will do it."*

This is speaking of when the sons of God are walking in fullness and no longer sin. It is like the bones in Ezekiel 37. They were in an <u>open</u> valley. Everybody sees the dry bones in the body of Christ. They see how dysfunctional we are. We talk all the time about freedom; and, we are in such bondage it is ridiculous. And they look at us and say, "You are free?" They walk past the valley of dry bones and mock us. But the day is coming when the wastes shall be built and the desert places shall be tilled. God will have worked in those places and gotten rid of the garbage in them.

Think about the areas of your life that are lacking, in which you struggle. Do not quit! The day comes when God says, "Enough is enough. He that has suffered in the flesh hath ceased from sin. I will pull that thing out of your life now." All you need to do is keep at it. Do not quit. Your own mind is going to condemn you. People are going to condemn you. Christians are going to line up and give you ungodly counsel and speak evil about you. The devil is always there. But it does not matter. Our God is a God ready to pardon, merciful, and forgiving.

This is our God. He knows everything about you and me. He understands that man is born unto trouble as the sparks fly upward. We are made this way. We are made of flesh. We are humans; we have issues. God does not say that we are not good enough; religion does. God is committed to us until we are cleansed from <u>all</u> our iniquity.

D.   The Hebrew Word For Eden Translated Differently

1.   Psalms 36:7-9 – "*⁷How excellent is thy lovingkindness, O God! therefore the children of men put their trust under the shadow of thy wings. ⁸They shall be abundantly satisfied with the fatness of thy house; and thou shalt make them drink of the river of <u>thy pleasures</u>. ⁹For with thee is the fountain of life: in thy light shall we see light.*"

   a.   Verse 8 – "thy pleasures" is the Hebrew word for "Eden."

   Out of the midst of Eden went a river. Out of the throne of God is a river (Revelation 22). Out of the midst of His people flows a river (John 7:37-39). That river is full of pleasure and full of paradise, because its origin is Eden.

2.   Genesis 18:9-14 – "*⁹And they said unto him, Where is Sarah thy wife? And he said, Behold, in the tent. ¹⁰And he said, I will certainly return unto thee according to the time of life; and, lo, Sarah thy wife shall have a son. And Sarah heard it in the tent door, which was behind him. ¹¹Now Abraham and Sarah were old and well stricken in age; and it ceased to be with Sarah after the manner of women. ¹²Therefore Sarah laughed within herself, saying, After I am waxed old shall I have <u>pleasure</u>, my lord being old also? ¹³And the Lord said unto Abraham, Wherefore did Sarah laugh, saying, Shall I of a surety bear a child, which am old? ¹⁴Is any thing too hard for the Lord? At the time appointed I will return unto thee, according to the time of life, and Sarah shall have a son.*"

   a.   Verse 12 – "pleasure" is the same word translated "Eden."

Even if we are old and well stricken in age, we can still experience the joy and pleasure of paradise, of Eden. And if we walk in the Kingdom of God, and God is restoring us back to that first dominion, just think what life is going to be like. God is not only restoring us spiritually and emotionally, but physically as well. Eventually, as we continue to walk in the kingdom, these bones that crack, that are well stricken and old – life is going to energize them. As it says in Romans 8:11, "*But if the Spirit of him that raised up Jesus from the dead dwell in you, he that raised up Christ from the dead shall also <u>quicken your mortal bodies</u> by his Spirit that dwelleth in you.*" This mortal body is going to be fashioned like unto his glorious body (Philippians 3:21).

So the Kingdom of God, when it comes in the earth as it is in heaven, is going to be exactly like the garden of God. No matter what we are going through right now, no matter what we have been through, no matter what the future may hold, do not quit. Do not give up. Do not surrender. He that endureth to the end shall be saved (Matthew 10:22). Put your eyes at the end of this race. Fix your eyes on the prize, and do not let any exit sign get you off. Because we are heading to Eden. The garden of the Lord is going to take over your soulish man. That old, rotten soul of yours is going to redound with purity, glory, joy, happiness. All of the waste places are going to be inhabited. God is going to fill everything in our lives that is lacking. God has an expected end for you; and ,that end is perfection, holiness, Eden.

Chapter 14

Pressing Into The Kingdom

In this lesson we want to look at pressing into the Kingdom of God. Pressing into the Kingdom of God means never giving up, never stopping and pressing through until we get into the Kingdom of God. It means pressing through our own carnal nature, pressing through this world that is constantly trying to keep us from God. It also means pressing through the temptations of the enemy. It would be great to think that everything was easy and things would just come to us. However, anything good in life will cost us something. There is a price to pay to go on with God and as the years go on, the price gets greater and the warfare increases. This is what ultimately separates the true disciples from the multitude. The multitude just wants to be blessed, ministered to and receive something from the Lord. They have little revelation about giving. God did not save us to just receive, though He is happy to give us everything. But He saved us and birthed us to be conformed into His image and take on His character and nature, which is simply one of giving, as John 3:16 *"For God so loved that He gave..."* When we take on His nature, our hearts will be completely given over to other people to bless them and see God come forth in their lives, to see the Kingdom of God begin to take form and shape in them.

I have learned in my life that if I were going to make it in God, it was going to take more than me just hanging around, waiting for something to happen. I have learned that I have to go do something about it, that I was responsible how far I went in God's kingdom. To be a part of His bride is something I must press into and that if I did not, I could miss out in what Jesus has truly destined for me. As David says in Psalms 27:4, *"One thing have I desired of the Lord, that will I seek after..."* It's not enough to just desire things of the Lord, we must seek after those very things. Proverbs 13:4 says, *"The soul of the sluggard desireth, and hath nothing: but the soul of the diligent shall be made fat."* Moreover, Proverbs 12:24 states, *"The hand of the diligent shall bear rule."* There is something to be said about diligence and continuing on in the Lord. We must continue on every day of our lives.

Let us bow our hearts and determine in our hearts that we will do whatever it takes to enter into the Kingdom of God. God may have to break us, deal with us and crush and remove many things in our lives. But, we must say in our hearts that we want Him and the things of God and press into His Kingdom.

I. Luke 16:16 – *"The law and the prophets were until John: since that time the kingdom of God is preached, and every man presseth into it."*

Jesus is basically saying here that up until this time we have had the law, the prophets and the dispensation of the Jews. But now a new day has dawned and it is time now for the Kingdom of God to come into operation. And as it does, every man must press into it.

A.   Word definition:

　　1.   Presseth in Greek – *biozo* – To force, to crowd oneself into, to seize, to suffer violence

B.   Other translations of verse 16:

"...and everyone strives violently to go in."
"...everyone is eager to get in."
"...and everyone is forcing his way into it."
"...everyone is pushing to get in."
"...everyone is urged to enter in."
"...everyone makes it into it by force."
"...and every man entereth violently into it."
"...and all classes have been forcing their way into it."
"...and everyone with the utmost earnestness and effort is pressing into it for his share in it."

C.   Companion scriptures:

　　1.   Matthew 11:12 – *"And from the days of John the Baptist until now the kingdom of heaven suffereth violence, and the violent take it by force."*

　　　　a.   *"Suffereth violence"* is the same Greek word *"presseth"* as found in Luke 16:16

　　　　b.   Other translations of verse 12:

　　　　"The kingdom of heaven has endured violent assault and violent men seize it by force, as a precious prize, a share in the heavenly kingdom is sought with the most ardent zeal and intense exertion."
　　　　"The kingdom of heaven has been forcefully advancing, and forceful men lay hold of it."
　　　　"The kingdom of heaven is being taken by storm and the strong and forceful ones claim it for themselves eagerly."

D.   Other words used in the King James Version translated as press:

　　1.   Greek for press – to pursue or follow after; to go forward, to persecute
　　2.   Hebrews 12:14 – *"*<u>*Follow*</u>* peace with all men, and holiness, without which no man shall see the Lord:"*
　　3.   Philippians 3:12-14 – *"12Not as though I had already attained, either were already perfect: but I* <u>*follow after*</u>*, if that I may apprehend that for which also I am apprehended of Christ Jesus..."*

E.   Other Passages Related To This

　　1.   Psalms 27:4 – *"One thing have I desired of the Lord, that will I seek after; that I may dwell in the house of the Lord all the days of my life, to behold the beauty of the Lord, and to inquire in his temple."*
　　2.   Genesis 32:24-30 – *"...26I will not let thee go, except thou bless me..."*

This is the story of Jacob wrestling all night with the angel, which I believe was Jesus; because, Jacob said at the end of the story in verse 30, *"I have seen God face to face, and my life is preserved."* It was not a physical wrestling match, but a wrestling match of the soul. Here is the thing about Jacob: God could not beat him initially. God did not seem to be able to break down Jacob's situation. In other words, God was testing Jacob's fortitude and Jacob did not give up. So Jacob said in verse 26, *"I will not let thee go, except thou bless me."* In all of his wrestling with God, Jacob realized he had a lot of problems; but, he never let go. Therefore, God gave Jacob a name change to Israel, signifying Jacob's character was changed. The word Israel means "prince with God, ruling with God; one that prevails with God." Jacob showed God that he was no longer Jacob, which means "deceiver and supplanter," but Israel.

There has to come in every one of us, that kind of attitude and fortitude that Jacob had, to press into that which God truly wants for us. We must not let God go until He blesses us.

Moreover, we must have this same fortitude when dealing with the devil and the sin in our lives. Every one of us has days where we are a little weak or a day when temptation wants to draw us away from Jesus and His presence. But there is always that space of time when we are drawn away by our lusts where we have a chance to walk away and resist by His grace that sin. James 1:14 states, *"But every man is tempted, when he is drawn away of his own lust, and enticed. 15Then when lust hath conceived, it bringeth forth sin: and sin, when it is finished, bringeth forth death."* At those times, we must, as Ephesians 4:27 states, *"Neither give place to the devil."* We must press through and begin to overcome in those areas in our lives. The devil always has a Delilah spirit lurking around to draw us away. If there are any weakness in our lives, satan will try to sift us as wheat (Luke 22:31) and exploit our weaknesses. There has to come something within us that says we love Jesus and His presence more than this momentary weakness of our flesh. Like Jacob, we might have many issues in our lives; but, we must never let Him go until He blesses us and makes us overcomers.

Even if we fall, we must repent and immediately arise and tell the Holy Spirit to never let us go. There has to be something within us that will press through it and fight again; because, the day will come when the grace of God, that divine influence upon our hearts, will take over. Sin will then become exceedingly sinful and we will walk free from that sin forever.

3. Mark 5:25-34 – Woman with issue of blood

This is the story of the woman with the issue of blood. It says in Mark 5:27, *"When she had heard of Jesus, came in the press behind, and touched his garment."* There were a lot of people crowding around Jesus. So the only way for her to get to Jesus was to press her way through all of the other people to get to Him. And all kinds of people were touching Jesus. Many people want to touch Jesus. However, this woman touched Jesus in a different way; because, when virtue went out from Jesus, He said in verse 31, *"Who touched me?"* The word for *"virtue"* in this verse is the same Greek word *dunamis*, which means miraculous power. Therefore, there has to come faith within us that wants to truly touch Him.

4. Matthew 15:22-28 – Woman of Canaan with a daughter vexed with a devil

This is the story of the woman of Canaan who cried out to Jesus and His disciples to heal her daughter, who was grievously vexed with a devil. Verse 23 states, *"But he [Jesus] answered her not a word. And his disciples came and besought him, saying, Send her away; for she crieth after us."* Moreover, Jesus answers all of the disciples' about her in verse 24, *"I am not sent but unto the lost sheep of the house of Israel."* Then she worshipped Jesus and asked again for His help. Jesus then answered, *"It is not meet to take the children's bread, and to cast it to dogs."* Nevertheless, that was not enough to stop the woman. She responds to Jesus in verse 27, *"Truth, Lord: yet the dogs eat of the crumbs, which fall from their masters' table."* Upon hearing this, Jesus tells the woman, *"O woman, great is thy faith: be it unto thee even as thou wilt. And her daughter was made whole from that very hour."*

In this story, Jesus tested the woman three times; yet, the woman did not get offended at what God said. I believe Jesus could not wait for that woman to pass that test. Jesus was ready to heal that child immediately, but was waiting for her to press through.

Sometimes Jesus will say something to us on purpose to offend us to see what our response will be. But He is really hoping that we will do the right thing and not get up and quit. Sometimes we have to pass through offense and through things that even Jesus says to us that we do not like.

5. Mark 10:46-52 – Blind Bartimaeus *"cried the more a great deal"*

Here is the story of blind Bartimaeus, begging by the highway side. Spiritually speaking, Bartimaeus has lost his vision in God, but notices Jesus walking by. He then begins to cry in verse 47, *"Jesus, thou Son of David, have mercy on me."* And everybody around him told him to be quiet. So, what does Bartimaeus do? He started screaming and shouting even louder, *"Thou Son of David, have mercy on me"* (verse 48). Sometimes when our needs or the needs of others is so great, we cannot allow anything or anyone keep us from pressing through to God.

So when Bartimaeus cries out the second time, it says in verse 49, *"And Jesus stood still."* Jesus then called Bartimaeus to Himself. It is interesting to note that nobody else got called to Jesus but him. I believe it was because nobody cared enough to shout and cry out, to violently press through into the Kingdom of God. Bartimaeus probably thought that he was never going to get this chance again. He knew Jesus was the pearl of great price. We must seize the moment when Jesus is passing by. As II Corinthians 6:2 states, *"Behold, now is the accepted time; behold, now is the day of salvation."* We must press through as he did.

Jesus himself has two natures. He is the Lamb of God as well as the Lion of the tribe of Judah. On the one hand, Jesus was the lamb who laid his life down for the sin of the world, humbling Himself, keeping His mouth, quietly doing the will of God. However, at other times, He is the Lion of the tribe of Judah, roaring out of Zion. I believe we have to take on these two natures of God as well. There are times we have to be passive, sweet and humble. But at other times, that lion nature must rise up within us when the enemies of God rise up against us to defy the armies of the living God. Just like David, he was the sweet Psalmist of Israel. But when Goliath defied the armies of the living God, David stood against him while the rest of Israel cowered in fear. Therefore, we must understand that at times, whatever kind of violence is needed to get this aspect of the Kingdom of God accomplished, we must press into it. We must force our way in to seize it.

6. Luke 5:1-4 – *"¹And it came to pass, that, as <u>the people pressed upon him to hear the word of God</u>, he stood by the lake of Gennesaret, ²And saw two ships standing by the lake: but the fishermen were gone out of them, and were washing their nets. ³And he entered into one of the ships, which was Simon's, and prayed him that he would thrust out a little from the land. And he sat down, and taught the people out of the ship. ⁴Now when he had left speaking, he said unto Simon, <u>Launch out into the deep</u>, and let down your nets for a draught."*

In this story, it says that the people pressed upon him to hear the word of God. So Jesus enters one of the ships and says to launch out into the deep. In other words, you and I need to press in to hear the Word of God. If we want the gospel of the kingdom to change our lives, we are going to need the Scriptures to do it.

What do we have to do to press into the Word of God? First we have to thrust out a little from the land, which means we have to thrust out from that which we are comfortable. We need to leave the place from where we are standing firm on ground, where we are always in control. When we go out into the water, we are not in control anymore. Then Jesus told them to launch out into the deep. I believe this means that if we want the deeper things of God, we must go further and follow the Lord. We must go that extra distance. We must go that stone's throw further, like Jesus in the garden of Gethsemane, *"And he was withdrawn from them about a stone's cast, and kneeled down, and prayed."* Jesus went a bit further. Paul, it says in Philippians 4:14, *"I press toward the mark for the prize..."* So there has to be something willing in us to press and go further for the Kingdom of God.

7. Luke 19:1-10 – Zacchaeus – "...*³And he sought to see Jesus who he was; and could not for the press, because he was little of stature. ⁴And he ran before, and climbed up into a sycamore tree to see him: for he was to pass that way...*"

Zacchaeus was a tax collector that stole from everybody. He hears about Jesus and wants to see Jesus, "*who he was.*" There was something in Zacchaeus that was hungry for something more and greater. But it says that the press was so great around Jesus that He couldn't get to Him. Instead of quitting and giving up, he climbed up a tree. Jesus then walks by that tree and says in verse 5, "*Zacchaeus, make haste, and come down; for today I must abide at thy house.*" After spending time with Jesus, Zacchaeus says in verse 8, "*Behold, Lord, the half of my goods I give to the poor; and if I have taken anything from any man by false accusation, I restore him fourfold.*" The Lord then replies, "*This day is salvation come to this house, forsomuch as he also is a son of Abraham*" (verse 9).

Why did salvation come to the house of Zacchaeus? I believe it was because he never gave up despite all of the people around Jesus. He did not get offended because he "*was little of stature*" (verse 3). He did whatever it took and Jesus saw him. Jesus always sees faith. Jesus always sees ardent desire and people who will always press in no matter what.

8. Mark 2:1-5 – "*¹And again he entered into Capernaum, after some days; and it was noised that he was in the house. ²And straightway many were gathered together, insomuch that there was no room to receive them, no, not so much as about the door: and he preached the word unto them. ³And they come unto him, bringing one sick of the palsy, which was borne of four. ⁴And when they could not come nigh unto him for the press, they uncovered the roof where he was: and when they had broken it up, they let down the bed wherein the sick of the palsy lay. ⁵When Jesus saw their faith, he said unto the sick of the palsy, Son, thy sins be forgiven thee.*"

Here is another example of those wanting to come near to Jesus and being unable to because of the press of people surrounding Him. Was this enough to make them turn around, give up and go home? Rather than giving up, they uncovered the roof where Jesus was. This story has great spiritual significance to us. The house in this story is a type of the house of God. And when it was noised that Jesus was in the house, they uncovered the roof. These brothers, knowing they needed a miracle, took away every obstacle to the blessing of the glory of God descending upon them. Sometimes, spiritually speaking, we need to take the roof off, so that the glory of God may descend upon His people. Jesus saw their faith, saw them pressing through and brought forth their healing.

9. II Chronicles 15:8-15 – Asa – "*...¹⁵And all Judah rejoiced at the oath: for they had sworn with all their heart, and sought him with their whole desire; and he was found of them: and the Lord gave them rest round about.*"
10. Psalms 63:1-2 – "*¹ O God, thou art my God; early will I seek thee: my soul thirsteth for thee, my flesh longeth for thee in a dry and thirsty land, where no water is; ²To see thy power and thy glory, so as I have seen thee in the sanctuary.*"

The day is going to come when we so long and desire to see the power and the glory of God, not just in church, but while we outside among the world. However, for this to happen, we must be thirsty and hungry for it.

11. Isaiah 41:17-20 – "*¹⁷When the poor and needy seek water, and there is none, and their tongue faileth for thirst, I the Lord will hear them, I the God of Israel will not forsake them...*"

If we are truly poor and needy for him, God will bring us into a place where the true glory and presence of God is. Ultimately, we must be willing to do whatever it takes. For example, when I am about to pray for people to be baptized in the Holy Ghost, I will ask them if they are ready to speak in tongues. So many will not be willing. I then bring them to this passage. You see, we must be willing to do what Jesus wants us to do. When we are poor and needy, we will do anything for His presence in our lives.

12. Isaiah 55:6-7 – "⁶*Seek ye the Lord while he may be found, call ye upon him while he is near:* ⁷*Let the wicked forsake his way, and the unrighteous man his thoughts: and let him return unto the Lord, and he will have mercy upon him; and to our God, for he will abundantly pardon.*"

13. Jeremiah 29:11-14 – "¹¹*For I know the thoughts that I think toward you, saith the Lord, thoughts of peace, and not of evil, to give you an expected end.* ¹²*Then shall ye call upon me, and ye shall go and pray unto me, and I will hearken unto you.* ¹³<u>*And ye shall seek me, and find me, when ye shall search for me with all your heart.*</u> ¹⁴*And I will be found of you, saith the Lord: and I will turn away your captivity, and I will gather you from all the nations, and from all the places whither I have driven you, saith the Lord; and I will bring you again into the place whence I caused you to be carried away captive.*"

14. Luke 11:5-13 – Ask, seek, knock

In this parable, a man is visiting his friend at midnight and asking for three loaves. Jesus says in verse 8, "*Though he will not rise and give him* [the three loaves], *because he is his friend, yet because of his importunity he will rise and give him as many as he needed.*" His importunity was the reason the man gave his friend the bread. In other words, the man was persistent and kept asking. He kept on pressing. Then Jesus concludes by exhorting us in verse 9, "*Ask, and it shall be given you; seek, and ye shall find; knock, and it shall be opened unto you.*" Sometimes it is not enough to just ask God. You must also seek and knock. We must do whatever it takes.

15. Acts 14:22 – "*…and exhorting them to continue in the faith, and that we must through much tribulation enter into the kingdom of God.*"

16. Luke 21:36 – "*Watch ye therefore, and pray always, that ye may be accounted worthy to escape all these things that shall come to pass, and to stand before the Son of man.*"

17. Matthew 26:46 – "*Rise, let us be going…*"

18. Hebrews 5:14 – "*But strong meat belongeth to them that are of full age, even those who by reason of use have their senses exercised to discern both good and evil.*" The word "*reason of use*" in this passage means "habitual using." We must press in to the Word of God continually in our lives. As we habitually use the Word of God every day and night, meditating upon it, we keep the Lord always before our face.

We must have a determination in our hearts that no matter what it takes, let us press and violently seize the Kingdom of God. Like Zacchaeus, we will climb a tree. Like Bartimaeus, we will shout even louder. Like those men, we will tear the roof off. Like that woman, we will press through all of those people and touch the hem of His garment.

Chapter 15
Called To His Kingdom And Glory

In relation to the Kingdom of God, I would like to look at the revelation that we have been called to His Kingdom and His glory and what that means. We have been called to more than just heaven. Most churches will tell us that heaven is the goal as a Christian. Their emphasis is just on getting people saved and then plugging them into some sort of ministry. However, there is so much more in which we have been called. We have been called to His glory and I have found that many Christians do not even know what His glory is.

When Jesus came into our lives, we were born again of incorruptible seed (I Peter 1:23), by the Word of God. That which is incorruptible cannot be corrupted. In our spirits now is the place where Jesus lives (I Corinthians 6:17, Romans 8:16, Hebrews 12:23, I John 3:9; 5:10). Jesus lives in our spirit and He cannot live with sin, demons or darkness. However, the problem we face is in our souls, which have not been completely sanctified yet. Our spirits are justified and made perfect when we are born again. Our true nature in God now can never sin again. The only thing I can do now is to let my soulish man, my carnal nature within me and those chambers of my soul where sin still dwells within, be sanctified and made holy by the Holy Spirit and the Word of God.

God, then, is in the process of sanctifying and redeeming, by the Holy Spirit and the Word of God, our souls, our carnal and adamic nature, to conform us into the image of His Son. We need, then, to be stirred every day and reminded, that we are to walk holy before God. We do not have the days anymore to give into sinful things or to take days off from walking with the Lord. We are called to something so holy, that the Bible calls it three different things: a high calling (Philippians 3:14), a holy calling (I Timothy 1:9) and a heavenly calling (Hebrews 3:1). We are called to His Kingdom and His glory. God is willing to share everything He is and has with a people. John 17:22 states, *"And the glory which thou gavest me I have given them."* Jesus wants to share His glory with a people. He just has to find that people. Deuteronomy 32:9 states, *"For the Lord's portion is his people; Jacob is the lot of his inheritance."*

A picture of this can be seen in the Tabernacle of Moses. When we first get saved, we are taken to the brass altar, where justification takes place. Then we move to the brass laver, which speaks of water baptism and the washing of water by the Word of God (Ephesians 5:26). We then slip through the first veil into the Holy Place, where the only light is shining from the golden candlestick, which is a type of the baptism of the Holy Ghost. Then, we are called ever onward to the table of shewbread, which contains rows of bread of His presence, which speaks of deeper revelation and truths. We stand around this table and eat it together. We learn about communion and fellowship together as a body and flowing together to the goodness of the Lord as we eat the revelation of God. Then, we approach the golden altar of incense and enter into deeper places of praise, worship and intercession. We begin to understand that we are a partaker of His divine nature and are becoming like Him. Our flesh and adamic nature is starting to diminish and get swallowed up by His holy nature. As we begin to worship, our worship becomes a heavenly and a high thing. The incense begins to ascend through that thin veil into that final place where destiny is calling us, wooing us ever onward, the Most Holy Place. At some point when we are worshipping before that golden altar, we are just going to be carried through that veil. We are going to be transformed, like what happened to Jesus on the Mount of Transfiguration, where God *"who shall change our vile body, that it may be fashioned like unto his glorious body, according to the working whereby he is able even to subdue all things unto himself"* (Philippians 3:21). Then, we will put on His divine nature while we walk on this earth.

The earth is going to see a representative of Jesus on this earth again for at least 3 ½ years. Jesus' ministry two thousand years ago was only 3 ½ years. Seven is the number for perfection. Therefore, I believe there is yet a 3 ½ year ministry of Jesus again. Jesus has already sat down on the right hand of the Father. He is interceding for us. So the only Jesus that is going to have that last 3 ½ year ministry is the many-membered Son. Not one Jesus on the shores of Galilee, but thousands of Jesus' all over the world, walking in His kingdom and His glory. We won't be Jesus; but, we will be like Him.

We have been called to His glory. Attaining to His glory is the highest calling in God. It is the pearl of great price. We must run after that prize, and not anything else. Even ministry and everyone serving the Lord must bow to the revelation that we have been called to His eternal glory. God is the treasure and He must be our utmost purpose in life. We must love and cherish and strive to walk in His glory everyday of our lives. It is the most priceless commodity in the universe. Zechariah 2:8 states, *"After the glory hath he sent me unto the nations."* We must run after the glory and desire it above all things. The glory of God must consume our lives. It must be everything to us. The glory is the beauty of who He truly is. It is His person and His presence. We have been called to it and to share in it. We have been called to His Kingdom and glory!

I.   I Thessalonians 2:11-12 – *"11As ye know how we exhorted and comforted and charged every one of you, as a father doth his children, 12That ye would walk worthy of God, who hath called you unto his kingdom and glory."*

A.   Other Translations

"To live lives worthy of God, who calls you into His own kingdom and the glorious blessedness."
"...for He called you to share in His kingdom and glory."
"...who is calling you to His own reign and glory."
"...who has given you a part in His kingdom and His glory."
"...who is inviting you to share His own kingship and glory."

B.   Word Definitions

1.   Kingdom in Greek – *basileia* – royalty, rule, a realm, to reign, sovereign. From a root – to walk

We are not just called to be kings, we are called to walk as kings.

2.   Glory in Greek – *doxa* – glory (as very apparent), used in a wide application (literal or figurative, objective or subjective). Also translated – dignity, honor, praise, worship. From a root – to think, to seem. Also translated as – be accounted, be of reputation.

3.   Glory in Hebrews – *kabod* – weight, spendor, copiousness. Root = to be heavy. His glory is like a weight, it can be felt. You know when it is there and you know when it is not there.

God's glory is the weight of His presence. It is the splendor, beauty and magnificence of God. His glory is who He is. The glory of God is God Himself being in a place, that divine heavy weight of His manifest presence.

C. Other Companion Scriptures That We Are Called To His Kingdom And Glory

1. II Timothy 4:18 – *"And the Lord shall deliver me from every evil work, and will preserve me unto his heavenly kingdom: to whom be glory for ever and ever. Amen."*

God is going to preserve us for His kingdom and His glory, if we let Him. Matthew 7:14 states, *"Because strait is the gate, and narrow is the way, which leadeth unto life, and few there be that find it."* The life in this verse means the life that God is living now. We must stay on that highway of holiness. All along this pathway, there are exits. We must continue walking even when facing those exit signs. There will be temptations, dealings and choices that will make us want to take an exit. When we takes exits, we go around in circles and stop going on with God; until, we decide to repent and get back on the road. We will be faced with those exits our whole life. Jesus wants to preserve us unto His heavenly kingdom and glory. He will perfect that which concerns us (Psalms 138:8). We will overcome by His grace.

2. Matthew 6:9-13 – *"⁹After this manner therefore pray ye: Our Father which art in heaven, Hallowed be thy name. ¹⁰Thy kingdom come. Thy will be done in earth, as it is in heaven. ¹¹Give us this day our daily bread. ¹²And forgive us our debts, as we forgive our debtors. ¹³And lead us not into temptation, but deliver us from evil: For thine is the kingdom, and the power, and the glory, for ever. Amen."*

The Kingdom of God and the glory of God (which are in heaven) God also wants to be in earth, in a people. The goal is to be conformed into the image of Christ.

3. I Chronicles 29:10-17 – *"¹⁰Wherefore David blessed the Lord before all the congregation: and David said, Blessed be thou, Lord God of Israel our father, for ever and ever. ¹¹Thine, O Lord, is the greatness, and the power, and the glory, and the victory, and the majesty: for all that is in the heaven and in the earth is thine; thine is the kingdom, O Lord, and thou art exalted as head above all. ¹²Both riches and honour come of thee, and thou reignest over all; and in thine hand is power and might; and in thine hand it is to make great, and to give strength unto all. ¹³Now therefore, our God, we thank thee, and praise thy glorious name. ¹⁴But who am I, and what is my people, that we should be able to offer so willingly after this sort? for all things come of thee, and of thine own have we given thee. ¹⁵For we are strangers before thee, and sojourners, as were all our fathers: our days on the earth are as a shadow, and there is none abiding. ¹⁶O Lord our God, all this store that we have prepared to build thee an house for thine holy name cometh of thine hand, and is all thine own. ¹⁷I know also, my God, that thou triest the heart, and hast pleasure in uprightness. As for me, in the uprightness of mine heart I have willingly offered all these things: and now have I seen with joy thy people, which are present here, to offer willingly unto thee."*
4. Psalms 145:10-13 – *"¹⁰All thy works shall praise thee, O Lord; and thy saints shall bless thee. ¹¹They shall speak of the glory of thy kingdom, and talk of thy power; ¹²To make known to the sons of men his mighty acts, and the glorious majesty of his kingdom. ¹³Thy kingdom is an everlasting kingdom, and thy dominion endureth throughout all generations."*

We must speak about the glory of His kingdom and talk of His power. We should be preparing ourselves in this life to go through the veil so that when that time comes, we are ready for Him to change our vile bodies and fashion it like unto His glorious body (Philippians 3:21). We will one day walk free from sickness, disease and sin. We will be His sons completely.

We are to make known to the world His mighty acts and the glorious majesty of His kingdom. We are called to manifest who He is and manifest His deeds in the earth.

5. Daniel 7:13-14 – "*13I saw in the night visions, and, behold, one like the Son of man came with the clouds of heaven, and came to the Ancient of days, and they brought him near before him. 14And there was given him dominion, and glory, and a kingdom, that all people, nations, and languages, should serve him: his dominion is an everlasting dominion, which shall not pass away, and his kingdom that which shall not be destroyed.*"

II. We've Been Called To Be Kings

Most people, I have found, do not have a high opinion of themselves. Proverbs 23:7 states, "*For as he thinketh in his heart, so is he.*" What a man believes about himself rules him. We must see ourselves, now, as God sees us. We at one time were just sinners saved by grace. But now are we the sons of God (I John 3:1). Now we are saints called to His Kingdom and glory. We have been called to be kings, to rule and reign with Jesus in His kingdom. Revelations 1:6 tells us that we have been made kings and priests unto God. We need to begin to walk in this revelation.

A. Kings in Greek – *basileus* – a sovereign (abstractly, relatively, or figuratively); to rule, reign; from a root that means to walk, the foot (through the notion of a foundation of power).

B. Scriptures

1. Job 36:7-11 – "*7He withdraweth not his eyes from the righteous: but with kings are they on the throne; yea, he doth establish them for ever, and they are exalted. 8And if they be bound in fetters, and be holden in cords of affliction; 9Then he sheweth them their work, and their transgressions that they have exceeded. 10He openeth also their ear to discipline, and commandeth that they return from iniquity. 11If they obey and serve him, they shall spend their days in prosperity, and their years in pleasures.*"
2. Proverbs 8:14-21 – "*14Counsel is mine, and sound wisdom: I am understanding; I have strength. 15By me kings reign, and princes decree justice. 16By me princes rule, and nobles, even all the judges of the earth. 17I love them that love me; and those that seek me early shall find me. 18Riches and honour are with me; yea, durable riches and righteousness. 19My fruit is better than gold, yea, than fine gold; and my revenue than choice silver. 20I lead in the way of righteousness, in the midst of the paths of judgment: 21That I may cause those that love me to inherit substance; and I will fill their treasures.*"
3. Proverbs 25:2 – "*It is the glory of God to conceal a thing: but the honour of kings is to search out a matter.*"

God calls those that search the Scriptures, kings. This is like those noble Bereans, who in Acts 17:11, "*received the word with all readiness of mind, and searched the scriptures daily, whether those things were so.*" Nobility comes from our character, from the Spirit of God within us, and what God is making us into. Therefore searching the Scriptures brings nobility and authority into our lives.

4. Revelation 1:5-6 – "*Unto him that loved us, and washed us from our sins in his own blood, 6And hath made us kings and priests unto God and his Father; to him be glory and dominion for ever and ever. Amen.*"

The first thing Jesus did for us was shed His blood to wash us completely from all uncleanness and perversion. Revelation 5:9 states, that Jesus "*hast redeemed us to God by thy blood out of every kindred, and tongue, and people and nation.*" We are cleansed from our past. Also, he has made us kings and priests unto God now that we might walk worthy of this calling. The glory of God now is what controls our life. It is what keeps us from sinning. The glory is the lawgiver and makes us to never want to do anything that upsets or grieves the Lord. We are called to walk like kings because God wants us to share in His kingship and His blessedness.

5. Revelation 5:10 – *"And hast made us unto our God kings and priests: and we shall reign on the earth."*

God wants us to reign in this life. I Timothy 2:12 states, *"If we suffer, we shall also reign with him."* We have been called to reign and be a king, to have a realm of authority. All we can say is to God be the glory; because, it is only by His grace this will ever happen.

6. Psalms 45:9-11 – *"9Kings' daughters were among thy honourable women: upon thy right hand did stand the queen in gold of Ophir. 10Hearken, O daughter, and consider, and incline thine ear; forget also thine own people, and thy father's house; 11So shall the king greatly desire thy beauty: for he is thy Lord; and worship thou him."*

The queen here speaks of God's bride. We were called to stand at the right hand of Jesus. The bride is a many-memebered bride. The day is going to come, when those who have despised the bride and did not think highly of her and set her at naught, will see her at the right hand of Jesus. But, the bride will act like Joseph did when he was despised by his own brethren. Joseph showed his brethren mercy. And like Joseph, the bride will have gone through the dealings of God, to break and deal with her, so that she will have the character and image like Jesus to rule and reign with Him. She will act nobly.

Therefore, in our lives today, we must learn to rule and allow the Kingdom of God to come forth within us. II Samuel 23:3 states, *"He that ruleth over men must be just, ruling in the fear of God."* God is not going to give us kingdom authority if we are not going to do it justly and honorably. We must walk worthy of the kingdom.

7. Matthew 16:17-19 – *"17And Jesus answered and said unto him, Blessed art thou, Simon Barjona: for flesh and blood hath not revealed it unto thee, but my Father which is in heaven. 18And I say also unto thee, That thou art Peter, and upon this rock I will build my church; and the gates of hell shall not prevail against it. 19And I will give unto thee the keys of the kingdom of heaven: and whatsoever thou shalt bind on earth shall be bound in heaven: and whatsoever thou shalt loose on earth shall be loosed in heaven."*

    a. Isaiah 22:22-23 – *"22And the key of the house of David will I lay upon his shoulder; so he shall open, and none shall shut; and he shall shut, and none shall open. 23And I will fasten him as a nail in a sure place; and he shall be for a glorious throne to his father's house."*
    b. Revelation 3:7 – *"And to the angel of the church in Philadelphia write; These things saith he that is holy, he that is true, he that hath the key of David, he that openeth, and no man shutteth; and shutteth, and no man openeth;"*

8. Psalms 132:11-18 – *"11The Lord hath sworn in truth unto David; he will not turn from it; Of the fruit of thy body will I set upon thy throne. 12If thy children will keep my covenant and my testimony that I shall teach them, their children shall also sit upon thy throne for evermore. 13For the Lord hath chosen Zion; he hath desired it for his habitation. 14This is my rest for ever: here will I dwell; for I have desired it. 15I will abundantly bless her provision: I will satisfy her poor with bread. 16I will also clothe her priests with salvation: and her saints shall shout aloud for joy. 17There will I make the horn of David to bud: I have ordained a lamp for mine anointed. 18His enemies will I clothe with shame: but upon himself shall his crown flourish."*
9. Jeremiah 17:12 – *"A glorious high throne from the beginning is the place of our sanctuary."*

We have been called to a glorious high throne. We are not called just to something of this life. We are called to have a realm of authority with Him. Walking as a king means walking in His glory.

10. Micah 4:6-8 – *"6In that day, saith the Lord, will I assemble her that halteth, and I will gather her that is driven out, and her that I have afflicted; 7And I will make her that halted a remnant, and*

her that was cast far off a strong nation: and the Lord shall reign over them in mount Zion from henceforth, even for ever. ⁸And thou, O tower of the flock, the strong hold of the daughter of Zion, unto thee shall it come, even the first dominion; the kingdom shall come to the daughter of Jerusalem." We are called to the first dominion, to have what Adam had from the beginning.

III. We've Been Called To His Glory

God's glory is for that in which we were born. It is the true reason for our existence. All that God is and has, He is willing and desperately wants to share it with His people. However, it must be a people who have been prepared by allowing the dealings of God to purge them and sanctify them so that they have the image of Christ.

In the last days, a great remnant of overcomers will have fought the good fight of faith and prevailed over the world, the flesh, and the devil. They will have done so only because the grace of God helped them and made them to become willing. These overcomers will then manifest forth His glory in the earth. They will shew forth the true nature of God in the last great day of visitation – the last great move of God.

    A. Called To Obtain God's Glory

        1. I Thessalonians 2:12 – *"That ye would walk worthy of God, who hath called you unto his kingdom and glory."*

        2. II Thessalonians 2:14 – *"Whereunto he called you by our gospel, to the obtaining of the glory of our Lord Jesus Christ."*

           a. Other translations:

              "...so that you may share in the glory of God."
              "...so that you may possess for your own the splendor of God."
              "...to gain the glory of God."

           b. Obtaining in Greek – acquisition of a thing, preservation, purchased, possession; from a root – to make around oneself, to acquire or buy.

You can be called to His glory; but, it does not mean you are going to get it. Matthew 22:14 states, *"For many are called, but few are chosen."* There is an obtaining, an accounting worthy of, and a buying and purchasing of the glory of God. We purchase the glory every day when we die to our flesh. Proverbs 23:23 states, *"Buy the truth, and sell it not."*

There are things in God in which there is a need to be attained. In David's army, there were those who attained to positions of honor within His army. II Samuel 23:19 states, *"Was he not most honourable of the three? Therefore he was their captain: howbeit he attained not unto the first three."* There are ranks within the body of Christ. I Corinthians 15:41-42 states, *"For one star differeth from another star in glory. ⁴²So also is the resurrection of the dead."* Some are going to shine brighter than others because of how much they attained the glory in this life.

We purchase and obtain glory by suffering. Romans 8:18 says, *"For I reckon that the sufferings of this present time are not worthy to be compared with the glory which shall be revealed in us."* When we go through suffering or the dealings of God, we buy the truth and allow the glory to be worked within us. We obtain things everyday by our choices. II Corinthians 4:17 states, *"For our light affliction, which is but for a moment, worketh for us a far more exceeding and eternal weight of glory."* Jesus said in Revelation 3:18, *"I counsel thee to buy of me gold tried in the fire, that thou mayest be rich."* Glory is obtained by our faith being tried in the fire. It is in the hard places of our lives, the things we have suffered and walked through that we see we have grown the most. That is when intimacy with God became a real factor in our lives, when we suffered, were broken, humbled, or went through loss. II Timothy 2:12 tells us, *"If we suffer, we shall also reign with him."*

      c.   Luke 21:36 – *"Watch ye therefore, and pray always, that ye may be accounted worthy to escape all these things that shall come to pass, and to stand before the Son of man."*

  3.   Hebrews 2:10 – *"For it became him, for whom are all things, and by whom are all things, in bringing many sons unto glory, to make the captain of their salvation perfect through sufferings."*

  4.   Isaiah 43:7 – *"Even every one that is called by my name: for I have created him for my glory, I have formed him; yea, I have made him."*

      a.   Another translation: *"...whom I have created and formed and made for my glory."*

Our destiny could not be conveyed any more clearly. We were created for His glory, as Colossians 1:26-27 states, *"The mystery which hath been hid from ages...which is Christ in you, the hope of glory."* Jesus came into us to give us a hope of glory.

  5.   I Peter 5:10 – *"But the God of all grace, who hath called us unto his eternal glory by Christ Jesus, after that ye have suffered a while, make you perfect, stablish, strengthen, settle you."*

We see here again to enter into this calling of His glory, we must first allow suffering and the dealings of God in our lives, which takes a lifetime. When Moses first experienced God's presence, He then asked the Lord in Exodus 33:18, *"I beseech thee, shew me thy glory."* But God told Moses that He could not see His face in the condition he was in, because to look at him in the state that he was in would destroy him. But, when we look at the book of Revelation 22:4, *"And they shall see his face."* There will be a people who will look fully into the face of Almighty God in all of His glory and nothing will happen to them, but more glory! They will have suffered and overcome and have been redeemed to a place where they can then handle the glory of God to the glory of God.

  6.   II Peter 1:3 – *"According as his divine power hath given unto us all things that pertain unto life and godliness, through the knowledge of him that hath called us to glory and virtue:"*

      a.   Other translations:

        "...who hath called us to His own glory and excellence."
        "...who hath called us to share His own glory and virtue."
        "...who called us by His own splendor and might."
        "...have been called to share in God's own excellence and glory."

His knowledge, which is the Word of God, is what causes us to partake in His divine nature and glory.

  7.   Romans 9:23 – *"And that he might make known the riches of his glory on the vessels of mercy, which he had afore prepared unto glory,"*

God has taken great preparation in the unfolding of His great mystery and purpose. From the beginning, we have been called to share in His glory.

      a.   Jeremiah 17:12 – *"A glorious high throne from the beginning is the place of our sanctuary."*
      b.   I Samuel 2:6-8 – *"⁶The Lord killeth, and maketh alive: he bringeth down to the grave, and bringeth up. ⁷The Lord maketh poor, and maketh rich: he bringeth low, and lifteth up. ⁸He raiseth up the poor out of the dust, and lifteth up the beggar from the dunghill, to set them*

among princes, and <u>to make them inherit the throne of glory</u>: for the pillars of the earth are the Lord's, and he hath set the world upon them."

8. Zechariah 2:8 – *"For thus saith the Lord of hosts; After the glory hath he sent me unto the nations..."* – This calling began with Israel who did not fulfill what God wanted for them. Now it has been passed on to us. We are to go after the glory, and then once we receive it and understand it, we are to take it to the nations.

9. Romans 8:18 – *"¹⁸For I reckon that the sufferings of this present time are not worthy to be compared with the glory which shall be revealed in us...³⁰Moreover whom he did predestinate, them he also called: and whom <u>he called</u>, them he also justified: and whom he justified, them <u>he also glorified</u>."* – Our ultimate destiny is to receive the final aspect of our salvation: We have been justified, we are being sanctified, we shall be glorified (II Corinthians 1:10).

10. Ephesians 1:18 – *"The eyes of your understanding being enlightened; that ye may know what is the hope of his calling, and what the riches of the glory of his inheritance in the saints,"* – Only by being enlightened can we begin to understand the glory of our inheritance. It is intended for all.

11. Colossians 3:4 – *"When Christ, who is our life, shall appear, then shall ye also appear with him in glory."* – To those for whom Christ is their life, we must know and believe that when He appears in glory, so shall we be in glory like Him (I John 3:2).

12. II Timothy 2:10 – *"Therefore I endure all things for the elect's sakes, that they may also obtain the salvation which is in Christ Jesus with eternal glory."* – Once again, we see that there is an enduring of sanctification and the dealings of God to obtain this precious glory.

13. I Peter 4:13 – *"But rejoice, inasmuch as ye are partakers of Christ's sufferings; that, when his glory shall be revealed, ye may be glad also with exceeding joy."* – Suffering and glory go hand in hand throughout the Scriptures – no suffering, no glory.

14. Philippians 3:20-21 – *"²⁰For our conversation is in heaven; from whence also we look for the Saviour, the Lord Jesus Christ: ²¹Who shall change our vile body, that it may be fashioned like unto his glorious body, according to the working whereby he is able even to subdue all things unto himself."* – Our destiny is to have these old earthly bodies changed and made like unto His new glorious body (I Corinthians 15:38-58).

15. II Corinthians 4:17 – *"For our light affliction, which is but for a moment, worketh for us a far more exceeding and eternal weight of glory;"* – There are degrees of glory and according to how much we allow God to sanctify us in this life will determine our degree or weight of glory.

16. II Corinthians 3:18 – *"But we all, with open face beholding as in a glass the glory of the Lord, are changed into the same image from glory to glory, even as by the Spirit of the Lord."* – It is the ministry of the glass ("glass" = mirror = The Word) and of the Holy Spirit that we are changed into His image from one realm of glory to another.

17. Isaiah 60:1-3, 7 – *"¹Arise, shine; for thy light is come, and the glory of the Lord is risen upon thee. ²For, behold, the darkness shall cover the earth, and gross darkness the people: but the Lord shall arise upon thee, and his glory shall be seen upon thee. ³And the Gentiles shall come to thy light, and kings to the brightness of thy rising...⁷and I will glorify the house of my glory."* – The glory of God is going to be revealed within a people.

18. Ephesians 3:16 – *"That he would grant you, according to the riches of his glory, to be strengthened with might by his Spirit in the inner man;"*

19. Isaiah 42:8 – *"I am the Lord: that is my name: and my glory will I not give to another, neither my praise to graven images."* (Isaiah 48:11)

This Scripture does not contradict the many other Scriptures that declare we have been called to obtain His glory. This Scripture says that God is not going to give His glory to another. But He is going to give His glory to the Jesus that is within His people. God's people who are conformed to His image will not be "another." They will have lost their identity in Jesus. Like Paul said in Galatians 2:20, *"I am crucified with Christ: nevertheless I live; yet not I, but Christ liveth in me."* When we have His image within us, we are then capable of receiving His glory.

Jesus said in John 17:22, *"And the glory which thou gavest me I have given them; that they may be one, even as we are one."* Jesus wants to give us His glory; but, He can't give it to us if we are still ourselves. God does not give His glory to another. We must not remain who we are but become conformed to the image of Christ Jesus. That means the death of every one of us is warranted. Who we are, our personality, our soulish nature and self must be swallowed up in the characteristics of God. Our lives should fulfill I Corinthians 13, which is the chapter on agape love. If it were not, then we are missing the mark. Love never fails. That is the image of Christ Jesus. Jesus said in Matthew 11:29, *"Learn of me; for I am meek and lowly in heart."* For most people, identifying with Jesus has been reduced to water baptism. But identifying with Christ involves so much more. It means not wanting our sinful nature anymore to have any place within our lives. God is out to destroy our carnal nature, as Psalms 116:15, *"Precious in the sight of the Lord is the death of his saints."* Jesus came into the world to die, so that others might live. As we die, others live and Jesus is truly manifested within us.

II Corinthians 5:21 states, *"For he hath made him to be sin for us, who knew no sin; that we might be made the righteousness of God in him."* He made an exchange for us, took our old dirty and nasty garments and exchanged them with the garments of righteousness and praise. He gave us the ability to share in all that He is, the glory of God.

So we see from all of the above passages of Scripture that we are called to obtain, receive, and walk in His glory!

B.   He Wants Us To Have It

1.   John 11:40 – *"Jesus saith unto her, Said I not unto thee, that, if thou wouldest believe, thou shouldest see the glory of God?"*

We must believe and receive this revelation of the glory of God, as I John 4:16 states, *"We have known and believed the love that God hath to us."* God has all of the love and glory to give us; but, if we don't believe it, we can miss it. If we believe, we can see His glory.

2.   Isaiah 58:8 – *"...the glory of the Lord shall be thy rearward."*
3.   Isaiah 43:7 – *"Even every one that is called by my name: for I have created him for my glory, I have formed him; yea, I have made him."*
4.   Psalms 84:11 – *"For the Lord God is a sun and shield: the Lord will give grace and glory: no good thing will he withhold from them that walk uprightly."*
5.   Psalms 149:5 – *"Let the saints be joyful in glory..."*
6.   Isaiah 4:5 – *"And the Lord will create upon every dwelling place of mount Zion, and upon her assemblies, a cloud and smoke by day, and the shining of a flaming fire by night: for upon all the glory shall be a defence."*
7.   Isaiah 60:1-2 – *"¹Arise, shine; for thy light is come, and the glory of the Lord is risen upon thee. ²For, behold, the darkness shall cover the earth, and gross darkness the people: but the Lord shall arise upon thee, and his glory shall be seen upon thee."*
8.   II Corinthians 3:7-10, 18 – *"⁷But if the ministration of death, written and engraven in stones, was glorious, so that the children of Israel could not stedfastly behold the face of Moses for the glory of his countenance; which glory was to be done away: ⁸How shall not the ministration of the spirit be rather glorious? ⁹For if the ministration of condemnation be glory, much more doth the ministration of righteousness exceed in glory. ¹⁰For even that which was made glorious had no glory in this respect, by reason of the glory that excelleth...¹⁸But we all, with open face beholding*

as in a glass the glory of the Lord, are changed into the same image from glory to glory, even as by the Spirit of the Lord."

C. His Glory Should Be Everything To Us

1. I Corinthians 10:31 – *"Whether therefore ye eat, or drink, or whatsoever ye do, do all to the glory of God."*
2. Psalms 138:5 – *"Yea, they shall sing in the ways of the Lord: for great is the glory of the Lord."*
3. Psalms 3:3 – *"But thou, O Lord, art a shield for me; my glory, and the lifter up of mine head."*

D. We Should Be Longing For The Glory And Him

1. Psalms 63:1-2 – *"¹O God, thou art my God; early will I seek thee: my soul thirsteth for thee, my flesh longeth for thee in a dry and thirsty land, where no water is; ²To see thy power and thy glory, so as I have seen thee in the sanctuary."*
2. Exodus 33:18 – *"And he said, I beseech thee, shew me thy glory."*
3. John 7:18 – *"He that speaketh of himself seeketh his own glory: but he that seeketh his glory that sent him, the same is true, and no unrighteousness is in him."*

E. Our Destiny Is All Wrapped Up In His Glory

1. Psalms 102:16 – *"When the Lord shall build up Zion, he shall appear in his glory."*
2. Romans 8:30 – *"Moreover whom he did predestinate, them he also called: and whom he called, them he also justified: and whom he justified, them he also glorified."*
3. Revelation 21:11 – *"Having the glory of God: and her light was like unto a stone most precious, even like a jasper stone, clear as crystal;"*
4. Haggai 2:7, 9 – *"⁷And I will shake all nations, and the desire of all nations shall come: and I will fill this house with glory, saith the Lord of hosts...⁹The glory of this latter house shall be greater than of the former, saith the Lord of hosts: and in this place will I give peace, saith the Lord of hosts."*
5. Isaiah 61:3 – *"To appoint unto them that mourn in Zion, to give unto them beauty for ashes, the oil of joy for mourning, the garment of praise for the spirit of heaviness; that they might be called trees of righteousness, the planting of the Lord, that he might be glorified."*
6. Isaiah 60:7, 9 – *"⁷All the flocks of Kedar shall be gathered together unto thee, the rams of Nebaioth shall minister unto thee: they shall come up with acceptance on mine altar, and I will glorify the house of my glory...⁹Surely the isles shall wait for me, and the ships of Tarshish first, to bring thy sons from far, their silver and their gold with them, unto the name of the Lord thy God, and to the Holy One of Israel, because he hath glorified thee."*
7. Psalms 45:13 – *"The king's daughter is all glorious within: her clothing is of wrought gold."*
8. Ephesians 5:27 – *"That he might present it to himself a glorious church, not having spot, or wrinkle, or any such thing; but that it should be holy and without blemish."*
9. I Samuel 2:8 – *"He raiseth up the poor out of the dust, and lifteth up the beggar from the dunghill, to set them among princes, and to make them inherit the throne of glory: for the pillars of the earth are the Lord's, and he hath set the world upon them."*
10. I Corinthians 15:49 – *"And as we have borne the image of the earthy, we shall also bear the image of the heavenly."*
11. Romans 8:18 – *"For I reckon that the sufferings of this present time are not worthy to be compared with the glory which shall be revealed in us."*
12. II Corinthians 4:17 – *"For our light affliction, which is but for a moment, worketh for us a far more exceeding and eternal weight of glory;"*
13. Philippians 3:21 – *"Who shall change our vile body, that it may be fashioned like unto his glorious body, according to the working whereby he is able even to subdue all things unto himself."*
14. II Thessalonians 1:10 – *"When he shall come to be glorified in his saints, and to be admired in all them that believe (because our testimony among you was believed) in that day."*

About The Author

Samuel Greene, Ph. D.

One of the callings the Lord gave Brother Sam years ago was to help write sound doctrine for the Charismatic movement and Spirit-filled believers. Since 1976, Brother Sam has been teaching the Word of God daily out of which has come dozens of teaching manuals and books which are part of an eight year Bible College curriculum taught at churches and Bible Schools all over the world.

For more information about Brother Sam, his ministry, or if you would like to order any of his books, please visit us online at www.Brother-Sam.org.

On this website, you will find:

- Devotionals
- Sermons/Podcasts, Videos
- Study Manuals & Bookstore
- Downloadable eBooks
- Worship CDs

A Biblical Reference Dictionary Every Minister & Disciple Must Have!

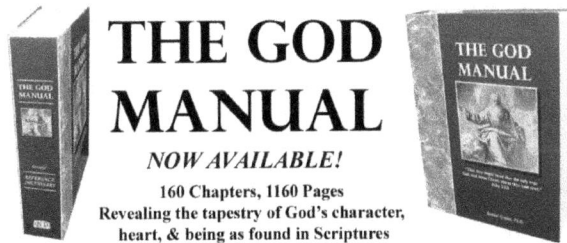

THE GOD MANUAL

NOW AVAILABLE!

160 Chapters, 1160 Pages
Revealing the tapestry of God's character, heart, & being as found in Scriptures

John 17:3 says, *"...that they might know thee the only true God, and Jesus Christ, whom thou hast sent."* The God Manual was written with hopes of seeking to reveal the correct Biblical image of who our precious Creator really is. With 160 lessons, it exhaustively teaches almost every aspect, characteristic, and attribute of God we can think of. In order to fulfill our calling to be conformed to Jesus' image, we must first know what that image is. Our prayer is that as you study these lessons your life will forever be changed, your worship increased, you realize that holiness is not an unattainable thing anymore, and most importantly you fall deeper in love with Jesus. (*ISBN 978-0-9831696-0-4*)

www.ingramcontent.com/pod-product-compliance
Lightning Source LLC
Chambersburg PA
CBHW080538090426
42733CB00016B/2621